Tradition and Creation

Essays in honour of Elizabeth Mary Wilkinson

Photograph by Andrew Ryle

TRADITION AND CREATION

Essays in honour of
Elizabeth Mary Wilkinson

EDITED BY

C. P. MAGILL, BRIAN A. ROWLEY
and CHRISTOPHER J. SMITH

LEEDS
W. S. MANEY & SON LIMITED
1978

The editors would like to express their gratitude for the generous financial assistance received from the Institute of Germanic Studies of the University of London and the Managers of the Bithell Bequest Fund, and from University College London. The editors would also like to offer their special thanks to Mrs Edda de Souza, of the School of European Studies of the University of East Anglia, and to the staff of the Institute of Germanic Studies of the University of London, for their very able secretarial and administrative assistance.

The styling adopted by the editors is that set out in the *MHRA Style Book, Notes for Authors and Editors*, edited by A. S. Maney and R. L. Smallwood, second edition (1978).

ISBN 0 901286 10 9

Printed and published in England by
W. S. MANEY AND SON LTD   HUDSON ROAD   LEEDS   LS9 7DL

Contents

v

Elizabeth Mary Wilkinson

ASKED FOR A SUMMARY DESCRIPTION of Mary Wilkinson, one could do worse than adapt a phrase from her early and memorable essay on Goethe's poetry: 'Feet on the ground, roots in the ground, head in the air'. Her own roots lie in Yorkshire, where warmth of heart, coolness of mind, and a liking for plain words are native characteristics. She was born, she gives us to understand, 'on the moors around Wuthering Heights' and if she forsook Yorkshire at an early age — she was schooled in Manchester — her origins are still discernible in her forthright ways and independent spirit. In her Inaugural Lecture, delivered at University College London in 1962 and entitled *In Praise of Aesthetics*, she gave us a sight of the principles which have governed her work as critic and teacher, and threw light, in passing, upon her induction into German studies at Bedford College — leaving us in the dark, however, about the unacademic motives which impelled her to abandon her earlier loves, biology, history, and English, and take to German. After her 'Lehrjahre', spent teaching modern languages at Clapham High School and Southampton Grammar School, and doing research after being awarded the Amy Lady Tate Studentship at Bedford College, she joined the German Department of University College London in 1940, during the Academic Diaspora. Improbable as it may seem, she gave her first lectures at Aberystwyth, doubtless against the uproar penetrating her lecture room from windswept Cardigan Bay — a partial explanation perhaps of her present incisive diction and style. After the return of University College from exile, London became her academic base, which she has only left to undertake those forays and excursions (as, for example, Visiting Professor or Professor-at-Large at Chicago, Columbia, and Cornell) which have helped to make her as well known across the Atlantic as in Great Britain and Germany.

Mary Wilkinson has, among her many gifts, a talent for wearing distinction lightly. Fortunately so, since by the time she retired, in 1976, from the Chair of German at University College, she was burdened by many honours and awards, her merit as a scholar and her practical services to German studies having been recognized on an international scale by the British Academy, the Akademie der Wissenschaften zu Göttingen, the Deutsche Akademie für Sprache und Dichtung, the Goethe-Institut, Smith College, Massachusetts, and the University of Kent at Canterbury. Her many friends feel, nevertheless, that another sort of tribute remains to be paid to her, of a kind particularly agreeable to scholars because it is rendered in the hard-earned currency of scholarship itself.

To read the list of Mary Wilkinson's publications is to realize how influential a critic she has been and to recall how often her remarkable blend of insight and articulateness has provided freshness and stimulus to our reading even of works long deemed familiar. Her clear vision, her ability to read a writer's mind, her gift for giving life to ideas, and her awareness, for all her concern with literary structures, of the human realities veiled by aesthetic semblance — these are some of the qualities which have made her an outstanding interpreter. But she has not stopped at interpretation; she has been no less concerned with the methodology of critical and scholarly investigation and with the presentation and (in the best sense) popularization of literature, informed and inspired by the aesthetics which has been for her, as she said in her Inaugural Lecture, 'a passion and a power'. She is expert at seeing familiar works in a fresh light, and as a pathfinder, opening up new routes to the heart of literary matters, she has few equals. To hear her deliver an address is to understand why she has been so successful a teacher: the arresting introduction, the taut argument, the eye-opening images, not to speak of the mischievous asides, affect the listener like a brisk walk on a Northern fell, from which we return with our muscles stretched, but unstrained.

Most people probably became aware of Mary Wilkinson as a textual critic, with her pioneering series of Goethe studies — on *Tasso*, *Egmont*, and the lyric poetry — published in the late 1940s, following on her much-loved edition of *Tonio Kröger*. Yet her first book, *Johann Elias Schlegel*, based on her doctoral dissertation, had shown her also as a historian. The alternatives of criticism and history have represented for her, not a dichotomy but a true Goethean polarity — of text and context, concentration and expansion — which finds its *Steigerung* in her own essays on 'Tasso — ein gesteigerter Werther' and on 'Goethe's Conception of Form', in her *Faust* essays of 1957, 1971, and 1973, and above all in the epoch-making edition, with translation, of Schiller's *Aesthetic Letters*. These works make up a significant proportion of the achievement of post-war *Germanistik* in England.

The list of publications also testifies to Mary Wilkinson's achievements in the art of successful and fruitful collaboration with others. If, as she told her audience in her 'Dankrede' to the Deutsche Akademie für Sprache und Dichtung, on the occasion of the award to her of the Foreign Scholar Prize, her extensive collaborations induced in her an unaccustomed feeling of 'Hochstapelei' in accepting the prize, those who know her well see her aptitude for collaboration as proof of true originality of mind. She herself, in this 'Dankrede', paid a generous tribute to her chief collaborator, the late Leonard Willoughby. Theirs was a classic partnership, notable not only for its range and endurance, but because of its quality, which was exceptional in the sense that the virtues which Mary Wilkinson attributed to collaboration — as a cure for the occupational ills of the solitary scholar and as a way of turning philology into the zestful science it ought to be and seldom is — show up so clearly in their joint enterprises. They are nowhere more clearly displayed than in their exemplary edition of Schiller's *Aesthetic Letters*. No undertaking could have been better suited to their dissimilar, yet congenial minds; it offered them the kind of challenge they relished most and was in precise accord with the view of scholarship they shared. 'The task of the scholar', they wrote in their Introduction, 'is far from being a purely "academic" activity. It is directly, and reciprocally, related to the personal and public challenge. For each new interpretation provokes a new kind of testing, and each kind of testing works back upon interpretation'.

It is doubtful whether Mary Wilkinson has ever thought of herself as dutiful, yet she has in the course of her 'Wanderjahre' always responded readily to 'die Forderung des Tages' — sometimes in markedly unacademic ways, as when she drove an ambulance during the war. She has combined her scholarly activities with much hard labour of a more practical kind: as Secretary for many years of the Board of Studies in Germanic Literatures and as a Head of Department she did much to promote the development, and shape the structure, of German studies in the University of London. Thanks no doubt to her experience as a schoolteacher, she has always been mindful of the problems of teaching German at pre-university level and has maintained close links with the Modern Language Association of Great Britain, of which she has been Honorary President. And for nearly twenty years she was the mainstay of the English Goethe Society, as its Secretary and Editor of its *Publications* (to whose printer she dedicated the translation of Karl Kraus's poem 'An meinen Drucker' reprinted below). She became President of the Society in 1974, to the pleasure and relief of its members, who know that they can still rely on her, however retiring her present disposition may be, to support their activities and enliven their meetings.

This volume of essays for Mary Wilkinson is not intended as an additional acknowledgement of her achievements, for that would be superfluous; it is simply an acknowledgement of our debt to her, our way of showing gratitude to one who has done so much to brighten our Germanistic lives. Its prime purpose is to give her pleasure: to entertain her, to exercise her ever-active intelligence, and to demonstrate to her the assured place she has in our hearts and minds. The contributors, who cover a broad span of generations, have chosen subjects which reflect some at least of her principal interests — aesthetics, pure and applied, the history of ideas, and Goethe; and in so far as the essays are not located in the Age of Goethe, they treat of matters and ideas which have played a significant part in her thinking about literature.

We are known, in part at least, by our recreations. In the latest edition of *Who's Who?* Mary Wilkinson gives hers as 'housekeeping and scholarship at a civilized pace at last'. We cannot all benefit from the first of these, for that would be to stretch hospitality beyond its natural limits, but we have great hopes of the second. The more Mary indulges her taste for leisurely scholarship, the less danger there is of *Germanistik* becoming one of the dismal sciences.

C. P. MAGILL, BRIAN A. ROWLEY, CHRISTOPHER J. SMITH

Tragic Guilt

A Germanist's Gleanings from Recent Interpretations of Aristotle's *Poetics*

By W. H. BRUFORD

MANY GERMANISTS must have wondered as I did what our Classical colleagues now think about the dramatic theory based on Lessing's reading of Aristotle's *Poetics* which was put before us as fundamental in our student days. They may welcome a few hints about where to turn for enlightenment on such questions in the now, alas, almost deserted Greek section of a university library.

The first thing the present inquirer discovered was that the whole conception of 'tragic guilt', so important in German theory since the later eighteenth century, is now generally considered to be altogether foreign to Aristotle. Over twenty years ago Kurt von Fritz described in a long essay the principal stages in the development of a moralistic theory of tragedy, from the Renaissance to our own day, out of a misinterpretation of Aristotle's notion of the great *hamartia* which brings calamity upon the tragic hero.[1] In the following year (1956) Humphry House's excellent lectures on the *Poetics* were published posthumously,[2] and here too we are told that in Aristotle's two uses of the word *hamartia* in Chapter 13 he is quite clearly and deliberately distinguishing the *hamartia* from the general moral failings in which the hero is said to fall short of being 'pre-eminently virtuous and just'. The word is translated by House as 'error of judgment', in agreement, as he points out, with Bywater's *Aristotle on the Art of Poetry*[3] and 'all serious modern Aristotelian scholarship', as reflected, for example, in Rostagni's editions (1927 and 1945), where the 'error' is said to result 'from ignorance of some material fact or circumstance'. D. W. Lucas takes

the same line in the latest English edition of the *Poetics*[4] in a
clear and concise appendix on *hamartia*. 'It is widely supposed',
Lucas writes, 'that *hamartia* is a flaw or frailty of character, a
conception which gives scope for developing the always
popular notion of poetic justice, and one which has found easy
application to Shakespeare's tragedies. This is due largely to
Butcher's influential essay *Aristotle's Theory of Poetry and Fine
Art*...[5] In fact "flaw" is a barely legitimate translation, and
those German writers who favour the same general interpretation use the more appropriate *Schuld*, equivalent to "fault".' An
illuminating re-examination of all the problems connected with
hamartia has recently been made by the Dutch scholar J. M.
Bremer, working in Cambridge under the supervision of
D. W. Lucas and Professor D. L. Page. In the resulting book,
'*Hamartia*',[6] the meaning of the term and earlier attempts at
its elucidation are systematically studied by means of a close
analysis of the *Poetics*, especially Chapter 13, backed by semantic
research into the history of the word and its cognates and by a
critical assessment of the relevance of Aristotle's ideas to the
understanding of a wide range of Greek tragedies.

When Greek tragedy and Aristotle's *Poetics* were rediscovered
at the Renaissance, Christian scholars not unnaturally gave to
hamartia the meaning 'sin' which it had come to have in the late
Greek of the New Testament, and it is this misunderstanding
which is the source of what Corneille for instance has to say in
his dramatic essays about the moral value of tragedy. In his
view, the audience expects poetic justice to be done. It wants to
see virtue rewarded and vice punished in tragedy. The same
view was given very wide currency from 1692 until well after
Lessing's time by André Dacier's *La poétique d'Aristote*. 'La
tragédie parfaite nous apprend à nous tenir sur nos gardes', he
wrote in his commentary, 'et à purger et modérer les passions
qui ont été la seule cause de la perte de ces malheureux. Ainsi
l'ambitieux y apprend à donner des bornes à son ambition,
l'impie à craindre Dieu, le vindicatif à renoncer à la vengeance.'
This view was fairly generally accepted in England in the
eighteenth century, as W. C. Greene, for example, reminds us in

the very informative chapter on 'The Idea of Tragedy' in his *Moira*.[7] Dryden supports it, for instance, in the prefaces to *All for Love* and *Troilus and Cressida*, in spite of the doubts he had expressed in his *Essay on Poetry* a decade earlier (1768). John Dennis even went so far as to declare that 'every tragedy should be a very solemn lecture'. Addison, however, had already strongly challenged the moralistic view in 1711 in the *Spectator* and been followed by Samuel Johnson. As D. W. Lucas has reminded us, however, the translation of *hamartia* by 'flaw' still continues to encourage the demand for poetic justice.

In Germany, according to Kurt von Fritz, Lessing had been the first to get back close to a true understanding of Aristotle. 'In den Ausführungen Lessings in der Hamburgischen Dramaturgie findet sich, wenn man genau aufmerkt, alles, was zu einem richtigen Verständnis der griechischen Tragödie gehört. Aber vieles ist nicht ausgeführt. Vor allem hat sich Lessing über die aristotelische *hamartia* und den modernen Begriff der tragischen Schuld nicht ausführlich geäußert' (von Fritz, p. 61). Max Kommerell, in his thorough study *Lessing und Aristoteles*, had already found clear indications 'daß Lessing *hamartia* als verzeihliche, nur halbfreiwillige sittliche Verfehlung aufgefaßt hat. Aber es ist auffallend', he continues, 'wie er die Erörterung dieses Begriffs umgeht',[8] in discussing Weisse's Richard III, for example. His ideas had been clearer in the correspondence on tragedy with Nicolai and Mendelssohn. It is surprising, von Fritz notes, to find that in the translation by M. C. Curtius used by Lessing the word 'Versehen' is used alongside 'Fehler' for *hamartia*, suggesting the interpretation 'Versagen der Erkenntnis' rather than 'sittliches Vergehen'.

When Schiller gave his address on 'Die Schaubühne als eine moralische Anstalt betrachtet' in Mannheim, he expected, says von Fritz, 'eine noch unmittelbarere moralische Wirkung des ernsten Dramas überhaupt auf die jeweilige Gegenwart, als sie Corneille je angestrebt hatte' (von Fritz, p. 63), but in his maturity he turned away from these ideas both in theory and practice. 'Die wohlgemeinte Absicht', he wrote in 'Über den Grund des Vergnügens an tragischen Gegenständen', 'das moralisch Gute überall als höchsten Zweck zu verfolgen, die in der Kunst schon so manches Mittelmäßige erzeugt und in Schutz nahm, hat auch in der Theorie einen ähnlichen Schaden angerichtet' (von Fritz, p. 64). Following the critical tendencies of the time, he was naturally drawn both towards the Greeks and towards Shakespeare, but his works finally 'nähern sich bis zu einem gewissen Grade der antiken Tragödie, ohne diese doch zu erreichen', as von Fritz (p. 64) shows in detail for *Die Braut von Messina*.

In the course of the joint reflections of Goethe and Schiller on the essential nature of drama and epic in 1797, prompted by the comparison of their respective problems with *Wallenstein* and *Hermann und Dorothea*, Greek tragedy and the *Poetics* were a continual source of fruitful ideas, as we see from the Goethe–Schiller correspondence. They are particularly struck by the empirical character of the *Poetics*, as a summary of Greek practice. Striking observations abound, but there is space here only for one of the best, in Goethe's letter to Schiller of 26 April 1797:

Im Trauerspiel kann und soll das Schicksal, oder welches einerlei ist, die entschiedene Natur des Menschen, die ihn blind da- oder dorthin führt, walten und herrschen; sie muß ihn niemals zu seinem Zweck, sondern immer von seinem Zweck abführen, der Held darf seines Verstandes nicht mächtig sein, der Verstand darf gar nicht in die Tragödie entrieren als bei Nebenpersonen zur Desavantage des Haupthelden usw. — Im Epos ist es gerade umgekehrt; bloß der Verstand, wie in der *Odyssee*, oder eine zweckmäßige Leidenschaft, wie in der *Ilias*, sind epische Agentien.

This seems to show how fully Goethe was already aware of the close connexion between the working out of destiny in Greek tragedy and the relationship between gods and men described by the Greeks as the work of what they called *ate* — '*bewilderment, infatuation, reckless impulse,* caused by *judicial blindness* sent by the gods, Hom.: hence *Ate* is personified as *the goddess of mischief*, or *reckless conduct*'.[9] One modern scholar has this to say of the *Agamemnon* of Aeschylus:

'La race', dit le Chœur (*Agamemnon* 1566), 'est rivée à l'Egarement'. Et ce que j'ai traduit 'Egarement', l'Até, c'est quelque chose qui ne vient pas de l'homme, c'est une sorte de brouillard tombé du ciel par lequel les Puissants d'en haut aveuglent l'insecte humain, puis l'emportent comme en un tourbillon, en sorte qu'il ne sait plus ce qu'il fait, qu'il agit comme un dément. 'Un daimôn aux lourdes serres nous a cruellement meurtris', dit Clytemnestre elle-même (*Agamemnon* 1660). Un *daimôn*, c'est à dire une Force surnaturelle, cette Force qui, pour chaque homme, détermine son destin.[10]

We must look here, surely for one important source of Goethe's ideas on 'das Dämonische'.

Goethe and Schiller were probably not aware that Hugh Blair, the first Professor of Rhetoric and Belles Lettres in Edinburgh, had begun in the early 1760s to draw a distinction in his lectures, first published in 1783, between two principal types of tragedy, the 'fate tragedy' of the Greeks and the modern 'theatre of passion', examples of which he took from Shakespeare and a wide range of English and French plays. The *Oedipus Rex*, he says, 'excites horror rather than pity . . . It leaves no impression favorable to virtue or humanity . . . Modern tragedy has aimed at a higher object, by becoming more the theatre of passion: pointing out to men the consequences of their own misconduct . . .',[11] exactly as Corneille and Dacier had said tragedy should. When Lenz wrote his *Anmerkungen über das Theater* in 1774, with its contrast between Greek fate tragedy and modern character tragedy like that of Shakespeare, he totally rejected the 'rules', ridiculed Aristotle and French classicism and advocated an episodic type of play like his own with a tendency towards social reform. It was left to Marmontel to draw a systematic contrast between the fate tragedy of the Ancients and the modern tragedy of passion, examples of which he drew from Corneille. This was in the long article 'Tragédie' in a supplement of 1777 to the great *Encyclopédie*. Contrasting the two 'systems', he sees several aesthetic advantages in the Greek type of tragedy, though he doubts whether it can be profitably imitated by the moderns, except in rehandling the old myths. Schiller came close to this view in 1797: 'Ich finde, je mehr ich über mein eigenes Geschäft und über die Behandlungsart der Tragödie bei den Griechen nachdenke, daß der ganze Cardo rei

B

in der Kunst liegt, eine poetische Fabel zu erfinden.'[12] What he writes about the *Trachiniae* of Sophocles anticipates much of what we shall find Karl Reinhardt saying about the same play:

> Ich habe diese Tage den Philoktet und die Trachinierinnen gelesen, und die letztern mit besonders großem Wohlgefallen. Wie trefflich ist der ganze Zustand, das Empfinden, die Existenz der Dejanira gefaßt! Wie ganz ist sie die Hausfrau des Herkules, wie individuell, wie nur für diesen einzigen Fall passend ist dies Gemälde, und doch wie tief menschlich, wie ewig wahr und allgemein. Auch im Philoktet ist alles aus der Lage geschöpft, was sich nur daraus schöpfen ließ, und bei dieser Eigentümlichkeit des Falles ruht doch alles wieder auf dem ewigen Grund der menschlichen Natur.[13]

What he goes on to say about the characters of Greek tragedy being 'mehr oder weniger idealische Masken', and not individuals in the same sense as in Goethe or Shakespeare, comes very close to what John Jones writes, as we shall see, about the difference between the Orestes of Aeschylus and Shakespeare's Hamlet.

The most striking expression which I have encountered of the view taken today by classical scholars of the essence of Greek tragedy is in a lecture with that title by the great French scholar A. J. Festugière, classicist and historian of religion. It begins as follows:

> Il n'y a qu'une tragédie au monde, c'est la grecque, celle des trois Tragiques grecs, Eschyle, Sophocle, Euripide. C'est la seule en effet qui conserve le sens tragique de la vie, parce qu'elle en maintient les deux éléments. D'une part les catastrophes humaines, qui sont constantes, de tous les temps et de tous les pays. D'autre part le sentiment que ces catastrophes sont dues à des puissances surnaturelles, qui se cachent dans le mystère, dont les décisions nous sont inintelligibles, si bien que le misérable insecte humain se sent écrasé sous le poids d'une Fatalité impitoyable, dont il cherche en vain à percer le sens. Supprimez l'un de ces deux facteurs, il n'y a plus de vraie tragédie. Et c'est le cas, par exemple, de la tragédie française du XVIIe siècle. Parce qu'on est alors — du moins officiellement — dans un âge de foi, le facteur surnaturel, ce facteur proprement tragique de la Fatalité, a été supprimé. Pour ces catholiques rationalistes du XVIIe siècle, tout est clair, il n'y a plus de mystère. Dieu a créé l'homme heureux. L'homme a péché. De ce péché résulte la misère humaine. Elle est rachetée par le Fils de

Dieu, dans lequel il suffit de croire . . . Il n'y a plus cette confrontation
antique de l'insecte humain qui se débat dans la nuit, avec des dieux
indifférents auxquels il ne comprend rien . . . On tombe . . . dans le
drame bourgeois, l'anecdote de tous les jours. Il n'y a plus de vraie
tragédie.

Even in Racine's *Phèdre*, that glory of the French stage, we find,
if we compare it with the *Hippolytus* of Euripides, that 'le
garçon n'est plus ce héros miraculeusement pur, ce dévot de la
déesse pure, Artémis. Il n'est plus qu'un gamin quelconque qui,
ayant trouvé sa "girl", n'a que faire d'une femme mûre. Et
Phèdre de son côté est simplement jalouse.'[14]

Festugière goes on to discuss the different ways in which the
three great tragic poets of the Greeks try to find some crack in
the wall which faces 'l'insecte humain', some hint at least of
justice in the ways of the gods to man. In the hero of the
Oedipus Rex and the heroine of the *Trachiniae* of Sophocles he
finds 'nulle faute', but an 'erreur tragique'. A similar interpretation of *hamartia* with regard to Aristotle's favourite example
is advanced in a lively article by E. R. Dodds,[15] where the then
Professor of Greek at Oxford, after a bout of examining,
analyses the interpretations of that work he has just encountered
in a number of scripts. The three most favoured were as follows.
To one group of candidates the tragedy justified the ways of the
gods to man, because Oedipus got only what he had deserved,
for some through his character, for others through his treatment
of Creon or for others again through his fatal *hamartia*, leading
to parricide and incest. Another group saw the work as a
tragedy of destiny, in which man is shown as a puppet manipu-
lated by the gods, and a third group saw Sophocles simply as
a pure artist, for whom the gods were just part of the poetic
machinery. Dodds expounds the interpretation of *hamartia* as
error, and traces the history of the 'moral flaw' theory. He
speaks of Dacier's 'puerile idea' of poetic justice and rejects also
Freud's view of the *Oedipus Rex* as a Tragedy of Destiny, in
which human freedom is denied. 'Neither in Homer nor Sophocles', he says, 'does divine foreknowledge of certain events
imply that all human actions are predetermined', quoting on this

point A. E. Gomme's formulation: 'The gods know the future, but they do not order it'. Similarly H. D. F. Kitto speaks several times in his *Greek Tragedy* of 'oracles that do not determine but only foresee'.[16] The cause of the hero's ruin, Dodds insists, is not fate, or the gods, but his own strength and courage, his loyalty to Thebes and his loyalty to the truth. There is no hereditary curse at work, as in the *Oresteia*.

In spite of the rejection by modern scholars of that interpretation of *Oedipus Rex* as a fate tragedy which was a commonplace of eighteenth-century criticism, the ordinary reader probably still shares the hero's own feeling that supernatural forces have brought calamity upon him, and not his own actions. In the rehandling by Euripides in his old age of the whole Theban legend in *The Phoenician Women*, he makes Oedipus, looking back on the whole series of catastrophes in his life after their culmination in the death of his two sons before Thebes, begin his monologue with the words, in Vellacott's translation:

> O Destiny! You created me, beyond all men,
>   For life-long wretchedness and pain,

and makes him speak of the 'divine malevolence' which has forced him to blind himself. The apparent jealousy of the gods for mortals, often for whole families, is a recurrent theme in Greek tragedy. It is well discussed by Festugière in the lecture from which we have quoted, where he points to other examples, not only in the tragedians but also in the historians, notably in Herodotus, in the dialogue, for instance, in *Histories*, 1, 32, in which Solon reminds Croesus, who is so sure of his own good fortune, that the gods are always envious of the happiness of men and delight in making them suffer, or in the story of Polycrates (III, 40), familiar from Schiller's ballad.

So too J. M. Bremer, discussing *Oedipus Rex* in his *Hamartia*, insists that the tragedy is not simply what Waldock has called 'an epigram in ill-luck'. 'It is of the essence of misfortune and ill-luck', he writes, 'for Sophocles and for all Greek consciousness before him, that it should come "from the gods" (theóthen). From our earliest account of the Oedipus story (*Odyssey*, 11, 271 ff.) two things are clear: not only that the incest is a *hamartia*, but also and most emphatically that the role of the gods is paramount: Oedipus is represented as suffering "nach der Götter verderblichem Ratschluß" (Voß).' Similarly 'his self-blinding cannot be dissociated from the activity of the gods', any more than his earlier 'blindness', 'the demonic aspect of which is as strongly stressed as the human aspect' (Bremer, pp. 161 ff.). Bremer discusses the *Trachiniae* on similar lines, as the tragedy of 'a noble person' who 'comes to ruin not because of any moral fault but because she commits a grave error by sending a present to her unfaithful husband: this present, instead of exercising its supposed magic power of renewing Heracles' love for her, turns out to be a trap laid by the dying centaur Nessus'. The 'demonic quality of her existence' as 'a victim of Aphrodite's power from her youth' is apparent throughout (Bremer, pp. 145–53). The fine passage quoted by Bremer from Karl Reinhardt's *Sophocles* strongly supports his view of Deianeira and is of special interest here as anticipating to some extent the ideas of Jones and Redfield about 'status-determined circumstances' in Greek tragedy:

Abgesondert und für sich betrachtet, müßte dieser Irrtum wie ein kläglicher, bedauerlicher Zufall wirken. Doch indem er sich in ihre Schicksalskurve einfügt, wie sie von Beginn, mit dem Prolog, vor uns schwankend zu erheben und auf ihren Fall zu steuern anfing, wird er zur notwendigen Vollendung ihres Wesens. Dadurch, daß der Irrtum, ihre Übereilung, ihr Unmaß, aus nichts anderem kommt als aus dem Willen, Maß zu halten, nicht sich zu verlieren, nicht Rache zu üben, nicht sich aufzulehnen, nicht die Schranken ihres Umkreises zu überschreiten: eben dadurch wird auch sie, nicht anders als der Aias [the Ajax of Sophocles], zum Ecce der menschlichen Verstrickung und Begrenzung. Die Vereinzelung und der Verlust der nährenden und hegenden Verbindungen, in die das Dasein eingelassen ist, nimmt hier die Form unschuldiger Verschuldung an, durch die die Schuldige sich selbst um ihres Lebens Sinn und Mitte bringt. (Bremer, p. 149)

It is not surprising that Blair and Marmontel, Lenz and Schiller should have contrasted Greek fate tragedy with modern character tragedy, though there is far more variety in Greek tragedy than this formulation implies. The emphasis on character expresses our modern psychological bias, our attempt to understand all action from within. Some recent writers on Greek tragedy have stressed the difference between this approach and what they now find in Aristotelian theory and the Greek tragedy down to his time on which it is based. James M. Redfield, in the introduction to his study of *Nature and Culture in the Iliad: the Tragedy of Hector*,[17] makes clear his strong agreement on this point with the view expressed by the Oxford scholar John Jones in his *Aristotle and Greek Tragedy*.[18] He quotes Jones as saying, in a comparison of the Orestes of Aeschylus with Shakespeare's Hamlet: 'The one is isolated by his status-determined circumstances, the other by his *psyche*-determined incapacity to act.' Aristotle's *Poetics* and the plays it describes are misread, according to this view, by moderns looking everywhere for the 'inward', for as Aristotle says: 'Tragedy is the imitation, not of human beings, but of action and life' (Chapter 6). As Jones sees it,

Aristotle is assaulting the now settled habit in which we see action issuing from a solitary focus of consciousness — secret, inward, interesting — and in which the status of action must always be adjectival: action qualifies; it tells us things we want to know about the individual promoting it . . . about the state of affairs 'inside' him . . . To our sense of characteristic conduct Aristotle opposes that of characterful action: the essence of conduct being that it is mine or yours; of action, that it is out there — an object for men to contemplate. (Redfield, p. 33)

One way of finding in action something interesting in itself, and not just a clue to psychical processes, is the sociological approach adopted by Redfield, an admirer of Claude Lévi-Strauss (e.g. of *La pensée sauvage*):

In telling a story the poet employs and persuades us to certain assumptions about the sources and conditions of action. He thus, in effect, takes a view of culture. And further: since he is telling his story to an audience, the meaning he conveys must be a meaning to *them*. So we can go on to ask: what sort of audience would have found this story meaningful? Here (and only here) we reach culture itself. (Redfield, p. 23)

It is in this way that Redfield illuminates the 'tragedy of Hector'. He sees tragedy — and aesthetic 'fictions' in general — as a means of enabling the audience (or reader) to view real-life situations and their attendant emotions at a certain 'psychical distance' — to use a term of Edward Bullough's, whose work has meant so much for Professor Wilkinson. The emotions people would normally experience in real life, by being made intelligible in a plot involving their own natural assumptions about life in society, about culture, may be purified — a novel explanation of 'katharsis'.

These brief notes on two very original works are of course too condensed to do more than point a finger, but a cultural approach of this kind to the problems of tragedy may seem to others, as it does to me, to have affinities with some *obiter dicta* of Goethe's about tragedy, and particularly with what he said, at widely separated periods of his life, about his own inability to write a real tragedy, if we take this as meaning something like a Greek tragedy as seen by Festugière.[19] The assumptions of Greek tragedy were impossible, he knew, for us moderns. 'Dergleichen ist unserer jetzigen Denkungsweise nicht mehr gemäß, es ist veraltet, überhaupt mit unseren religiösen Vorstellungen in Widerspruch', as he said to Eckermann in the last month of his life. 'Verarbeitet ein moderner Poet solche frühere Ideen zu einem Theaterstück, so sieht es immer aus wie eine Art von Affektation. Es ist ein Anzug, der längst aus der Mode gekommen ist, und der uns, gleich der römischen Toga, nicht mehr zu Gesichte steht.' Goethe could never have simulated so stark a view of life and culture as would have been required. The traditions he inherited were fundamentally Christian despite the Enlightenment, which still thought of God — and man — as good. Humane ideas of this kind, Festugière tells us, were unknown in Greece before Plato:

Il faut avoir ressenti jusqu'au fond de l'être la misère humaine pour comprendre le secret ressort du tragique dans la tragédie grecque. Et il faut avoir compris ce secret ressort pour se rendre compte de ce qu'ont eu vraiment de révolutionnaire, de totalement neuf, d'inouï, les paroles de Platon dans le Timée (29 E 1) ... 'Dieu est bon. Or, en qui est bon, jamais, à propos de rien, ne se forme aucune pensée de jalousie.'

Reminding his audience, by examples like those quoted above, of the almost universal belief of the Greeks before Plato that the gods were powerful indeed, but not good and not well-disposed towards men, he calls Plato's pronouncement in the *Timaeus* 'un prodigieux *acte de foi*' and concludes: 'Et l'on mesure, dès lors, tout ce que le christianisme doit à Platon.'[20] In Goethe's late conversation with Eckermann we see how firmly, in spite of appearances, the enlightened view of our common humanity was still founded in Christian ethics, and perhaps it is not fanciful to find in it also a reminder of his firm belief that to understand a foreign country's literature one must have as wide an acquaintance as possible with its whole culture.

REFERENCES

[1] Kurt von Fritz, 'Tragische Schuld und poetische Gerechtigkeit in der griechischen Tragödie', *Studium Generale*, 8 (1955), 194–237, reprinted in his *Antike und moderne Tragödie* (Berlin, 1962), pp. 1–112. Further references relate to this reprinted version, henceforth cited as 'von Fritz'.

[2] Humphry House, *Aristotle's Poetics: A Course of Eight Lectures*, revised with a preface by Colin Hardie (London, 1956).

[3] *Aristotle on the Art of Poetry*, translated and edited by Ingram Bywater (Oxford, 1909).

[4] Aristotle, *Poetics*, edited by D. W. Lucas (Oxford, 1968), Appendix IV, pp. 299–307.

[5] *Aristotle's Theory of Poetry and Fine Art*, translated and edited by Samuel H. Butcher (London, 1895).

[6] J. M. Bremer, '*Hamartia*': *Tragic Error in the Poetics of Aristotle and in Greek Tragedy* (Amsterdam, 1969), henceforward cited as 'Bremer'.

[7] W. C. Greene, *Moira: Fate, Good and Evil in Greek Thought* (Cambridge, Massachusetts, 1944).

[8] Max Kommerell, *Lessing und Aristoteles* (Frankfurt/Main, 1940).

[9] *An Intermediate Greek–English Lexicon* (Oxford, 1972), p. 129.

[10] A. J. Festugière, *De l'essence de la tragédie grecque* (Paris, 1969), p. 15.

[11] Hugh Blair, *Lectures on Rhetoric and Belles Lettres*, tenth edition (London and Edinburgh, 1806), III, 305 ff. (Lecture xlvi).

[12] Letter to Goethe, 4 April 1797.

[13] Ibid.

[14] Festugière, pp. 11 ff.

[15] E. R. Dodds, 'On misunderstanding the *Oedipus Rex*', in his *The Ancient Concept of Progress* (Oxford, 1973), pp. 64–77.

[16] H. D. F. Kitto, *Greek Tragedy*, paperback edition (London, 1973), p. 298.

[17] James M. Redfield, *Nature and Culture in the Iliad: The Tragedy of Hector* (Chicago, 1975), henceforward cited as 'Redfield'.

[18] John Jones, *Aristotle and Greek Tragedy* (Oxford, 1962).

[19] See E. Grumach, *Goethe und die Antike* (Berlin, 1949), I, 241 f.

[20] Festugière, pp. 26 ff.

Lessing and Pierre Bayle

By H. B. NISBET

IT IS NOT easy for us to understand the immense popularity which the *Dictionnaire historique et critique* of Pierre Bayle, the philosopher of Rotterdam, enjoyed throughout Europe for much of the eighteenth century. By the time it reached its second edition in 1702, it contained between seven and eight million words.[1] And in the third, posthumous edition of 1720, it filled four folio volumes, with a total of well over 3,000 pages.[2] On the face of it, it was a massive reference work, strictly for the learned. It is a biographical dictionary, with alphabetical articles, and concentrates not on crowned heads and illustrious figures of public life, but on scholars, writers, and men of religion, often of the most obscure identity. There are no articles, for example, on Homer, Plato, Sophocles, Augustus, Aquinas, Montaigne, Racine, or Richelieu. A few Old Testament figures and semi-legendary saints are included, but there are no articles on New Testament figures, apart from St John. Even Moses and Jesus Christ are absent, although Mohammed is treated at length.

The presentation likewise scarcely seems calculated to ensure instant popularity. The terse and strictly factual articles refer the reader at once to enormous footnotes, often filling over three-quarters of the page, for the most diverse information on sources and earlier authorities; and the footnotes frequently expand into long digressions of a historical, philosophical, theological, or scientific nature, interspersed with bizarre anecdotes, and with polemical sallies against Bayle's now forgotten adversaries among the Calvinist refugees in Holland. Further footnotes are appended to the footnotes themselves.

Nevertheless, few works in the eighteenth century achieved such wide circulation and popular resonance as the *Dictionnaire*,

13

whose formative influence on the Enlightenment can scarcely be overestimated. Gerhard Sauder, in his article 'Bayle-Rezeption in der deutschen Aufklärung', gives some idea of the work's impact in Germany, where it was studied by all the leading writers of the century.[3] The situation was similar in France, where students queued outside libraries to read it (Sauder, p. 86*), and in England, where a greatly enlarged ten-volume edition appeared between 1734 and 1741.[4] Voltaire, Gibbon, Hume, and Diderot were all decisively influenced by it.[5]

The reasons for Bayle's success were manifold. They lay in the temper of the work as a whole, and in the sheer diversity of its contents. As the title indicates, its temper was critical. And after a century of dogmatic metaphysics and warring confessions, each of which had claimed exclusive truth for its own doctrines and the certain perdition of its enemies, the age was ready for it. It reviewed the accumulated learning of the past with remorseless scrutiny, subjecting not only historical reports, but also all major philosophies and — more important still — the central doctrines of Christianity, to penetrating and destructive examination. For Pierre Bayle was as complete a sceptic as any thinker in modern times. He maintained that reason, having devoured all dogmatic systems, must in turn devour itself. Its enquiries must end in contradiction and absurdity, followed by suspense of judgement; and the only defence against total uncertainty lies in unreasoning faith in the truths of revelation.

Despite his protestations of faith, Bayle was soon attacked from several quarters as a dangerous heretic. The notoriety he thereby incurred was an essential ingredient of his success. The angry clergyman quoted in Sauder's article (p. 94*) was typical of many critics when he warned the public 'daß wann sie lange genug dieselben durch geblättert / sie sich endlich in einen verdammlichen *Scepticismum* und folgends in den *Atheismum* selber gestürzet siehet. Von solchen *Scriptis* sauget die Jugend . . . den ersten Gifft in sich / weil sie von ihren alten Lehrern unterm Vorwand der *Novitäten* / aufs allerbeste *recommendirt* werden'. But the fulminations of such diehards merely lengthened the queues at the bookshops; and when Bayle, in reply to

his critics, added to his work four apologetic *Éclaircissements* —
on atheists, on Manicheans, on Sceptics, and on the obscene
passages in the *Dictionnaire* — these simply helped readers to
track down the objectionable passages more quickly. (As
Lessing once said of an index of ribaldries in Plautus's works
which one editor added for the benefit of delicate readers:
'Dieses werden die Keuschen, so wie die Unkeuschen, zu
gebrauchen wissen'.[6])

As to the contents of the work, what to us today is at worst
a fundamental fault and at best a deterrent — Bayle's haphazard
approach and readiness to leap from one subject to another
— from the subtleties of Calvinist theology to the reliability of
ancient Greek texts, from Cartesian cosmogony to Roman law,
from the genealogies of the patriarchs to disputed details in the
lives of medieval schoolmen — was to his age of integral culture
a recommendation and an inspiration. The schoolboy in search
of basic facts, the scholar looking for out-of-the-way information, and even the country squire in pursuit of racy stories to
entertain his male companions after dinner — none of them
returned empty handed.[7] As one reviewer put it, Bayle was 'ein
Mann vor alle Leute' (Sauder, p. 93*).

And lastly, for all his infuriating pedantry — what a later
admirer, Ludwig Feuerbach, described as his 'ermüdende
Unermüdlichkeit'[8] — Bayle's style is enlivened by a subtle
humour and a pervasive irony. His irony not only conveys his
tolerant amusement at the foolishness of mankind. It also fur-
nished his successors, in an age of censorship, with an infallible
means of undermining dogma without exposing themselves
to accusations which could be made to stick. In short, the
Dictionnaire is as good an introduction to the *Aufklärung* as any.

This, then, was the work to which the young Lessing, soon
after he left Leipzig university, formed a lasting addiction, and
which supplied him with so many of his tools as a critic, antiquarian, and controversialist. The full extent of his knowledge
of and debt to Bayle's works has not hitherto been explored in
detail. Apart from a few pages in T. W. Danzel's biography of
Lessing, first published in 1850,[9] a general chapter in H. E.

Allison's *Lessing and the Enlightenment*,[10] and Sauder's recent article, there are only brief references to the question in the secondary literature. (I shall return later to the reasons for this neglect.)

It is possible that Lessing first heard of Bayle from his father, whose dissertation of 1717 included criticisms of the French thinker.[11] Or he may have first encountered Bayle's ideas through Leibniz, whose *Théodicée* of 1710 is directed against Bayle's doubts concerning the ability of reason to defend the Christian mysteries and to justify the role of evil in the best of possible worlds. What is certain is that Lessing was using the *Dictionnaire* by 1749 or 1750 at the latest. His essay on Plautus, published in 1750, is not only written in Bayle's manner, but expressly refers to Bayle (LM, IV, 78). In 1749, Lessing's drama *Die Juden*, with its Bayle-like message of religious tolerance, had also appeared. And the first of his theological writitings, probably of 1750, the *Gedanken über die Herrnhuter*, has rightly been described as a 'Bayle-inspired analysis of the relation between religious belief and moral action' (Allison, p. 52).

In 1751, Lessing began to study the *Dictionnaire* intensively. Bayle had at first conceived of his project as a dictionary of errors — of the errors he had discovered in earlier biographical compendia — and Lessing now adopted a similar role, in various reviews and essays, in relation to reference works which had appeared since Bayle's death. This soon grew into the ambitious project of a general criticism of C. G. Jöcher's *Allgemeines Gelehrten-Lexicon*, to consist of alphabetical biographical articles, parallel to those of Jöcher, but correcting Jöcher's countless mistakes. Nine of the articles were published in Lessing's collected *Schrifften* of 1753 (LM, V, 127–42), but at Jöcher's request, Lessing had already — uncharacteristically — agreed to abandon the plan and to place his materials at Jöcher's disposal. In the articles he did complete, Lessing models his approach on Bayle, and repeatedly cites the *Dictionnaire* as a means of correcting Jöcher's deficiencies. By this time, Lessing was using both Gottsched's German translation of the *Dictionnaire* and the third or a subsequent French edition.

I do not have space to go into all his many borrowings from it, or into the other writings by and on Bayle which he consulted; but I do have evidence to show that he knew a good deal more about Bayle's life and works than has hitherto been suspected. I should, however, point out that his reception of Bayle was by no means uncritical. His attitude towards Bayle fluctuated from the start, and was modified by other influences, especially that of Leibniz. But the main point I wish to make here is that the *Dictionnaire* was a work on which Lessing relied throughout his career, and which played a decisive part in his intellectual development (see Danzel, 1, 219).

Before I turn to the main areas of Lessing's thought on which the ideas of Bayle impinged, I should like to mention briefly some of the characteristics the two thinkers have in common.

Similarities are evident even in their lives and basic attitudes. Both were sons of Protestant clergymen, who early learned to question their inherited faith. Both devoted much time to journalism in the first half of their careers as writers, and Bayle's periodical *Nouvelles de la république des lettres* shows the same breadth of interest as do Lessing's reviews for the Berlin periodicals. Both, for all their intellectual friendships, were ultimately solitary figures, who preferred the life of private scholarship to academic appointments.[12]

Lessing, of course, unlike Bayle, was a creative writer. But in his non-literary works — the antiquarian, theological, and theoretical writings — his affinities with the French writer are striking. There is the same erudition and delight in apparently insignificant facts. There is the same preoccupation with the classics, and Lessing's studies of Plautus (1750) and Sophocles (1760) were intended to fill gaps in the *Dictionnaire*. The thought of both writers is occasional in character (see Danzel, 1, 223), and such unity as their writings possess is one of personality, of characteristic responses, rather than clearly formulated ideology (see Feuerbach, p. 189). For Bayle, in his ceaseless criticism of received doctrines, his defence of the persecuted and pleas for universal tolerance, and Lessing, the seeker after truth who refuses to compromise with any dogma, are kindred spirits, and both are morally impressive characters.

Among the main characteristics they have in common that of style must come high on the list. More than once, Lessing speaks with admiration of Bayle's style (LM, v, 146 and viii, 293), which he at first attempted to imitate directly. The essay on Sophocles is a good example, with its terse, three-page text, accompanied by two alphabets of notes, with further alphabets of notes on the notes themselves, outdoing even Bayle in its discursiveness. The formula 'Man erlaube mir . . . eine kleine Ausschweifung' (LM, viii, 349), followed by a long and erudite note, is characteristic. But it is in the *Laokoon*, although its plan is philosophical rather than biographical, that Lessing succeeds best in capturing Bayle's studied informality, his agreeable discursiveness, and his variety of tone and subject-matter. We know, of course, that the *Laokoon* began as a piece of rigorous deduction from the concepts of space and time, of motion and rest;[13] but Lessing then went out of his way to give it as casual an appearance as possible. Like Bayle, he played down the importance of abstract reasoning in favour of empirical fact, with numerous concrete examples and references to sources. And his footnotes and calculated digressions, like Bayle's, are long and varied, containing historical reflections, criticism of sources, philosophical arguments, polemics, and curious anecdotes, sometimes of a scurrilous nature. Here, Lessing adopts some of those features of Bayle's style which made the *Dictionnaire* so popular a work. But Lessing, when he chooses, has a gift for economy and precision which the French thinker lacked, for at his worst, Bayle can be verbose, repetitive, and conscientious to the point of pedantry.

Another activity in which both thinkers excel is in drawing distinctions between related, but often confused, conceptual areas (see Danzel, 1, 235). For the two are first and foremost analytical intellects; and just as Bayle draws sharp distinctions between religion and ethics, reason and faith, and theory and practice, so also does Lessing differentiate between hitherto confused areas, such as poetry and the visual arts, and, like

Bayle, reason and revelation, religion and ethics. Bayle's thought, however, is almost entirely analytical. Indeed, he delights in demonstrating that certain modes of knowledge are irreconcilable. But Lessing at times follows Leibniz, whose influence constantly modifies that of the French philosopher, in seeking to harmonize apparently irreconcilable opposites, such as reason and revelation.

Not surprisingly, Bayle delights in paradoxes, for he continually seeks to show that rational thought is inherently paradoxical. In analysing the doctrine of original sin, for example, he likens the God who permitted it to a mother who allows her daughter to go unescorted to a ball, knowing all the while that she is certain to be seduced (*Dictionnaire*, III, 2206, article 'Pauliciens'). And in defending all acts done in good conscience, he did not hesitate to apply this to acts of apparent immorality, citing the example of justified adultery between a married woman and a stranger whom she in good conscience believes to be her husband (OD, II, 468). Lessing revelled in such paradoxes, of course. His fragmentary essay of 1763 or 1764, *Von der Art und Weise der Fortpflanzung und Ausbreitung der christlichen Religion*, is a good example, with the typically Baylean paradox that the Romans were entirely justified in persecuting the early Christians, not because they were Christians, but because they were lawbreakers (LM, XIV, 324–25). Bayle had similarly declared 'toute Secte qui s'en prend aux loix des sociétez, et qui rompt les liens de la sûreté publique, ... mérite d'être incessament exterminée par le glaive du Magistrat' (*Commentaire philosophique*, in OD, II, 412).

Provocative statements such as these ensured that Bayle and Lessing were both constantly involved in controversies and polemics. Since Bayle saw the role of reason as essentially negative, his arguments in the *Dictionnaire* are governed more often by a desire to refute his opponents than by any constructive purpose, as Leibniz disapprovingly noted.[14] Lessing's first major polemical foray, the critique of Jöcher, was undertaken in direct imitation of Bayle. And indeed, the *Dictionnaire* is his model in all his early attacks on careless scholarship, faulty translations, and inadequate historical research, particularly in his journalistic and antiquarian writings. Most of his later polemics, of course, are in the field of theology. His feud with Goeze is remarkably similar to that of Bayle with his arch-enemy and fellow-refugee Jurieu, who eventually succeeded in having Bayle removed from office. Lessing and Bayle, then, both spent their last years in a series of disputes with theologians; and both confessed that they derived considerable enjoyment from so doing (LM, xviii, 265; cf. OD, iv, 883 f.).

I should like to devote the latter part of this paper to the main issues in Lessing's thought on which Bayle's influence made itself most strongly felt: the questions of *religious and Biblical criticism*, of *scepticism*, and of *morality and universal tolerance*.

Firstly: religious and Biblical criticism. Whether Bayle was a sincere Christian, as he claimed he was, or a man who set out to undermine Christianity while claiming to defend it, is still uncertain. (The problem is, of course, precisely the same with Lessing.) Bayle scholars today include several who defend him as a sincere Calvinist,[15] but the majority of Bayle's readers since his death in 1706 — and this includes most of the leaders of the Enlightenment — have regarded him as a freethinker and remorseless enemy of the dogmatists. For although Bayle claimed that, by showing up the irrationality of Christian doctrines and exposing the immorality of Old Testament heroes such as King David, he could then elevate faith upon the ruins of reason, it seemed to many that his true aim was to elevate reason upon the ruins of faith.

Lessing certainly saw him as a critic of religion and alternately condemned and imitated his procedures. For in the early 1750s, soon after he first encountered Bayle's works, he warns his readers against Bayle as one of 'die fürchterlichsten Bestreiter unserer Religion' (LM, v, 146), and criticizes Bayle's favourite tactic, as in the notorious article 'David', of dwelling on the crimes of Old Testament heroes (LM, iv, 372 f.). Yet before long, Lessing was himself employing Bayle's tactics with considerable skill. For example, in the fragment mentioned above,

Von der Art und Weise der Fortpflanzung und Ausbreitung der christlichen Religion, he sets out to refute one of the traditional proofs of the divine origin of Christianity, from the speed and success with which it triumphed, against all odds, in the Roman Empire. Lessing replies that it in fact arose and spread by a perfectly natural process, and under highly favourable circumstances. This is simply a variation of Bayle's argument, in the article 'Mahomet' in the *Dictionnaire*, that the proof of a religion's authenticity from the speed of its propagation would favour Mohammedanism more than Christianity. Lessing's opening sentence, in fact, is closely modelled on a parallel passage in that article in Gottsched's German translation of the *Dictionnaire*. Lessing's sentence reads:

Unter den Gründen für die *Wahrheit der christlichen Religion* ist derjenige keiner von den geringsten, der von der Art und Weise *ihrer Fortpflanzung und Ausbreitung* hergenommen wird. (LM, xiv, 314)

And Bayle, in Gottsched's translation, runs as follows:

Hierdurch erhalten wir der christlichen Religion einen von den Beweisen ihrer Göttlichkeit: nämlich denjenigen, der aus ihrer schleunigen Fortpflanzung durch die ganze Welt hergenommen wird.[16]

To quote only one further example, Lessing's late fragment *Meines Arabers Beweis, daß nicht die Juden, sondern die Araber die wahren Nachkommen Abrahams sind*, is modelled on Bayle's ironic and destructive articles 'Abraham', 'Abimelech', and 'Sarah'. In it, Lessing argues that Isaac was probably the son not of Abraham, but of Abimelech, which would explain the alacrity with which Abraham obeyed God's command to sacrifice him (LM, xvi, 302 f.).

But in Lessing's later years, Bayle's influence on his Biblical criticism makes itself felt more indirectly, through the controversial fragments from H. S. Reimarus's *Apologie oder Schutzschrift für die vernünftigen Verehrer Gottes* which Lessing published in 1774–77 and which led to his controversy with Hauptpastor Goeze. Reimarus's critique of the Bible as a catalogue of crimes, contradictions, and absurdities draws heavily on the English

c

deists and on Bayle, whom he cites in the *Apologie* and emulates in his own chapter on King David.[17] The following ironic remark from Bayle's article 'David' is an example of the kind of thing which Reimarus, Voltaire, and many others in the eighteenth century learned to exploit:

[on Saul's failure to recognise David, his former retainer and harpist, at the Goliath incident] Si une Narration comme celle-ci se trouvoit dans Thucydide ou Tite Live, tous les Critiques concluroient que les Copistes auroient transposé les pages, oublié quelque chose en un lieu, répété quelque chose dans un autre, ou inséré des morceaux postiches dans l'Ouvrage de l'Auteur. Mais il faut se garder de pareils soupçons lors qu'il s'agit de la Bible. (*Dictionnaire*, II, 963*)

Lessing, in his late conflict with Goeze, became a master of such devious tactics, as the many discrepancies between his public professions of orthodoxy and his private utterances to his brother and to Elise Reimarus confirm.

Secondly, the question of scepticism. Bayle's scepticism extended to all metaphysical dogmas, but it was his religious scepticism which made the greatest impact on Lessing. His principal onslaught on the mysteries of Christian revelation occurs in a footnote to his article 'Pyrrho', in an imaginary dialogue between two Abbés, one of whom is a Pyrrhonian sceptic. The Pyrrhonian Abbé argues that Christianity actually supports Pyrrhonism, for as he says, the dogma of the Trinity refutes the idea of reason that two things which do not differ from a third do not differ from each other; the Incarnation refutes our conviction that a body and a rational soul are sufficient to constitute a person; the Eucharist refutes our rational belief that a body cannot be in several places at the same time; and the doctrine of original sin confounds all rational views of God, and supports rather the Manichean conception of two equally powerful deities, one good and the other evil, but neither omnipotent (*Dictionnaire*, III, 2306–8; see also IV, 3001–7). It was these objections, particularly that against original sin, which Leibniz took as the starting point of his *Théodicée*, in which he tries to show that the existence of evil is quite compatible with his own rationalistic picture of the best of possible worlds.

Again and again, Lessing was to return to these questions. He repeatedly attempted to rationalize the Christian mysteries, only to fall back on the conclusion that they are either above or contrary to reason. For example, in the early essay *Das Christentum der Vernunft*, he offers a detailed rationalization of the Trinity (LM, xiv, 175 ff.); yet in the essay *Über den Beweis des Geistes und der Kraft* of 1777, he says that his reason revolts against the proposition that God has a Son of the same nature as himself (LM, xiii, 6). But in *Die Erziehung des Menschengeschlechts* of around the same date, he attempts a new rationalization of the Trinity, and of the doctrines of the atonement and of original sin (LM, xiii, 430 f.). And finally, in *Die Religion Christi* of 1780, he concludes in sceptical tones that Christian doctrine is 'so ungewiß und vieldeutig, daß es schwerlich eine einzige Stelle gibt, mit welcher zwei Menschen, so lange als die Welt steht, den nämlichen Gedanken verbunden haben' (LM, xvi, 518). This same inconsistency can be found in his attacks on the German neologists who tried to reduce Christianity to the rational articles of natural religion (see LM, xii, 96 and xviii, 82 and 102 f.), that is, to reconcile reason and revelation, and his own readiness to do much the same thing himself.

What are we to make of such inconsistencies, running as they do throughout Lessing's life? They even occur within the compass of a single work, *Die Erziehung des Menschengeschlechts*, in the well-known discrepancy, real or apparent, between paragraphs 4 and 77, in the first of which we are told that revelation teaches us no more than reason could eventually discover on its own, and in the second, that revelation may teach us things which reason could never attain by its own devices. I have argued in an earlier paper that such inconsistencies are in keeping with Lessing's temperament, which demanded constant change and intellectual excitement, and with his declaration of 1777 that he preferred the search for truth to its possession.[18] But I would go further here, and argue that such inconsistencies are part of the sceptical tradition; that they do not conflict with an underlying scepticism; and that Lessing, even in his inconsistencies, was following a procedure which had been sanctioned by Pierre Bayle.

Lessing's former teacher Kästner wrote in 1786: 'Lessing
fand überhaupt mehr Vergnügen an Untersuchung und Beschäftigung des Verstandes als am ruhigen Besitze der Wahrheit,
ohngefähr wie Baile mit dem er soviel Aehnliches hat' (*Lessing
im Gespräch*, p. 334). What Kästner is referring to is Lessing's
habit of adopting theories provisionally, only to abandon them
for new and equally provisional ones, even at the price of
repeated inconsistency. This procedure has the approval of
Sextus Empiricus, the father of all systematic scepticism; for
Sextus points out, in his *Outlines of Pyrrhonism*, that the end of
scepticism is not cessation of enquiry, because to stop enquiring
on the grounds that all problems are rationally insoluble would
itself constitute a new form of dogmatism. Sextus declares:

to continue the investigation of problems is not inconsistent in
those who confess their ignorance of their real nature, but only in
those who believe they have an exact knowledge of them; since for
the latter the inquiry has already, as they suppose, reached its goal,
whereas for the former the ground on which all enquiry is based
— namely, the belief that they have not found the truth — still
subsists.[19]

But how am I to reconcile my contention that, in trying again
and again to rationalize the Christian mysteries, Lessing was
following not only the sceptical tradition, but Pierre Bayle
himself? For had not Bayle declared that these same mysteries
are *incompatible with reason*?

The answer, I think, lies in a passage from Leibniz's *Théodicée*
which Lessing quotes in 1773 in an essay on Leibniz and the
Trinity (LM, XII, 90). Leibniz, seeking as always to defend his
own belief that the world is the creation of a rational God
against Bayle's scepticism, points out that Bayle himself, in a
posthumous work, had admitted that reason may *one day* be able
to make rational sense of the Christian mysteries, such as that of
original sin. Bayle had said that, while reason may *at present* be
unable to resolve such mysteries, his work may stimulate someone *in the future* to devise a hitherto unknown solution. 'Il
semble donc', says Leibniz, 'qu'il [Bayle] ne prend les objections
pour invincibles, que par rapport à nos lumières présentes, et il

ne désespère pas . . . que quelqu'un ne puisse un jour trouver un dénouement peu connu jusqu'icy' (*Théodicée*, p. 66; cf. also p. 99).

What Lessing found here was a loophole in Bayle's scepticism, which allowed him to reconcile it in his own mind with the rationalism of Leibniz. Lessing then took it upon himself to attempt those rationalizations of the mysteries which Bayle had said might one day be possible, but which had hitherto eluded the rationalists. His final attempt is in *Die Erziehung des Menschengeschlechts* — but the very form in which he puts forward his rationalizations of the Trinity, etc., in that work — as *rhetorical questions* — makes it clear that he regarded them, in the sceptical tradition, not as dogmas, but only as provisional statements. And the same is true, I am convinced, of his apparent conversion to Spinoza's pantheism in the last years of his life. The ironic and jocular tone in which he expounded his Spinozism to Jacobi suggests that it too was no more than provisional, as in a remark reported by Jacobi after they had discussed whether the God of Spinoza might not be eternally expanding and contracting: 'Einmal sagte Leßing, mit halbem Lächeln: Er selbst wäre vielleicht das höchste Wesen, und gegenwärtig in dem Zustande der äussersten Contraction' (*Lessing im Gespräch*, p. 508). Lessing's brother Karl certainly thought that his Spinozism was just as provisional as his earlier speculations (*Lessing im Gespräch*, p. 589). And it is particularly significant that, in those same conversations with Jacobi, we find Lessing recommending his friend to read the *Dialogues Concerning Natural Religion*, the testament of the foremost British sceptic, David Hume.

It appears, then, that Lessing tried in his later years to unite the rationalism of Leibniz and Spinoza with the scepticism of Pierre Bayle; and in so doing, he was following precedents within the sceptical tradition itself. He was able to do so by insisting that the line which separates mystery from established truth, revelation from reason, is not a clear one, but rather a vaguely defined, and possibly receding, frontier. It is in this spirit that we should interpret the verdict of the judge in the parable of the rings in *Nathan der Weise*. For it tells us not what the true religion is, but only that the question of religious truth is unanswerable, or — and here is that same reservation that Bayle made in the posthumous work quoted by Leibniz — that it may possibly be answered at some indeterminate time in the future.

The truths of the main religions, therefore, are at most relative. Since each religion is relative to the customs and culture of the country it originates in, the only reasonable course to adopt is to follow the ways of our fathers. Or as Sextus Empiricus expressed it: 'we follow a line of reasoning which, in accordance with appearances, points us to a life conformable to the customs of our country and its laws and institutions, and to our own instinctive feelings' (Loeb edition, I, 13). Bayle, too, believed that custom and habit, rather than rational evidence, determine our beliefs, and says that, in view of the uncertainty of all dogmas, it is enough that we should cling to what appears true to us in the light of our own circumstances (see OD, II, 396 and 543).

Since, then, it is impossible to discover which, if any, of the religions is the true one, some other criterion must be found if we are to assess the merits of the believers. Both Bayle and Lessing find this criterion in *morality*, that is, they distinguish between religious *beliefs*, and the *actions* of believers. We do not know whether Lessing ever read Bayle's principal work on religion and morality. It is the *Commentaire philosophique* on the words of Christ in the parable of the Great Supper, as reported by St Luke: 'Go out into the highways and hedges, and compel them to come in, that my house may be filled'. *Compelle intrare*: words which were used for centuries to justify religious persecution and conversion by force. Lessing must at least have known of the work, for Bayle often refers to it in the *Dictionnaire*. It is in the *Commentaire* that Bayle puts forward his celebrated defence of the 'rights of the erring conscience': 'la conscience erronée doit procurer à l'erreur les mêmes prérogatives, secours, et caresses, que la conscience orthodoxe procure à la vérité (OD, II, 425). That is, the Mohammedan or heretic who follows what he sincerely believes to be true, is as worthy of respect as the most orthodox Christian (see OD, II, 439 and LM, XVI, 371). Bayle argues that Christ's words 'compel them to come in' *cannot* be interpreted literally, and the criterion he applies is that of morality. Any literal interpretation of the Bible which enjoins us to commit crimes — such as compelling the conscience of others — simply cannot be true.

Here we encounter one of the limits of Bayle's scepticism, in which Lessing is once again in agreement with him. For despite his questioning of every received dogma, Bayle only rarely — and that only in his last years — questions the truths of moral reason, which he holds to be self-evident (OD, II, 368). Lessing is likewise inclined, from an early date (LM, XIV, 159), to rate sincerity and moral rectitude more highly than orthodoxy. And the following words from one of his polemics of 1778 are simply a restatement of Bayle's principle of the rights of the erring conscience:

Ein Mann, der Unwahrheit, unter entgegengesetzter Überzeugung, in guter Absicht . . . durchzusetzen sucht, ist unendlich mehr werth, als ein Mann, der die beste edelste Wahrheit, aus Vorurtheil, mit Verschreyung seiner Gegner, auf alltägliche Weise vertheidiget. (*Eine Duplik*, LM, XIII, 23)

By the time he writes *Nathan der Weise*, Lessing has put aside the question of religious truth completely, in favour of that of morality, for it is by their actions alone that men may be judged. Morality is the test of a religion's worth, if not of its truth, and not vice versa. Bayle too refused to make morality dependent on religious faith,[20] and stressed that even atheists may lead virtuous lives (*Dictionnaire*, IV, 2987–89). And both he and Lessing repeatedly defended heretics as men who followed their individual conscience (see *Dictionnaire*, III, 2058, and Lessing's 'Rettungen' of Cochläus, Lemnius, Adam Neuser, etc.).[21]

In short, Bayle was one of the earliest and most powerful advocates of universal tolerance, of which Lessing became the most eloquent spokesman in eighteenth-century Germany.

I have outlined some of the main affinities between Lessing and Bayle, several of them suggesting a direct influence. I have not stressed their many and obvious differences — the main one being that Lessing, unlike Bayle, was a creative writer. And we should not forget that the legacy of Leibniz and rationalism remained with Lessing all his life, modifying and counteracting that of the French philosopher.[22] But this must not blind us to the fact that some of his central attitudes, particularly in his later years, are integral parts of the sceptical tradition.

As the years went by, however, fewer and fewer people could share the well-tempered scepticism of Lessing and his era, or attain that peculiar state of unperturbedness or *ataraxia* which, according to the Pyrrhonists, is the fruit of the suspensive philosophy. It is remarkable how quickly the picture of Lessing as a 'Wahrheitsheld' took shape after the Restoration. One recent critic, Ernst Gombrich, does describe him as 'a Pyrrhonist at heart',[23] but Gombrich is very much in the minority. One of the reasons for this neglect, I am sure, is that scepticism never took root in Germany to the extent that it did in France and Britain. Throughout the eighteenth century in Germany, it was regarded as a dangerous force. Gottsched ventured to publish his translation of Bayle only after he had added numerous editorial notes, refuting Bayle's sceptical arguments with the aid of Leibnizian metaphysics; as late as 1785, Adam Weishaupt was dismissed from his professorship at Ingolstadt for urging his University Library to purchase the *Dictionnaire*;[24] and in Prussia, the limited freedom which writers had enjoyed to question religious dogma ended with the death of Frederick the Great, which was shortly followed by the notorious Wöllner Edict of 1788. The failure of scepticism to establish a firm tradition in Germany may help to explain why the German critics have been reluctant to concede its importance for one of their greatest writers, and their persistent attempts to reduce his ideas to a closed and self-contained system.

REFERENCES

[1] See Richard H. Popkin, 'The High Road to Pyrrhonism', *American Philosophical Quarterly*, 2 (1965), 18–32 (p. 26).
[2] Subsequent references to the French text are to this edition (Rotterdam, 1720), henceforth referred to as '*Dictionnaire*'.

[3] In *DVjs* (1975), Sonderheft, pp. 83*–104*.

[4] *A General Dictionary, Historical and Critical* (London, 1734–41).

[5] See Popkin, article 'Pierre Bayle', in *The Encyclopedia of Philosophy*, edited by Paul Edwards, 8 vols (New York, 1967), I, 257–62 (p. 259); also E. C. Mossner, *The Life of David Hume* (Edinburgh, 1954), p. 78.

[6] G. E. Lessing, *Sämtliche Schriften*, edited by Karl Lachmann and Franz Muncker, 23 vols (Stuttgart, 1886–1924), IV, 76 (henceforth referred to as 'LM').

[7] I have in my possession a mid-eighteenth-century MS from my copy of the English edition, purchased from the library of Callendar House, Falkirk, in the early 1960s. It consists of a long list of page references, nearly all of them to scurrilous anecdotes.

[8] *Pierre Bayle nach seinen für die Geschichte der Philosophie und Menschheit interessanten Momenten dargestellt und gewürdigt* (Ansbach, 1838), p. 157.

[9] T. W. Danzel and G. E. Guhrauer, *Gotthold Ephraim Lessing: Sein Leben und seine Werke*, second edition, edited by W. von Maltzahn and R. Boxberger, 2 vols (Berlin, 1880–81), I, 219–27.

[10] Ann Arbor, 1966, pp. 16–24.

[11] See Georges Pons, *G. E. Lessing et le Christianisme* (Paris, 1964), p. 100.

[12] On their distaste for academic life see Bayle, *Œuvres diverses* (referred to henceforth as 'OD'), 4 vols (The Hague, 1727–31), IV, 703 f., letter of 8 March 1694; and *Lessing im Gespräch*, edited by Richard Daunicht (Munich, 1971), p. 331.

[13] See *Lessings 'Laokoon'*, edited by Hugo Blümner, second edition (Berlin, 1880), pp. 77 ff.

[14] G. W. Leibniz, *Essais de Théodicée sur la bonté de Dieu, la liberté de l'homme et l'origine du mal*, in *Die philosophischen Schriften*, edited by C. J. Gerhardt, 7 vols (Berlin, 1875–90), VI, 324.

[15] For example, Walter Rex, *Essays on Pierre Bayle and the Religious Controversy* (The Hague, 1965), pp. 35, 65, 203, etc. and Elisabeth Labrousse, *Pierre Bayle*, 2 vols (The Hague, 1963–64), II, 314–16 and 608 f.

[16] *Historisches und Critisches Wörterbuch*, translated by J. C. Gottsched, 4 vols (Leipzig, 1741–44), III, 258.

[17] Reimarus, *Apologie . . .*, edited by Gerhard Alexander, 2 vols (Frankfurt, 1972), I, 233 and 600.

[18] H. B. Nisbet, 'Lessing and the Search for Truth', *PEGS*, N.S., 43 (1973), 72–95.

[19] In *Sextus Empiricus*, Loeb Classical Library, 4 vols (London, 1933–49), I, 157–59.

[20] Compare Harald Schultze, *Lessings Toleranzbegriff* (Göttingen, 1969), p. 42.

[21] Lessing himself describes his *Rettung des Hieronymus Cardanus* (1754) as a supplement to Bayle's article on that figure (LM, V, 310).

[22] On Lessing's combination of scepticism with an optimistic faith in reason and humanity — in contrast to Bayle's pessimism — compare E. M. Wilkinson's remark 'der Skeptizismus der Aufklärung ist dadurch gekennzeichnet, daß er trotzdem konstruktiv, daß er hoffnungsvoll geblieben ist', in 'Schiller und die Idee der Aufklärung', *Jahrbuch der deutschen Schiller-Gesellschaft*, 4 (1960), 42–59 (p. 45).

[23] E. H. Gombrich, 'Lessing: Lecture on a Master Mind', *Proceedings of the British Academy*, 43 (1957), 133–56 (p. 151).

[24] See Klaus Epstein, *The Genesis of German Conservatism* (Princeton, 1966), p. 102. I am grateful to Dr M. Kay Flavell for this reference.

On the Nature and the Delineation of Beauty in Art and Philosophy

Lessing's Responses to William Hogarth and Edmund Burke

By E. M. BATLEY

HOGARTH's *Analysis of Beauty* (1753), according to its sub-title 'written with a view to fixing the fluctuating Ideas of Taste',[1] was first brought to Lessing's attention in the form of Christlob Mylius's German translation to which he refers briefly on 7 March 1754, some weeks before it was advertised in the Easter edition of the Leipzig *Catalogus Universalis*.[2] Mylius's preface is dated 11 December 1753 although Lessing cannot have read either the preface or the translation until shortly before writing an appreciative review which appeared in the *Berlinische Privilegierte Zeitung* on 30 May 1754.[3]

In Lessing's estimation Hogarth was one of the greatest painters ever produced by England and his admiration is so expressed as to reflect the young critic's conviction that the purpose of art is to give pleasure, its social function is to educate, and its appeal is through the senses to the heart. He attributes Hogarth's fame to his ability 'in alle seine Gemählde eine Art von satyrischer Moral zu bringen ..., die das Herz an dem Vergnügen der Augen Theil zu nehmen, nöthiget'. The reflectiveness and learning which characterized the *Zergliederung der Schönheit* were for him additional proof that Hogarth's paintings and engravings were more than simply the products 'eines glücklichen Genies'. Lessing's review is descriptive and, occasionally, rhetorical rather than critical. He is content to accept Mylius's reputation as a man of letters and his statement of having been advised personally by Hogarth as indications that there is little fault to be found with the translation. By extending the applicability of Hogarth's linear principles beyond fashion, furniture design, dancing, oratory, acting (including the movement of head, arms and hands), all of which were described in Hogarth's work, to philosophy and music, Lessing reveals his dependence on Mylius's preface at this stage. Yet although he distinguishes only inaccurately between the waving line ('die wellenförmige Linie'), the line of beauty ('die Linie der Schönheit') and the line of grace ('die Linie des Reitzes'), he does succeed in identifying for his readers the core of Hogarth's system of beauty and its implications.

It was probably Lessing's recognition of the relevance of Hogarth's system to all those arts and sciences concerned with formal beauty (as he specified on 25 June and 4 July, philosophers, naturalists, antiquaries, orators, preachers, painters, sculptors and dancers) and to the contemporary debate on the 'Nachahmung der schönen Natur', which induced him to provide the German reading public with a new edition at a subscription price of one fifth the cost of Mylius's. Since Mylius had died on 6 March 1754 Lessing took upon himself the task of revising the translation and the style, where clarity seemed to be lacking, and of adding a German translation of Monsieur Rouquet's explanations of Hogarth's satirical paintings. The engravings were also to be better produced.

The last entry in the *Berlinische Privilegierte Zeitung* to refer to Hogarth, dated 4 July, is signed by the new printer, Christian Friedrich Voß. It consists of material drawn verbatim from Lessing's earlier entries of 7 March, 30 May and 25 June, together with a new observation which prefigures the view of aesthetics as defined by C. F. Nicolai in the following year:[4] 'Ihm [Hogarth] werden wir es also zu verdanken haben, wenn man bey dem Worte *schön*, das man täglich tausend Dingen beylegt, künftig eben so viel denken wird, als man bisher nur empfunden hat' (LM, v, 416).

In the *Analysis of Beauty* Hogarth had enumerated those

fundamental principles of art which were generally allowed to give elegance and beauty: fitness, variety, uniformity, simplicity, intricacy and quantity, 'all of which co-operate in the production of beauty, mutually correcting and restraining each other occasionally'. The two figures to which Michelangelo had referred, the 'triangular form of the glass' and the 'serpentine line', signified for Hogarth not only beauty and grace but the whole order of form (H, p. xvii). The basic line of beauty, representing the principles listed above, was a two-dimensional line following the simple contour of a serpent. The line of grace, three-dimensional in its effect (although Hogarth does not refer to this property), had the power of 'super-adding grace to beauty':

... the serpentine line, by its waving and winding at the same time different ways, leads the eye in a pleasing manner along the continuity of its variety ... and which by its twisting so many different ways, may be said to inclose (tho' but a single line) varied contents; and therefore all its variety cannot be express'd on paper by one continued line, without the assistance of the imagination, or the help of a figure; (see Fig. 26. Tp. 1.) where that sort of proportion'd, winding line, which will hereafter be call'd the precise serpentine line, or *line of grace*, is represented by a fine wire, properly twisted round the elegant and varied figure of a cone. (H, pp. 38–39)

In proposing his theory of the 'pyramid of sight', which was composed of visual rays as the foundation for linear perspective, Leonardo da Vinci had had recourse to mathematics.[5] In the Haydocke translation of Lomazzo's *Tracte containing the Artes of curious Paintings, Carvings, Buildings*, Hogarth had found the belief expressed 'that Painting is subordinate to the Perspectives, to naturall Philosophy, and Geometrie'.[6] Yet in the *Analysis of Beauty* Hogarth deliberately makes no attempt to discover a mathematical or a geometrical prescription for the line of beauty. He even explains in the introduction that his illustrations were merely intended to appeal to the imagination, to *suggest* what to look for:

My figures, therefore, are to be consider'd in the same light, with those a mathematician makes with his pen, which may convey the idea of his demonstration, tho' not a line in them is either perfectly straight, or of that peculiar curvature he is treating of. Nay, so far was I from aiming at grace, that I purposely chose to be least accurate, where most beauty might be expected, that no stress might be laid on the figures to the prejudice of the work itself. (H, p. 2)

Hogarth was criticized for this omission in the *Monthly Review* of 1754 and for the same reason by Edmund Burke in 1758.[7] But in 1760 C. L. Hagedorn tempered his own criticism of Hogarth's lack of precision with the aesthetically much more important question: 'ob eine solche Bestimmung für die Künste thulich, und eine einzige in der Anwendung auf alle Fälle angemessen sey?', for he too understood the relative nature of visual beauty and the irrelevance of absolute prescriptions for art.[8] Instead, Hogarth had chosen to identify the mean among seven graded serpentine lines, each varying in its degree of curvature, as the most beautiful. Hagedorn, who published three substantial and critical essays on Hogarth between 1760 and 1762, had appreciated his point of view, yet Lessing, upon whose preface to his revised edition of the *Zergliederung der Schönheit* Hagedorn had depended for some of his critical insights, does not at first sight seem to have done so.[9]

Some of the material for Lessing's preface to the new German edition is drawn from the reviews in the *Berlinische Privilegierte Zeitung*, but most of it is new and, for the first time, critical. By now he had read Mylius's translation, although not the English original, carefully enough to have detected a number of minor errors.[10] Much more important for Lessing was Hogarth's apparent failure to specify which of the seven lines was the line of beauty. Whether Lessing's own oversight in this matter was attributable to a cursory reading of the appropriate chapter or to the fact that the illustrations were missing from the edition he had before him, he proceeded to complain that the 'fluctuating Ideas of Taste' had *therefore* not been 'fixed' according to the intention stated in the sub-title, merely circumscribed more narrowly. Although Hagedorn wilfully chose to regard No. 6 of the seven waving lines as the most beautiful, he acknowledged with his own reservations what Lessing did not, that Hogarth had indeed designated No. 4 as *the* line of beauty

(Hagedorn, vi, i, 10–11). Hogarth had described Nos. 5, 6 and 7 as 'gross and clumsy' and Nos. 3, 2 and 1 as 'mean and poor' and further demonstrated 'a still more perfect idea of the effects of the precise waving-line' by reference to a female under-garment:

Every whale-bone of a good stay must be made to bend in this manner: for the whole stay, when put close together behind, is truly a shell of well-varied contents, and its surface of course a fine form; so that if a line, or the lace were to be drawn, or brought from the top of the lacing of the stay behind, round the body, and down to the bottom peak of the stomacher; it would form such a perfect, precise, serpentine line, as has been shown, round the cone, figure 26 in plate 1. For this reason all ornaments obliquely contrasting the body in this manner, as the ribbons worn by the knights of the garter, are both genteel and graceful . . . (H, pp. 49–50)

It was this *apparent* oversight of Hogarth's which persuaded Lessing to consider whether recourse to higher mathematics may allow limits to be set for the degree of curvature beyond which the waving line ceased to be beautiful. Consequent upon his references to Hogarth in the 'Betrachtungen über die Quellen und Verbindungen der schönen Künste und Wissen-schaften' and upon his reading of Burke, Moses Mendelssohn embarked upon this very course early in 1758, having received some albeit lighthearted exhortation to do so from Lessing towards the end of January (LM, xvii, 134–35). The search proved fruitless when the equation which Mendelssohn drew from the work of J. François Blondel on the problem of the degree of curvature in pillars was found to produce only a multiplicity of answers.[11] Lessing's conjecture in the 'Vorbericht' of 1754 that higher mathematics may provide a geometrical prescription for the line of beauty, that a science may offer the solution to a problem derived from art, had, however, been accompanied by significant qualifications which bring him closer to Hogarth's aesthetic viewpoint than his speculation suggests.

While Hogarth had failed, in his opinion, to prescribe a precise line which was neither too shallow nor too curved, Lessing had to concede that this was, in any case, virtually impossible for the artist. His understanding for the kind of aesthetics implicit in Hogarth's *Analysis of Beauty* (and later in Hagedorn's *Betrachtungen über die Mahlerey*) is, moreover, expressed in the reasons he attributes to Hogarth for his omission:

Er sahe es vielleicht ein, daß in dieser Untersuchung ohne Hülfe der höhern Mathematik nicht fortzukommen sey, und daß weitläuftige und schwere Berechnungen sein Werk wohl gründlicher, aber nicht brauchbarer machen könnten. Er ließ also seinen Faden, als ein Künstler, da fahren, wo ich wollte, daß ihn ein philosophischer Meßkünstler ergreiffen und weiter führen möchte. (H, p. 3)

Indirectly, this amounts to an acknowledgement that beauty is derived from, and relative to, its artistic context. Lessing implied that even the discovery of a geometrical formula for the precise line would not have enhanced the usefulness of Hogarth's *Analysis* for art: yet, constrained by the 'metaphysische Gründe der Schönheit', mathematics could have identified those properties of the true line of beauty which can be grasped more swiftly and more easily than the properties in other lines of this kind. The underlying *philosophic* concept of beauty is formulated precisely: 'Die Vollkommenheit bestehet in der Uebereinstimmung des Mannichfaltigen, und alsdann wenn die Uebereinstimmung leicht zu fassen ist, nennen wir die Vollkommenheit Schönheit' (H, p. 3).

The critical discussion in the 'Vorbericht' reveals Lessing's conviction that whereas it is for philosophy, with the aid of mathematics, to discover *why* the line of beauty exerts such a pleasant force over our emotions, it is for the artist to exploit the fact that it does so.

Despite variations in what Mendelssohn would have described as the 'willkürliche Zeichen', the words describing the concepts, Aristotle, Hogarth and Lessing shared the same fundamental philosophic idea of beauty. In *De Poetica*, which Lessing possibly knew as early as 1750,[12] Aristotle had shown that his concept of beauty, like Hogarth's, was related to the manner of man's perception of order: 'whatever is beautiful, whether it be a living creature or an object made up of various parts, must necessarily not only have its parts properly ordered, but also be of an appropriate size, for beauty is bound up with size and order.'[13]

The unity of plot is derived less from Aristotle's belief that tragedy should represent some action than from his concept of beauty. For this reason a plot should be able to be encompassed in a single vision and be of such length as may be easily held in the memory: 'With regard to the limit set by the nature of the action, the longer the story is, the more beautiful it will be, provided that it is quite clear.'[14] The notions of size, order and ease of overview are implicit in Lessing's review in the *Berlinische Privilegierte Zeitung* of Mendelssohn's *Briefe über die Empfindungen* (1755) although here his main concern is to show how Mendelssohn distinguishes clearly between perfection ('die Uebereinstimmung des Mannigfaltigen'), which produces in us a sense of pleasure in God, being based on the positive powers of our soul, and beauty ('die Einheit im Mannigfaltigen'), which produces a pleasure dependent upon the limiting of those mental powers (LM, VII, 52–53). Perfection, he infers, is of infinite, beauty of finite proportion. These comments heralded the distinction which Edmund Burke was to make in 1757 between the production of the sublime by 'greatness of dimension', and of beauty by objects which are 'comparatively small', 'smooth', 'of delicate frame' (Burke, p. 117).

Burke's *Philosophical Enquiry into the Origin of our Ideas of the Sublime and Beautiful* was published in London on 21 April 1757.[15] Muncker estimates Lessing's reflections on this work to have been written between April 1758 and 1759, although they may have been jotted down at the time of his initial, enthusiastic response to Burke expressed in a letter to Friedrich Nicolai on 25 November 1757 (LM, XVII, 127–28). Despite Burke's conviction that perfection was not the cause of beauty, Lessing fuses his notion of the distinction between sublimity and beauty with Mendelssohn's notion of the distinction between perfection and beauty. In so doing he both adapts and develops the philosophic concept which he had seen as the bedrock for any mathematical inquiry into the properties of Hogarth's line of beauty:

Alle angenehmen Begriffe sind undeutliche Vorstellungen einer Vollkommenheit.

Die Vollkommenheit ist die Einheit im Mannigfaltigen.

Bei der unendlichen Vorstellung der Einheit im Mannigfaltigen, ist entweder der Begriff der Einheit, oder der Begriff der Mannigfaltigkeit der klärste.

Die undeutliche Vorstellung einer Vollkommenheit, in welcher der Begriff der Einheit der klärste ist, nennen wir *schön*.

Die undeutliche Vorstellung einer Vollkommenheit, in welcher der Begriff der Mannigfaltigkeit der klärste ist, nennen wir *erhaben*.

Daher heißt in dem ganzen Umfange der schönen Wissenschaften und Künste nichts schön, was sich nicht auf einmal übersehen läßt, und nichts erhaben, was sich auf einmal aus einem Gesichtspunkte ganz betrachten läßt. (LM, xiv, 220–21)

Lessing's definition of beauty seems to have become an amalgam of ideas echoing several sources: 'Die undeutliche ['dunkle' in Mendelssohn; 'dark' in Burke] Vorstellung [Aristotle, Hogarth, Mendelssohn] einer Vollkommenheit [Wolff, Mendelssohn], in welcher der Begriff [Mendelssohn, Burke] der Einheit [Aristotle, Hogarth] der klärste [Aristotle, Hogarth] ist, nennen wir *schön*.' Determining the derivation of this construct is at best a hazardous undertaking, yet the applicability of its essence to art is clarified by recalling Lessing's implicit beliefs, in his reviews of Hogarth and Mendelssohn, that pleasure (and indeed all emotions) arises from an unclear perception of perfection, that beauty provides pleasure, and that the task of art is the production of beauty. In his review of Burke's *Philosophical Enquiry* which was especially critical of the Englishman's lack of a system, Mendelssohn had agreed with his view that the very difficulty for the imagination of ordering the parts of an object described in words induces a 'darkness' which allows poetry much greater power in evoking passion than does the clarity of painting.[16] This reversed Dubos's contention that painting was superior to poetry in rousing the emotions.[17]

The fragmentary notes on Burke also contain a number of comments on the emotions of love and hate. Burke had believed in the existence of a reciprocal relationship between

D

the physical attitude of the body and the experience of emotion. Of the physical cause of love he had written:

... that as a beautiful object presented to the sense, by causing a relaxation in the body, produces the passion of love in the mind; so if by any means the passion should first have its origin in the mind, a relaxation of the outward organs will as certainly ensue in a degree proportioned to the cause. (Burke, p. 151; cf. section XIX, pp. 149–51)

Adapted to the stage and specifically to the representation of anger, this principle had provided Lessing with the cornerstone for his defence of the 'indeclamable' parts of the dialogue in *Miss Sara Sampson* in which he had purposely employed 'sinnliche Bilder' as aids to evoke emotion in the actor.[18] In the *Dramaturgie* he was to advise actors how to move their limbs, even their lips, teeth and eyebrows, in order to arouse within them the emotion of anger (8 May 1767; LM, IX, 194–95). He found the same principle confirmed later in J. G. Noverre's *Lettres sur la danse et sur les ballets*, the first ninety-six pages of which he translated in 1769.[19] In practice and in theory Lessing anticipates Burke's belief in the interrelationship between emotion and the physical movement of the body.

Inspired by Burke's observations, Lessing argued that the basis for love was 'die Ähnlichkeit der Denkungsart, die Identität der Urtheile', to which Mendelssohn added the qualification 'die Ähnlichkeit der Urtheile über Vollkommenheiten und Unvollkommenheiten, die mich oder ihn angehen' (LM, XIV, 220–25). Such a conception of love is undramatic by its very nature, yet although Lessing therefore chose not to depict it on stage in its romantically affirmative aspect, he did allow the idea of mutual 'like-mindedness' to provide the basis for the emotional relationship between Minna and Tellheim (generosity) and Emilia and Appiani (respectability). Lessing derived his comments on hate, the reverse of love, from the concept of perfection:

Da ich mir nun die Person, die ich hasse, als eine solche denke, die von mir völlig unterschieden ist, so kann es nicht fehlen, daß nicht der Begriff einer Vollkommenheit in ihr, in mir den Begriff einer

Unvollkommenheit, und umgekehrt der Begriff einer Unvollkommenheit in ihr, in mir den Begriff einer Vollkommenheit
erwecken sollte. Geschähe dieses nicht, so würde ich die gehaßte
Person mir gleich und nicht von mir unterschieden denken, welches
wider die Voraussetzung ist.

Wir freuen uns folglich nicht über des Feindes Unvollkommenheit, sondern über unsere Vollkommenheit, die wir uns bey jener
gedenken. Und so auch mit unserm Verdruße über die Vollkommenheit des Feindes. (LM, xiv, 225)

He implies that the cure for hate is to appreciate that the
imperfections we observe in others may be perfections to them.
This is the tolerance towards the three positive religions as it
is embodied in *Nathan*. Moreover, procedures are indicated by
which one progresses from hate (hostility, prejudice), that is,
from a state of ignorance about the 'imperfections' of others, to
understanding. Reflected in terms of dramatic technique, it is
the progression from caricature to character, from Tellheim
the redundant Prussian officer to Tellheim the lover, from
Nathan the Jew to Nathan the Wise.

The capacity for 'Sympathie' is described in Lessing's responses to Burke's section on love as the means by which one
person can become confused with another even when the
similarities between them are few and slight. In this context,
sympathy is seen as a derivative of love. In his review of the
Philosophical Enquiry Mendelssohn's paraphrase of the Englishman's notion of sympathy had restricted it to an emotional
identification: 'das Vermögen, uns an die Stelle einer andern
Person zu setzen, und mit ihr zu fühlen, was ihr widerfährt'.[20]

However, although writing under the heading 'Von der
Liebe', Lessing includes the potential identification of *mental*
attitudes and judgements as well as of emotional experiences
in his concept of 'Sympathie'. It is this more embracing concept
which is at the heart of his advocacy of tragedy over history
and of 'bürgerliches Trauerspiel' in particular, however much
the arguments in the *Dramaturgie* may be indebted to Aristotle
and Marmontel. His comments on Burke's work are characterized by an implicit belief in man's perfectibility and through him
in the perfectibility of society. As Mendelssohn had stated

explicitly in his *Briefe über die Empfindungen* and as Lessing was to repeat later in his rejoinders to Reimarus, God was the ultimate perfection towards which men moved. Toleration of the imperfections of others ('perfections' from their point of view) is engendered, as Lessing's fragmentary comments imply, by the practice and extension of 'Sympathie'. He had already argued in 1756 that the purpose of tragedy was to develop this human capacity for the advantage of others:

Sie soll uns nicht blos lehren, gegen diesen oder jenen Unglücklichen Mitleid zu fühlen, sondern sie soll uns so weit fühlbar machen, daß uns der Unglückliche zu allen Zeiten, und unter allen Gestalten, rühren und für sich einnehmen muß . . . *Der mitleidigste Mensch ist der beste Mensch*, zu allen gesellschaftlichen Tugenden, zu allen Arten der Großmuth der aufgelegteste. (Letter to Nicolai, 13 November 1756; LM, xvii, 66)

It was therefore socially desirable for tragedy to arouse the emotion of sympathy in the audience. Burke's belief that the passions were divided into those aimed at self-preservation and those which were directed towards society thus echoed Aristotle and Lessing. Moreover, they were, in similar fashion, derived from his conception of the state of sympathy in which, according to Burke, we experience the 'self-preserving' passions of others, which are the source of the sublime, and their 'social' passions which, being the source of beauty, afford us the most lively sense of pleasure. Pleasure derived from sympathy arising from an actual event was greater, argued Burke, than in the imitative arts, however close to nature the imitation may be.[21]

In the same month as the *Philosophical Enquiry* had been published in London, April of 1757, Lessing had been more discriminate when he wrote to Nicolai that the pleasure derived from believing an object to be real preceded the pleasure derived from the imitation itself. Differentiating between our emotional perception of life and of art in February of the same year, he had drawn on a figure from Aristotle to argue: the observer of a serpent produced by a painter, believing it to be real on account of the excellence of the imitation, experiences fear; only when he perceives that it is an imitation will he feel pleasure. Lessing concluded 'Daher gefallen uns alle unangenehmen Affekte in der Nachahmung' (letter to Mendelssohn, 2 February 1757; LM, XVII, 91). Lessing's and Mendelssohn's deeper and more systematic appreciation of the social function and effect of the 'schöne Künste' was derived from their belief in perfectibility: despite Burke's philosophical insights, they found the *Philosophical Enquiry* unsystematic. Nor was it as appreciative as they had been of the nature and function of beauty in art.[22]

Another fundamental difference between Burke and Lessing was that Burke believed the soul to be the seat of the emotions, and Lessing the heart. For Lessing the soul was the seat of all mental activity which itself precipitates the experience of emotion and passion. In this process the 'Vorstellungen' ('perceptions') have an important catalytic effect. In the fragments on Burke, Lessing had written: 'Die undeutliche Vorstellung einer Vollkommenheit, in welcher der Begriff der Einheit der klärste ist, nennen wir *schön*.' Burke had denied that perfection was a constituent of beauty. Mendelssohn was also critical of him for not allowing that proportion, fitness and perfection were at least to some extent the causes of beauty, and for failing to provide a proper account of the nature of beauty. To describe it as 'some merely sensible quality', and relative size as one of its attributes, was not enough. Burke had also discounted the validity of Hogarth's theory of 'gradual variation', the cornerstone for his advocacy of the serpentine-line, on the grounds that 'though the varied line is that alone on which complete beauty is found, yet there is no particular line which is always found in the most completely beautiful; and which is therefore beautiful in preference to all other lines. At least I never could observe it' (Burke, pp. 115 f.).

Burke's lack of a systematic foundation for his understanding of art, and of linear art in particular, induced him to expect an absolute prescription for the line of beauty which, even in 1754, Lessing had not thought either useful for art, or possible. The philosophic concept for beauty which had then served

Lessing as the premiss for any such geometrical quest had undergone slight modification in his recorded responses to Burke. However, it continued to fulfil the useful purpose of being equally applicable to painting, sculpture, poetic and dramatic art. It provided the basis for the literary criticism of the *Briefe, die neueste Litteratur betreffend*, in which the achievement of 'ein schönes Ganze' becomes the hallmark of artistic merit, even of genius; for his appreciation of acting as a 'transitorische Malerei' — as a result of which he applied the principles of linear beauty to stage-action in the advice he gave in the *Dramaturgie* (LM, IX, 197 ff; see also 8, 12, 15 May, LM, IX, 193–206); for the importance he attached to actors and the stage as the visual mediators between idea and emotional response, and for his sensitivity both to the visual aspect of his own dramas, even in the process of their creation, and to the interplay between spatial and temporal dimensions in art. In Hogarth and Burke, in Mendelssohn's responses to their writings, and in the latter's own essays, the dimensional aspects of art had been manifoldly discussed. In 1753 Hogarth had recommended the study of stage-action from the point of view of linear movement and had observed how rest in movement and space in painting contributed to the production of 'infinite variety'. The authority for this had been Shakespeare: 'and so plain space makes a considerable part of beauty in form, so cessation of movement in acting, is so absolutely necessary; and in my opinion much wanted on most stages, to relieve the eye from what Shakespeare calls, *continually sawing the air*' (H, p. 152).

In his criticism of the Hamburg production of Cronegk's *Olint und Sophronia* in 1767 Lessing had also recommended Hamlet's advice as 'eine goldene Regel für alle Schauspieler'; at the same time he elaborated upon his own view that acting consisted of both 'sichtbare' and 'transitorische Malerey'. Moreover, these observations are contained in the very next article after he has advocated Hogarth's serpentine lines as a guide for practising movements of the hand, and they echo the aesthetic premisses of *Laokoon* (8 May and 12 May 1767; LM, IX, 197–206).

On 21 January 1758 Lessing referred for the first time to his current work on *Emilia Galotti* in a letter to Nicolai. On the same day he wrote to Mendelssohn, mentioning his own translation of Burke's *Philosophical Enquiry*, of which the first sections were already at press, and asking to be informed, in simple terms, of whatever he might discover in geometry of the mathematical nature of Hogarth's line of beauty.[23] It is therefore not surprising to discover in the text of *Emilia Galotti* ironic echoes of the Anglo-German debate on the nature of beauty which serve the aesthetic purpose of demonstrating Hettore Gonzaga's restricted view of beauty divorced from the concepts of morality or social responsibility, his inability to observe the distinction between beauty expressed in art and beauty expressed in life, and, indirectly, his misconceived belief in the attainability of an absolute prescription:

Der Prinz: (*mit einer erzwungenen Kälte*): Also, Conti, rechnen Sie doch wirklich Emilia Galotti mit zu den vorzüglichsten unserer Stadt? *Conti:* Also? mit? mit zu den vorzüglichsten? Und den vorzüglichsten unserer Stadt? — Sie spotten meiner, Prinz. Oder Sie sahen, die ganze Zeit, eben so wenig, als Sie hörten.
Der Prinz: Lieber Conti, — (*die Augen wieder auf das Bild gerichtet*) wie darf unser einer seinen Augen trauen? Eigentlich weiß doch nur allein ein Maler von der Schönheit zu urtheilen.
Conti: Und eines jeden Empfindung sollte erst auf den Ausspruch eines Malers warten? — Ins Kloster mit dem, der es von uns lernen will, was schön ist! (1. 4; LM, II, 384)

REFERENCES

[1] William Hogarth, *Analysis of Beauty* (London, 1753). References to and quotations from this edition are cited as 'H'.

[2] *Catalogus Universalis oder Verzeichniß Derer Bücher, welche in der Frankfurter und Leipziger Oster-Messe, entweder ganz neu gedruckt, oder sonsten verbessert, wieder aufgelegt worden sind, auch ins künftige noch herauskommen sollen* (Leipzig, 1754), p. 479: 'Hogarts, Wilh. Zergliederung der Schönheit, die schwankenden Begriffe von dem Geschmack festzusetzen, aus dem Engl. übersetzt von C. Mylius und mit dem Original Kupferstichen versehen, — gr. 4. London, Hannover in Commißion, bey Joh. Wilh. Schmidt'. An almost identical entry was made for the Michaelmas edition of the same year (p. 532).

It was apparently reported in 'Nichols Anecdotes of Hogarth' that the translation was undertaken to amuse Marshal Broglio and the King of Prussia to whom he dedicated his March to Finchley: see the handwritten comment facing the frontispiece of the first English edition.

[3] Gotthold Ephraim Lessing, *Sämtliche Schriften*, edited by K. Lachmann, third edition, revised by Franz Muncker (Leipzig, 1904), v, 405–07. References to and quotations from this edition are cited as 'LM'.

[4] See *Briefe über den itzigen Zustand der schönen Wissenschaften in Deutschland* (Berlin, 1755). Defending Baumgarten's *Aesthetica* and Meier's *Ästhetik* against attacks by J. B. Carpzov, Nicolai asserted the distinctiveness of aesthetics without seeming to focus as sharply as J. E. Schlegel or Hogarth did on the nature of art itself: for him aesthetics was to be defined as 'die Wissenschaft des empfindenden Verstandes', emotional responses to works of art being tempered by the intellect.

[5] *The Literary Works of Leonardo da Vinci*, edited by J. P. Richter, 2 vols (New York, 1970), I, 126 (*Trattato della pittura*, 1721).

[6] Io Paulo Lomazzo, *Tracte containing the Artes of curious Paintings, Carvings, Buildings*, translated by R. Haydocke (Oxford, 1598), Book I, 'Of Proportion', p. 14.

[7] *The Monthly Review or Literary Journal*, 10 (1754), 100–110 (p. 101). See also Edmund Burke, *A Philosophical Enquiry into the Origin of our Ideas of the Sublime and Beautiful*, edited by J. T. Boulton (London, 1958), pp. 115 f. References to and quotations from this edition are cited as 'Burke'.

[8] Christian Ludwig von Hagedorn, *Betrachtungen über die Mahlerey*, 2 parts (Leipzig, 1762). The essay 'Betrachtungen über die Stellung nach der sogenannten Wellenlinie' first appeared anonymously in the *Bibliothek der Schönen Wissenschaften und der Freien Künste*, edited by C. F. Nicolai, 9 vols (Leipzig, 1757–63), VI, i (1760), 1–15 (pp. 4–6). References to this edition are cited as 'Hagedorn'.

[9] 'Vorbericht zu diesem neuen Abdrucke', in William Hogarth, *Zergliederung der Schönheit, die schwankenden Begriffe von dem Geschmack festzusetzen*, translated by C. Mylius, second edition (Berlin and Potsdam, 1754).

[10] According to Lessing, Mylius translated Hogarth as having stated that the heart was 'eine Art des ersten Grundes der Bewegung': Lessing would have preferred 'eine Art des ersten Bewegungsgrundes' ('Vorbericht', pp. 2 f.). He did not comment on Mylius's translation of 'elegant' as 'schön' or of 'the continuity of its variety' as 'durch den beständigen Zusammenhang'.

[11] Letter of 17 February 1758, in Moses Mendelssohn, *Gesammelte Schriften*, Volume XI, *Briefwechsel*, I, 1754–1762, edited by B. Strauß (Berlin, 1932), pp. 175 f. Mendelssohn was presumably referring to Jacques François Blondel's *Discours sur la manière d'étudier l'architecture, et les arts qui sont relatifs à celui de bastir: Prononcé par M. Blondel . . . à l'ouverture de son deuxième cours publique sur l'architecture, le 16. Juin 1747* (Paris, 1747).

[12] 'Fülleborn fand nur "hin und wieder auf einzelnen Blättern Perioden aus Aristoteles Poetik übersetzt", die Fülleborn später in der "Dramaturgie" weit richtiger und deutscher wiedergegeben habe. Wahrscheinlich fallen diese Versuche vor das Jahr 1753, in welchem die Verdeutschung des Aristotelischen Werkes von Curtius erschien . . . vielleicht reichen sie bis in die Zeit der Arbeit an den "Theatralischen Beiträgen" (1750) oder gar in die Studienjahre zurück' (LM, XIV, 164).

[13] *Aristotle, Horace, Longinus: Classical Literary Criticism*, edited by Betty Radice and R. Baldick, translated by T. S. Dorsch (London, 1965), p. 42. Mr Parent, to whose essay 'De la Nature de la Beauté Corporelle' (*Journal des Sçavans*, 28 (1700), 394 ff.) Lessing had referred in the preface to his own edition of Hogarth's work, had not insisted on the relationship between the parts or on both simplicity and variety being apparent in the perception of beauty: the most appropriate location for beauty was 'les figures courbes mêlées de convexités, de concavités, et d'inflexions . . . en un mot dans toutes les figures courbes, simples ou composées, soit qu'on y distingue une varieté [sic] ou une uniformité de parties, soit qu'on connoisse les rapports de ces parties, ou qu'on ne les connoisse pas' (p. 398).

[14] *Aristotle, Horace, Longinus*, p. 42.

[15] Since the second edition was not printed until 10 January 1759, Lessing must have had a first edition in his possession which did not include the 'introductory DISCOURSE concerning TASTE and several other Additions' which went some way to meeting the criticisms in the *Literary Magazine*, and the *Critical* and *Monthly Reviews* (see Burke, pp. xxiii and 180).

[16] *Bibliothek der Schönen Wissenschaften und der Freien Künste*, III, ii (1758), 290–320.

[17] *Bibliothek der Schönen Wissenschaften und der Freien Künste*, III, i, 1–29: 'Des Abts du Bos Anmerkungen über das Genie der Dichter und Mahler'; and III, ii, 215–27: 'Fortsetzungen der Anmerkungen des Abts du Bos, über die Beschaffenheit des Genies der Dichter und Maler'.

[18] Letter to Mendelssohn, 14 September 1757, LM, XVII, 120–22; cf. Burke, p. 133: 'I have often observed, that on mimicking the looks and gestures, of angry, or placid, or frighted, or daring men, I have involuntarily found my mind turned to that passion whose appearance I endeavoured to imitate; nay, I am convinced it is hard to avoid it; though one strove to separate the passion from its correspondent gestures. Our minds and bodies are so closely and intimately connected, that one is incapable of pain or pleasure without the other.'

[19] J. G. Noverre, *Briefe über die Tanzkunst und über die Ballette* (Hamburg and Bremen, 1769). The first 6 'Bogen' (pp. 1–96) were translated by Lessing, the rest by J. J. C. Bode.

[20] *Bibliothek der Schönen Wissenschaften und der Freien Künste*, III, ii (1758), 296.

[21] Section XIV, 'The effects of SYMPATHY on the distress of others'; Section XV, 'Of the effects of tragedy', Burke, pp. 45–48. Compare *Bibliothek der Schönen Wissenschaften und der Freien Künste*, III, ii (1758), 296.

[22] This is probably one of the reasons why Lessing never apparently completed a German translation of Burke, which was left to Christian Garve; see *Burke's Philosophische Untersuchungen über den Ursprung unserer Begriffe vom Erhabenen und Schönen* (Riga, 1773).

[23] LM, XVII, 132–35. Muncker gives the following comment on the dating of the second letter: 'Der undatierte Brief war vermutlich dem vorausgehenden Schreiben Nr. 88 beigeschlossen und stammt vom gleichen Tag wie dieses' (p. 134).

Sublime Manliness and Lovely Femininity in the Age of Goethe

By Raymond Immerwahr

SCHILLER's philosophical and aesthetic writings abound in polarities: naive and sentimental, grace and dignity, inclination and will, necessity and freedom, to mention a few. It was an aspect of his feeling for life to see everything as a kind of mythic drama[1] with personified antagonists, but, as in his own dramas, he sought to resolve the conflicts in some kind of synthesis. As long as aesthetic thought is focused upon the human being, it is difficult to think in terms of dynamic antithesis without some association with the basic human experience of sexuality, and we need not be surprised to find this association in the aesthetics of Schiller.[2] I shall consider here the one major essay in which sexual dichotomy becomes explicit, *Anmut und Würde*, then look back to the tradition from which it derives, consider briefly sexual connotations in aesthetic writings of a few contemporaries, and conclude with a few examples from Novalis and Friedrich Schlegel.

The most striking illustrations offered by Schiller are in the central passage of *Über Anmut und Würde* which concludes the examination of grace and turns to that of dignity:

Man wird, im ganzen genommen, die Anmut mehr bei dem *weiblichen* Geschlecht (die Schönheit vielleicht mehr bei dem männlichen) finden, wovon die Ursache nicht weit zu suchen ist. Zur Anmut muß sowohl der körperliche Bau als der Charakter beitragen; jener durch seine Biegsamkeit, Eindrücke anzunehmen und ins Spiel gesetzt zu werden, dieser durch die sittliche Harmonie der Gefühle. In beiden war die Natur dem Weibe günstiger als dem Manne. Der zärtere weibliche Bau empfängt jeden Eindruck schneller und läßt ihn schneller wieder verschwinden. Feste Konstitutionen kommen nur durch einen Sturm in Bewegung, und wenn starke

Muskeln angezogen werden, so können sie die Leichtigkeit nicht
zeigen, die zur Grazie erfordert wird . . . So wie die Anmut der
Ausdruck einer schönen Seele ist, so ist *Würde* der Ausdruck einer
erhabenen Gesinnung.[3]

This passage and its context unequivocally demonstrate
Schiller's conscious association of the physical and tempera-
mental qualities of the human female with grace and those of the
male with dignity. This is less clear in the case of his discussion
of beauty and sublimity. The general drift is to imply that
beauty has more of the feminine, sublimity more of the masculine, but in the one parenthetical phrase qualified by a 'vielleicht' Schiller seems to move in the opposite direction. If he
is thinking here of beauty as an ideal synthesis more likely to be
approximated in an artistic conception of the male figure, he is
consciously or unconsciously paying homage to Winckelmann,
who saw the highest manifestation of human beauty in some
ancient statues of the youthful Apollo and Dionysos and whose
monistic approach to beauty and sublimity will be considered
later.

The term *sublime* and its German equivalent *erhaben* can be
traced back to the Latin title of a work originally written in
Greek about A.D. 40, *Peri Hypsous* (*De Sublimitate*), formerly
attributed to the third-century philosopher Longinus. It is
essentially a short textbook on rhetoric. *Hypsou* or *sublimitas*
denotes the quality of a passage which makes it have a profound
impact on the listener or the reader. The Latin *sublimitas* has
an added connotation of height, justifiable in the translation by
the large number of examples the author has selected for their
loftiness or grandeur. In this work the sublime is repeatedly
characterized in terms of masculine boldness, force, and
aggressiveness. Beauty is mentioned only incidentally, and there
is no occasion to contrast the masculine and the feminine. The
concern is rather with the kind of qualities that single out
mature, forceful men from fat, ineffectual ranters on the one
hand and from boys on the other.[4] Generally speaking, one can
say that this ancient work moves in a man's world of struggle
and conflict, in which the boldest and strongest win out, but

the ideal is the sophisticated, controlled masculinity of Roman civilization.

Although the *Peri hypsous* itself did not become directly influential again until its authority was invoked by Boileau in his *Art poétique* of 1674,[5] it epitomized ancient rhetorical thought and may be said to have started the concept of sublimity on a two-thousand-year career in philosophy, aesthetics, and ethics. The qualities which the 'pseudo-Longinus' recognized in public speaking and poetry, and in nature as a source of images for the speaker and poet, were sought after by Renaissance artists even before the first printings of *De Sublimitate* shortly after the middle of the sixteenth century. Loftiness, grandeur, striking impact, and heroic struggle are salient qualities of Baroque art and literature, and we may say that from the late sixteenth century well into the eighteenth, the ideal human personality was conceived as sublime. The concept really came into its own in the eighteenth century, when it was extended directly to the aesthetic realm apart from rhetoric or literature, to the moral, to the metaphysical, and to the direct impact of the natural landscape on the observer. But these extensions were already implicit in the ancient text, which compares sublimity with thunder, lightning, and conflagrations.[6]

Some other eighteenth-century connotations of the sublime and its relation to the beautiful were anticipated in ancient rhetorical literature as well. Cicero and Quintilian associate sublimity with moral grandeur, particularly virtue steadfast against fate, and with pathos. Their usage and its relevance for European Romanticism (in the person of Wordsworth) are examined in a collection of essays by Klaus Dockhorn.[7] The ancient rhetoricians distinguished three techniques of persuasion: *pedein*, or rational argument; *ethos*, which is the evocation of a bond of common humanity between speaker or writer and audience; and *pathos*, or overpowering emotion. Because *pedein* (Latin *persuasio*) is the least effective approach, rhetorical tradition has concentrated on non-rational *ethos* and *pathos*, or in modern terms the humane and the sublime. The technique of *ethos* convinces us that the speaker or writer is an ordinary

human being like you or me and in so doing subtly flatters us
into agreement. This approach appeals to that part of the non-
rational side of human nature which is calm, temperate, satisfied
with familiar, every-day experience. *Pathos* bursts through the
familiar to stir up intense passion and convey a feeling for some
infinite transcending power.

The history of the sublime in European thought has been
traced by Karl Vietor.[8] Concerned as we are here only with the
sublime in its polar relationship to the beautiful and with a few
other currents of thought that came together in the aesthetic
essays of Schiller, we may turn now to Lord Shaftesbury. The
concept occurs in his *Characteristics* both with and without the
actual word. He distinguishes between true 'inspiration' as a
real feeling of the Divine Presence and 'enthusiasm' as 'a false
one', but concedes that they both are associated with the image
of something prodigious or super-human, 'something vast,
immane'.[9] The word 'sublime' is applied to disinterested friendship without hope of reward. Shaftesbury further anticipates
Schiller's interest in the relation of beauty to grace and that of
physical to moral beauty. 'Beauty of sentiments' and 'grace of
actions' are mysteriously expressed 'in the turn of outward
features' (Shaftesbury, II, 68 f., 90 f.). Shaftesbury also
approaches Keats in declaring that 'the most natural beauty
in the world is honesty and moral truth. For all beauty is
truth' (I, 94).

Edmund Burke published his *Philosophical Enquiry into the
Origin of Our Ideas on the Sublime and Beautiful* at the age of 39
in 1756.[10] His concern is not with rhetoric, as might have been
expected from so brilliant an orator, but with aesthetic and
philosophical implications of sublimity. Like the author of
Peri Hypsous, Burke associates the sublime with power, force,
and the terror these arouse in the percipient, in short with
aspects of masculine combat. But an equally important element
of the sublime for Burke is the confrontation with overwhelm-
ing or mysterious and hence terrifying powers of nature:

I know of nothing sublime which is not some modification of
power . . . Strength, violence, pain and terror are ideas that rush in

upon the mind together. Look at a man, or any other animal of prodigious strength, and . . . the emotion you feel is [fear] . . . Power derives all its sublimity from the terror with which it is generally accompanied. (Burke, pp. 110 ff.)
In short, wheresoever we find strength, and in what light soever we look upon power, we shall all along observe the sublime the concomitant of terror . . . (Burke, p. 115)

Unlike the ancient Greek author of the textbook on rhetoric, who admired balanced and controlled power, this eighteenth-century English gentleman is fascinated by power in the raw. Even when he extends the concept of the sublime far beyond human or animal ferocity in combat, he retains the connotations of fear and the threat of pain. When he attributes sublimity to God, it is only in so far as the Divinity is contemplated 'under the arm, as it were, of almighty power', so that we 'shrink into the minuteness of our own nature, and are, in a manner, annihilated before him' (Burke, p. 119). It is the association of the sublime with fear that leads Burke into the domain of the dark and gloomy, the mysterious, and the obscure (Burke, pp. 99 ff., 275 ff.) and to qualities like sudden contrast, irregularity and roughness which were starting to evoke mixed horror and fascination when contemplated in the landscape.[11]

Burke's association of the beautiful with the female as viewed from a male perspective is all too obvious. Beauty is a 'quality of Venus', just as strength and the impression of sublimity are qualities of Hercules (Burke, p. 195). Beauty is defined as 'that quality or those qualities in bodies by which they cause love, or some passion similar to it' (Burke, p. 162). Although Burke ranges far beyond the domain of eroticism and takes care to distinguish love from sexual desire, a sexual orientation remains discernible, at times even glaringly conspicuous:

When we have before us such objects as excite love . . . , the head reclines something on one side; the eyelids are more closed than usual, and the eyes roll gently with an inclination to the object, the mouth is a little opened, and the breath drawn slowly, with now and then a low sigh, the whole body is composed and the hands fall idly to the sides. All this is accompanied by an inward sense of melting and languor. (Burke, pp. 286 f.)

The elements into which Burke attempts to resolve beauty in any object of perception — smallness, smoothness, gradual variation, delicacy, grace (Burke, pp. 209–32) — are at least implicitly, and not infrequently explicitly, sexual:

Observe that part of a beautiful woman where she is perhaps the most beautiful, about the neck and breasts; the smoothness; the softness, the easy and insensible swell; the variety of the surface . . . ; the deceitful maze, through which the unsteady eye slides giddily, without knowing where to fix, or whither it is carried. (Burke, p. 216)

The English work on aesthetics which was most widely read and quoted by German writers of the late eighteenth century was the *Elements of Criticism* by Henry Home, Lord Kames.[12] The chapters dealing with the relation of beauty to sublimity combine the basic aesthetic theory of Burke with the textbook approach of *Peri Hypsous*, from which Lord Kames frequently quotes. He not only defines and differentiates beauty and sublimity but shows how authors may best achieve either of these effects. For Lord Kames, beauty is that which is agreeable, hence associated with sweetness and gaiety; grace is agreeable movement (Kames, 1, 317 f.). A chapter-heading in the first edition contrasts the positive quality of dignity, for Kames close to grace, with the negative quality of meanness. Subsequent editions changed the title of the chapter to 'Dignity and Grace'. These two concepts remain closely associated, though not quite synonymous. The concept of grace is elaborated at the end of the chapter in a passage which begins: 'It is undoubtedly connected with motion; for when the most graceful person is at rest, neither moving nor speaking, we lose sight of that quality.'[13] Schiller, in a footnote to *Anmut und Würde*, quotes this passage from the latest German edition (Schiller, v, 446 n.) and argues that a graceful person will be so even in sleep. It is clear that he was challenged and stimulated by Lord Kames's argument and that the chapter title in the later editions of *Elements of Criticism* and in the German translation inspired both the title of Schiller's entire essay and a polarity never intended by the Scottish author.

Lord Kames is in essential agreement with Burke in associating sublimity with power and beauty with love. But he directs his attention much more than Burke to the experiencing subject, and it is in this sense that he quotes the old adage, 'Beauty is not in the countenance but in the lover's eye' (Kames, 1, 261). The same tendency is manifest in his varying illustrations of sublimity, quite a few of which exhibit the subject confronted by a more powerful enemy (e.g. Kames, 1, 266). But for Lord Kames the subjective reaction to the sublime is no longer cringing terror but an impulse toward emulation (Kames, 1, 265, 282 f.). Kames's idealization of the percipient's reaction to the sublime object was seized upon by Kant and Schiller and developed into their much more refined and complex aesthetics. Although they removed the beautiful and the sublime farther from the attraction to feminine beauty and the struggle against an overpowering adversary, they did not abandon the implicit reference to these primal experiences. On the other hand, they re-established in a very idealized sense the criterion of utility, fitness, or functionality which had been rejected by Burke and Lord Kames alike.

Kant's first work on the beautiful and the sublime, *Beobachtungen über das Gefühl des Schönen und Erhabenen*,[14] dates from 1764, just two years after the *Elements of Criticism*. The sexual reference remains clear enough: '*Freundschaft* hat hauptsächlich den Zug des *Erhabenen, Geschlechterliebe* aber des *Schönen* an sich' (Kant, II, 830). An entire chapter 'Von dem Unterschiede des Erhabenen und Schönen in dem Gegenverhältnis beider Geschlechter' (Kant, II, 850–68) contrasts feminine beauty with masculine nobility, dignity, and sublimity, but the ideal held up for each sex is the kind of union of both sets of qualities that will heighten the beauty of woman and the sublimity of man (Kant, II, 850). Kant's ethical orientation leads him to prefer the sublime 'Bezwingung [der] Leidenschaften durch Grundsätze' over that 'Weichmütigkeit' which he associates with beauty and charm (Kant, II, 834 f., cf. 839 f., 852 ff.).

This exaltation of sublimity over beauty is still evident in the otherwise much more profound argument of the *Kritik der*

Urteilskraft, published in 1790. The new kind of functionalistic rationalism that Kant had shortly before established for ethics in his *Kritik der praktischen Vernunft* is here extended to aesthetics. Each human being and each human act and creation were there viewed as part of the moral universe, intended to work freely for the good of the whole. The *Kritik der Urteilskraft* considers a corollary of that categorical imperative which guides us as parts of a greater moral society: the exercise of examining the effects of an act or the function of a work under the categorical imperative to judge its contribution to the greater whole takes on value and enjoyability for its own sake. We can practise upon an individual personality, act, or work, even an object in nature, to admire its embodiment, within itself, of the same kind of organization that characterizes the moral universe as a whole. Kant does not believe in a work of art so disinterested as to have no moral purpose, but he recognizes that man is able, in the moment of aesthetic experience, to view an object apart from its outward functionality, from its interest to us as responsible members of the moral order. In that longer or shorter moment of aesthetic contemplation we enjoy for its own sake the embodiment of a complete and harmonious order within the object itself.

Thus defined, beauty would appear to be a purely formal quality, but sexual polarity becomes apparent in Kant's differentiation of beauty from sublimity: In the beautiful object we recognize a form that is directly favourable, not just to the moral order, but to life itself. The sublime object at first sight appears rather to obstruct or threaten our vital energies, but in so doing it stimulates them to greater vigour and activity. Kant's statement that beauty evokes 'ein Gefühl der Beförderung des Lebens' (Kant, VIII, 329) may well be the most forward-looking pronouncement in his entire aesthetics, for it goes beyond ethical functionalism to recognize the organic principle stressed by his younger contemporaries, especially Goethe and the Romantics. But Kant remains more conservative in linking beauty in this context to the charm and playfulness emphasized by Burke and Lord Kames and in his insistence on the superiority of the

E

sublime, associated with power, fear, and the countervailing confidence in man's moral destiny.

Here Schiller's *Über Anmut und Würde* departs radically from Kant by arguing that the harmonious spontaneity of beauty represents a more advanced stage of aesthetic and ethical development than the triumphant moral struggle of sublimity. For Schiller the sublime and the beautiful as well as the concomitant dignity and grace still carry sexual but not — if we may resort to a catchword of our own day — 'sexist' connotations. Schiller repudiates Kant's preference for stern self-discipline over spontaneous harmony. In Kant's presentation of the idea of duty he finds a 'Härte . . ., die alle Grazien davon zurückschreckt und einen schwachen Verstand leicht versuchen könnte, auf dem Wege einer finstern und mönchischen Asketik die moralische Vollkommenheit zu suchen' (Schiller, v, 465). In so far as man obeys the imperative of reason by an effort of the will he is sublime; in so far as he does so freely and spontaneously he partakes of beauty and grace.

In some other passages of *Über Anmut und Würde* and in such later aesthetic writings of Schiller as his letters *Über die ästhetische Erziehung des Menschen* one notes a striving towards an ultimate synthesis of grace and dignity and of the beautiful and the sublime. The idea of masculine and feminine aesthetic elements requiring balance and synthesis in a higher ideal of beauty is most clearly expressed by Schiller's disciple Wilhelm von Humboldt. In two contributions to Schiller's journal *Die Horen*, 'Über den Geschlechtsunterschied und dessen Einfluß auf die organische Natur'[15] and 'Über die männliche und weibliche Form' (Humboldt, 1, 335–69), Humboldt sums up the dualistic concept of a masculine and feminine ideal of human beauty and explains how we strive to synthesize it in a common human ideal. The following passage is from the second essay:

In beiden [Geschlechtern] . . . ist die Menschheit ausgedrückt, denn jedes stellt die beiden, in ihr vereinten Naturen dar; nur daß in jedem eine dieser beiden Naturen das Uebergewicht hat . . . Denn ihrer charakteristischen Verschiedenheiten ungeachtet, nähern sich die männliche und weibliche Bildung dadurch einander, daß in jeder

dem besondern Ausdruck des Geschlechts der allgemeine Ausdruck
der Menschheit zur Seite steht. (Humboldt, 1, 351 ff.)

Although we are concerned here primarily with the tendency
of some eighteenth-century thinkers to regard the sublime and
the beautiful as a polarity, this is by no means true of all of them.
For Winckelmann the sublime was simply a heightened manifestation of the beautiful: 'Durch die *Einheit* und *Einfalt* wird
alle Schönheit *erhaben*', he declares in his *Geschichte der Kunst des
Altertums*.[16] Yet it was precisely Winckelmann to whom the
argument for sexual associations has first been applied. I am
referring to an article published a few years ago by Max
Baeumer.[17] Winckelmann was notoriously homosexual and his
favourite examples of supreme beauty are taken from the figure
of the boy at puberty, whose body still manifests some of the
softer and more gentle outlines (Winckelmann, IV, 64 f.), from
ancient statues modelled after castrated youths (Winckelmann,
IV, 73 f.), from hermaphrodites (Winckelmann, IV, 75 f.), and
from ancient figures of Bacchus and Apollo which united
qualities of the two sexes (Winckelmann, VII, 111 f.). Baeumer
charges that Goethe, Schiller, Wilhelm von Humboldt, in short
the whole of German Classicism, took over Winckelmann's
ideal of beauty while deliberately ignoring or even concealing
('geflissentlich übersehen oder vielleicht auch bewußt unter-
schlagen') its homoerotic character (Baeumer, p. 74). Influential
as Winckelmann undoubtedly was, he is not a source from
which German Classicism surreptitiously took over the sexual
associations of its aesthetic concepts. In Schiller and von
Humboldt these take the form of a dichotomy, which is absent
in Winckelmann and is, as we have seen, readily traced to
Burke and Lord Kames. Goethe, to be sure, does accept to a
degree the monistic approach of Winckelmann to the beautiful
and the sublime, but Goethe's own application of these concepts is utterly free of homoeroticism or, indeed, of significant
sexual overtones of any kind, and his own essay of 1805 on
Winckelmann discusses the latter's homosexuality with an
admirable combination of charitable discretion and candour.[18]
In this essay Goethe takes Winckelmann's approach to beauty

as a starting point from which to approach the relation of art to the fleeting quality of beauty in the human figure. Precisely because human beauty is so transitory, we need art to objectify and perpetuate it in its ideal reality. The experience of art is comparable to the feelings of the ancients who caught sight of the Olympian Jupiter: 'Der Gott war zum Menschen geworden, um den Menschen zum Gott zu erheben. Man erblickte die höchste Würde und ward für die höchste Schönheit begeistert.' (HA, xii, 103). Elsewhere, in *Italienische Reise* and *Dichtung und Wahrheit*, it is the sublime which makes the impression, whereas beauty orders and unifies the experience of the sublime so as to lend it permanence (HA, ix, 222 f., 382 f.; xi, 545). Goethe tends to associate the sublime, somewhat like Burke, with obscurity and night and with the expansive feelings of youth and primitive peoples; it thus has connotations of indefinite grandeur and mystery and needs the clarity and order which can be imparted by beauty.[19] We find a somewhat similar approach in Herder, who declares: 'Gefühl für Erhabenheit ist ... die Wendung meiner Seele' and compared his life with a walk through Gothic vaults or a green shaded lane: 'Die Aussicht ist immer Ehrwürdig und erhaben'; but when he comes out into the open he needs the sun to make the best use of these impressions.[20]

Whereas Kantian idealism and German Classicism oriented their aesthetics upon the human form and man's struggle between impulse and reason, in the new generation of Romanticism man lost his primacy. For the Romantics the frame of reference becomes the entire universe seen as a living whole reflecting and animated by the Divine spirit. The sublimity which they find in man is in reference to something vastly greater. In Novalis and Friedrich Schlegel the concept of sublimity therefore overshadows or absorbs the beautiful. With the former it becomes an elevation ('Erhebung') to an all-encompassing mystic vision. This vision was originally inspired by his love–death relationship to Sophie von Kühn, who becomes transfigured into a cosmic principle of wisdom and is frequently identified with both Christ and the Blessed Virgin.

But while elevating his original human love to a mystic level, Novalis retains its erotic aspect. Indeed eroticism becomes a mystic sacrament while simultaneously the Body and Blood of Christ are trans-substantiated into an object of ardent passion.[21] One cannot separate Novalis's use of the adjective 'erhaben' from the infinitive 'erheben' and its modern past participle 'erhoben'. But for Novalis elevation, 'Erhebung' — rather like the English 'sublimation' in the physical sciences — is one side of that two-fold process for which he also uses the terms 'potenzieren' and 'logarythmisieren'. As the concrete, physical, erotic is transfigured with mystic, spiritual significance, the universal is crystallized into something individual, even mundane.[22] The side of the process represented by 'Erhebung' is illustrated in two entries of *Das allgemeine Brouillon*:

Die *Erhebung* ist das vortrefflichste Mittel, was ich kenne, um auf einmal aus fatalen Collisionen zu kommen. So z. B. d[ie] allg[emeine] Erhebung in Adelstand — die Erhebung aller Menschen zu *Genies* — die Erhebung aller Phaenomene im *Wunderstand* — der Materie zu Geist — des Menschen zu Gott aller Zeit zur goldnen Zeit etc. (Novalis (1960), III, 440)
Der Busen ist die in *Geheimniß-Stand erhobne* Brust — die moralisirte Brust... So z. B. ist ein gestorbner Mensch ein in abs[oluten] Geheimnißzustand erhobener Mensch. (Novalis (1960), III, 290)

In Novalis's two fragmentary novels, *Die Lehrlinge zu Saïs* and *Heinrich von Ofterdingen*, we find sublimity attributed to conscience and virtue. *Die Lehrlinge* presents the terrifying aspect of nature as a reflection of human nightmares, passions, and weakness. The wakeful person who recognizes them as such 'wird in Ewigkeiten über diesem endlosen Wechsel erhaben schweben' (Novalis (1977), I, 90). Again in the conversation between Heinrich and Sylvester after the death of Mathilde in the Second Part of *Ofterdingen*, sublimity appears as a reaction to terrifying storm clouds reflecting man's inner self:

Wenn dann die verderblichen Strahlen herunterzucken und mit höhnischem Gelächter die schmetternden Donnerschläge hinterdrein fallen, so werden wir bis ins Innerste beängstigt, und wenn in uns dann nicht das erhabene Gefühl unsrer sittlichen Obermacht entsteht, so glauben wir den Schrecknissen der Hölle, der Gewalt böser Geister überliefert zu seyn.[23]

Here Novalis has brought sublimity back to the ethical connotations of Schiller, Kant, and ancient Rome, but as Sylvester shortly reminds us, the 'sublime, far-reaching, personal idea' of conscience goes beyond conventional ethics. It is the innate mediator of every human being, the representative of God on earth (Novalis (1977), I, 332). But this same principle is likewise the constitutive force of all nature:

Vom Sternhimmel, diesem erhabenen Dom des Steinreichs, bis zu dem krausen Teppich einer bunten Wiese wird alles durch ihn erhalten, ... und durch ihn die unbekannte Bahn der unendlichen Naturgeschichte bis zur Verklärung fortgeleitet. (Novalis (1977), I, 333)

The counterpart of conscience in the mineral and stellar realm is expressed here in the metaphor of a sublime cathedral. Novalis has 'elevated' the sublime far beyond its connotations in Longinus, Burke, Kant, and German Classicism, but in raising it to ultimate mystic import he has kept it true to its origins in that courage which stands fast against the terrors of thunderbolt and nightmare.

The transformation of the sublime is more gradual in Friedrich Schlegel, but the direction is similar. He starts from a dichotomy of the sublime and beautiful, with greater lip service to the latter, but gradually shifts his emphasis toward the sublime. In his early studies of Greek literature, his contributions to the *Athenäum* and in the novel *Lucinde*, even the early descriptions of painting written in Paris, he pays homage to the beautiful while half concealing a greater attraction to the sublime. In his antiquarian studies he attributes beauty primarily to the uncultivated 'Naturpoesie' of Homer at the beginning of the cycle of Greek civilization and to the conscious artistry of Sophocles at its crest, but he pays greater attention to the sublime work of Pindar, other lyric poets, and Aeschylus between them, and of such writers as Aristophanes in the subsequent period of decline; and some, like Aristophanes and the Ionic lyricists, win praise for their synthesis of beauty and sublimity.[24] Schlegel's references to post-antique literature at this time, to authors like Dante, Shakespeare, and Goethe, to characters like Hamlet and Faust, emphasize either sublimity alone or its synthesis with beauty. Despite his insistence on the emulation of the ancients he can affirm: 'Die erhabne Bestimmung der modernen Poesie ist . . . nichts geringeres als das höchste Ziel jeder möglichen Poesie.'[25]

A common element of this early period and that of Schlegel's journal *Athenäum* is the association of sublimity with the Platonic concept of a common human ideal to be approached in either sex. It is a major theme of the two writings of this second period in which the term 'sublime' appears in its most interesting contexts: the letter 'Über die Philosophie' addressed to Schlegel's mistress Dorothea and the novel *Lucinde*. In the letter Schlegel maintains that the womanly figure is aesthetically inferior because it is too obviously designed for the single purpose of motherhood, whereas the male figure displays a variety of functions:

Ist aber die männliche Gestalt reicher, selbständiger, künstlicher und erhabener, so möchte ich die weibliche Gestalt *menschlicher* finden. In dem schönsten Manne ist die Göttlichkeit und Tierheit weit abgesonderter. In der weiblichen Gestalt ist beides ganz verschmolzen, wie in der Menschheit selbst. Und darum finde ich's auch sehr wahr, daß die Schönheit des Weibes eigentlich nur die höchste sein kann: denn das Menschliche ist überall das Höchste und höher als das Göttliche. (F. Schlegel, VIII, 46)

In short, the beauty of woman is more human (as might be expected from the traditional association of beauty with *ethos*), the sublimity of man more Divine, but as (and to the extent that!) the human surpasses the Divine, the beauty of woman surpasses that of man.

In the context of the passage just quoted Schlegel calls the male figure 'unbestimmt' because of the multiplicity of functions for which it is destined. In the passage of *Lucinde* entitled 'Eine Reflexion' we find that 'das Bestimmende oder das Bestimmte' has switched over to become an innate, self-evident quality ('das Namenlose') of the male, whereas the feminine is now 'das Unbestimmte'. (It would appear that in the letter 'bestimmt' was used in the sense 'destined' or 'designed', here in the sense 'definite'.) Feminine indefiniteness is 'geheimnisreicher, aber das Bestimmte hat mehr Zauberkraft. Die reizende Verwirrung des Unbestimmten ist romantischer, aber die erhabene Bildung des Bestimmten ist genialischer' (F. Schlegel, v, 72). We are left unsure whether the sublime, clearly defined male or the beautiful, charming, romantic, and misty female has carried off the prize.

From 1802 on Schlegel applies the sublime to a great variety of objects: in art, painting, the landscape, history, and religion, but no longer with clear sexual reference. As he moves toward Catholicism he comes to regard the primal Divine revelation that is dimly remembered from a pre-historical past and will be renewed in an eschatalogical future as the ultimate sublime object of human longing.[26] The most striking evidence of the triumph of sublimity over beauty is found in a description of the hills overlooking the Rhein opposite Bonn in the travel journal which Schlegel published in 1806.[27] He lets himself be carried away by his enthusiasm for the lofty crags, for the equally rugged knights who inhabited them in the Middle Ages, and for their origin in a violent geological past. He praises the 'erhabene und edle Neigung' of the Germans to live on heights like these and concludes that for him 'sind nur die Gegenden schön, welche man gewöhnlich rauh und wild nennt; denn nur diese sind erhaben, nur erhabene Gegenden können schön sein, nur diese erregen den Gedanken der Natur' (F. Schlegel, iv, 187).

Novalis in elevating earthly experience to ultimate mystic significance, Schlegel in directing his longing to primal revelation and to the heroic past of human and geological history have left far behind them the purely human *ethos* of antiquity and of German Classicism and exalted sublime *pathos* to the level of the Divine.

REFERENCES

[1] S. S. Kerry, *Schiller's Writings on Aesthetics* (Manchester, 1961), pp. 1–13; Herbert Cysarz, *Schiller* (Halle, 1934), p. 195.

[2] Male and female connotations in *Über Anmut und Würde* have been pointed out by Max L. Baeumer, 'Winckelmanns Formulierung der klassischen Schönheit', *Monatshefte*, 65 (1973), 61–75 (p. 74).

[3] Schiller, *Sämtliche Werke*, edited by Gerhard Fricke and Herbert G. Göpfert, second edition (Munich, 1960), v, 469 f. This edition is henceforward cited as 'Schiller'. Emphasis throughout this article is from the sources.

[4] *Longinus on the Sublime*, translated by A. O. Prickard (Oxford, 1906), pp. 5 ff.

[5] Karl Vietor, 'Die Idee des Erhabenen in der deutschen Literatur', in his *Geist und Form* (Bern, 1952), pp. 235–66 (pp. 238 f.).

[6] *Longinus on the Sublime*, pp. 3, 28.

[7] *Macht und Wirkung der Rhetorik* (Bad Homburg, 1968), especially pp. 10 f., 15 ff.

[8] See note 5 above.

[9] Anthony Earl of Shaftesbury, *Characteristics of Men, Manners, Opinions, Times*, etc., edited by John M. Robertson, 2 vols (New York, 1900), I, 37 f. This edition is henceforward cited as 'Shaftesbury'.

[10] Quoted here from the second edition (London, 1759, reprinted New York, 1971), henceforward cited as 'Burke'.

[11] See my book, *ROMANTISCH: Genese und Tradition einer Denkform* (Frankfurt, 1972), pp. 38 ff.

[12] 3 vols (Edinburgh, 1762, reprinted Hildesheim and New York, 1970), henceforward cited as 'Kames'.

[13] Sixth edition (Edinburgh, 1785, reprinted New York, 1972), I, 363.

[14] Kant, *Werke in zehn Bänden*, edited by Wilhelm Weischedel (Darmstadt, 1956–64, reprinted Wiesbaden, 1968), II, 821–84. This edition is henceforward cited as 'Kant'.

[15] Wilhelm von Humboldt, *Werke*, edited by A. Leitzmann (Berlin, 1903), I, 311–34. This edition is henceforward cited as 'Humboldt'.

[16] Winckelmann, *Sämtliche Werke*, 12 vols (Donaueschingen, 1825–35, reprinted Osnabrück, 1965), IV, 60. This edition is henceforward cited as 'Winckelmann'.

[17] See note 2 above.

[18] *Goethes Werke*, Hamburger Ausgabe, edited by Erich Trunz, 14 vols (Hamburg, 1948–60), XII, 96–129. This edition is henceforward cited as 'HA'.

[19] See also his letter to Frau von Stein, *Goethes Briefe*, Hamburger Ausgabe, edited by Karl Robert Mandelkow, 4 vols (Hamburg, 1962–67), I, 275 (3 October 1779).

[20] Herder, *Sämmtliche Werke*, edited by B. Suphan, 33 vols (Berlin, 1877–99), IV, 438 ff.

[21] See *Hymnen an die Nacht*, 5 and 6, and *Geistliche Lieder*, VII ('Hymne'), Novalis, *Schriften*, edited by Paul Kluckhohn and Richard Samuel, third edition (Stuttgart, 1977–), I (1977), 150 ff., 166 ff. This edition is henceforth cited as 'Novalis (1977)'.

[22] *Schriften*, edited by Paul Kluckhohn and Richard Samuel, second edition (Stuttgart, 1960–75), II (1965), 545 ('Logologische Fragmente', No. 105). This edition is henceforward cited as 'Novalis (1960)'.

[23] Novalis (1977), I, 330. There are slight textual differences between the second and third editions in this passage. I have taken 'mit höhnischem' from the second edition; the third edition reads 'mit höhnischen Gelächter'.

[24] Friedrich Schlegel, *Seine prosaischen Jugendschriften*, edited by Jakob Minor, 2 vols (Vienna, 1882), I, 14, 243 (with footnote 4), 351. An implicit preference in this early period for the poets designated as sublime is brought out more clearly in Schlegel's private lectures of 1803–04, *Kritische Friedrich-Schlegel-Ausgabe*,

edited by Ernst Behler, Hans Eichner and Jean-Jacques Anstett (Munich, Paderborn, Vienna and Zurich, 1958–), xi, 77 ff. This edition is henceforward cited as 'F. Schlegel'.

[25] *Prosaische Jugendschriften*, i, 111.

[26] F. Schlegel, vi, 292 (in reference to the dim recollection in Shakespeare of man's original sublimity); viii, 207 ff. (vestiges of the primal revelation in the religions of India); xix, 89 f. (note 70, dating from 1805); iii, 316 f. (eschatological longing in the poetry of Lamartine).

[27] *Briefe auf einer Reise durch die Niederlande, Rheingegenden, die Schweiz und einen Teil von Frankreich*, F. Schlegel, iv, 153–204.

The Dramatic Image

Observations on the Drama with Examples from Schiller and Lessing

By Frank M. Fowler

OF THE many aspects of E. M. Wilkinson's work which I have long admired, not the least important is her unfailing faithfulness to the nature of the object under scrutiny: the poem to which she opens our eyes, our minds, and our hearts, is perceived and communicated in all its suggestiveness as poem — and the play as play. Perhaps in an ideal world of scholar-critics such a fundamental virtue could be taken for granted; but in reality it is still rare enough to merit explicit comment.

If any one of the three main literary 'kinds' has suffered excessively from critical distortion of the object, it must surely be the drama; and the German drama has, I believe, suffered more than either the English or the French. That the issue has, however, not always been a specifically German one may perhaps be best illustrated by the one short paragraph in Wellek and Warren's well-known *Theory of Literature* in which the matter is brought up:

One awkwardness, to be sure, is the fact that in our time drama stands on a different basis from epic ('fiction', novel) and lyric. For Aristotle and the Greeks, public or at least oral performance was given the epic: Homer was poetry recited by a rhapsode like Ion. Elegiac and iambic poetry were accompanied by the flute, melic poetry by the lyre. Today, poems and novels are eye-read to oneself, for the most part. But the drama is still, as among the Greeks, a mixed art, centrally literary, no doubt, but involving also 'spectacle' — making use of the actor's skill and the play director's, the crafts of the costumer and electrician.[1]

Now with all due respect to electricians (though I abhor their intermittent attempts to turn dramatic performances into a kind of *son et lumière* in which the *lumière* totally dominates and distracts from the *son*), this formulation would seem to describe the theatre in a way that is somewhat crude and distinctly unsympathetic. By contrast, nothing whatever is said here of performed drama as communal celebration or communal experience — whereas a recent critic has pointed out that the dramatic performance 'creates, albeit briefly, a sense of communal experience which is perhaps the nearest most people can come today to a shared ritual'.[2] Nor is anything said of the audience's unique sense of immediacy, of something that is *happening now*, something that cannot be stopped or accelerated, something with an assertive rhythm and dynamic of its own, something that normally demands to be experienced whole, well-nigh uninterrupted, commanding undivided attention from a body of people temporarily freed from the distractions of over-tired children, hungry dogs, shrilling telephones, and persons from Porlock. Of course, the invention of printing has made it possible for us to have it both ways: we may, before or after a performance, re-read a favourite speech or passage of dialogue, or even choose to study the verbal text in detail, looking before and after, pausing to reflect and to compare. Yet here we face the central paradox of drama: careful reading is seldom if ever an adequate substitute for the experience of an inspired performance in the theatre; while the best individual performance will never exhaust all the imaginative potential of a rich and suggestive text. And the richer the texture (in symbolic action, in poetry, and in thought), the more acute the problem becomes.

The matter of the theatrical dimension of drama is in fact brushed aside by Wellek and Warren, who continue their discussion thus: 'If, however, one avoids that difficulty by reducing all three [basic kinds] to a common literariness . . .'. But it is precisely the reduction to a mere literariness that has in my view hampered the study of the German drama more than any other single factor. Even today, so one-sided is the concentration of many critics of the drama on the verbal text alone that they seem to have been corrupted by Mephisto's notorious advice to the freshman: 'Im ganzen — haltet euch an Worte!'. But the fact that a play possesses a rich poetic texture does not mean that the text on the page is complete in itself; and the fact that the theatre regularly enters into alliances with texts that are, from a literary point of view, manifestly mediocre or even execrable does not mean that it is therefore unable to receive and wondrously transform into a living reality what is best in dramatic literature.

A fairer account of the matter than that of Wellek and Warren was in fact provided by W. H. Hudson, who, writing almost half-a-century before them, offered the basis for a markedly more constructive approach:

It may of course be assumed that the essential difference in technique between the novel and the drama is commonly recognised in theory by every reader of the one or the other. But its practical bearings for the student of literature are, I believe, very seldom appreciated to the full, and to these, therefore, some attention should be given.

The novel is self-contained; that is, it provides within its own compass everything that the writer deemed necessary for the comprehension and enjoyment of his work. The drama, on the other hand, when it reaches us in the form of print, and when we read it as literature, in the same way as we read a novel, is not in this sense self-contained. It implies everywhere the co-operation of elements outside itself, and for the moment these elements are lacking. What we read is, in fact, little more than a bare outline which the playwright intended to be filled in by the art of the actor and the 'business' of the boards — a literary basis for that stage-representation upon which he calculated for the full execution of his design. In the mere perusal of a play, therefore, we labour under certain drawbacks and and difficulties, for much of its effect is likely to be lost upon us for want of those continual appeals to the imagination, those descriptions, explanations, and personal commentaries, which in a novel help us to visualize scenes, understand people, estimate motives, grasp the ethical import of actions. For this reason, the comprehension and enjoyment of a play as a piece of literature must always make immeasurably greater demands upon us than the comprehension and enjoyment of a novel. — In ordinary practice — and particularly in our study of Shakespeare, whose works we persist in treating as 'pure' literature, and rarely regard in their primary qualities as plays written expressly for the stage — we are too apt to neglect these simple but far-reaching considerations. It is worthwhile, therefore, to insist that in our study of any drama we should do our utmost to recreate its proper theatrical circumstances and surroundings, and thus to make our private reading of it so far as possible an adequate substitute for public performance.[3]

Hudson's dated reference to Shakespeare may serve to remind us of some of the major developments in Shakespeare studies that have taken place since his day: our century has seen not only the establishment of more accurate texts and the careful detailing of Shakespeare's sources, but also the general discovery of the immense importance of imagery, *and* a sustained attention precisely to the theatrical dimension of the plays — including the playwright's stagecraft and the specifically dramatic impact of his works. Now in Shakespeare scholarship — to a degree unparalleled in the study of Germany's classical dramatists — the attention to verbal imagery has, as it were, been counterbalanced by enhanced awareness of the specifically dramatic dimension. And indeed the two should surely go hand-in-hand. For the imagery of the drama, in contrast to that of the poem or the novel, is not purely verbal. It is also visual.

One might, however, read several thousand pages on Germany's classical dramatists without ever lighting on a hint of the attitude displayed by Wolfgang Clemen when he draws explicit attention in Shakespeare's plays to 'moments of great theatrical power ..., tableaux which, interpreted in each case by the text, compress the essence of a figure, and sometimes of a whole play, into a single visual image ..., symbolic moments on the stage often more eloquent than many speeches'.[4] Yet such moments are by no means peculiar to Shakespeare; they recur as a persistent feature of the drama throughout the ages, and are to be found in the German tradition from the *Osterspiel* to Dürrenmatt. If — for whatever reason — we ignore or underestimate them in the great writers of the eighteenth century, we perpetuate a dangerously blinkered attitude which must hamper both interpretation and evaluation.

A case in which greater attention to visual detail might have helped to prevent unwarranted accusations of unsatisfactory construction and inconsistent character-portrayal is that of Schiller's first historical tragedy, *Die Verschwörung des Fiesko zu Genua*. For here the playwright has not only been charged with failing to link the political theme of the play with Fiesko's personal problems; he has repeatedly been accused of vacillating between two contradictory views of his protagonist, uncertain whether to make him an autocratic villain or a self-sacrificing republican: indeed the near-juxtaposition in the middle of the play of the two crucial soliloquies in which Fiesko comes to diametrically opposite conclusions about his ultimate political intention has even been pilloried by one critic as 'eine dramatische Unmöglichkeit'.[5] In fact there is nothing dramatically — or psychologically — impossible about the sequence of scenes in question (II.19; III.1; III.2), though it is on this sequence that the charge of faulty construction principally depends.

The first of these soliloquies is spoken by Fiesko immediately after he has been visited by the small band of republicans who need to claim him for their cause since he alone commands the respect of the common people and the nobility alike. At first apparently untouched by their pleas, he finally reveals — in a highly histrionic manner — that he has secretly organized a *coup* down to the last detail, having obtained practical support from France and from the Pope; whereupon three of the four conspirators fall to their knees before him in admiration and awe. From this moment of glory young Fiesko derives the greatest satisfaction ('Mein ungeheuerster Wunsch ist befriedigt'); yet as soon as the republicans have bidden him goodnight he finds that 'Befriedigung' has given way to emotional turmoil within him: 'Welch ein Aufruhr in meiner Brust?'.[6] Even at this point he cannot refrain from imagining the immense power which is now within his grasp; he sees himself as ruler of all Genoa — the position that his earlier address to the common people and his consistently autocratic behaviour had suggested as his inevitable goal. But under the influence of the republicans' tribute he ends by imagining himself renouncing the ducal purple — an action which he sees as not merely great but divine: 'Ein Diadem erkämpfen ist *groß*. Es wegwerfen ist *göttlich*. (*Entschlossen*) Geh unter, Tyrann! Sei frei, Genua, und ich (*sanft geschmolzen*) dein *glücklichster* Burger!' The last stage-direction clearly indicates a moment of sentimentality, such as we shall see again in his interview with Leonore in IV.14; but such moments Fiesko never allows to interfere with the realization of his political ambitions. And, ironically, in the ensuing scene — on a deserted heath outside the city where even walls have ears — Verrina, the perceptive man of the world who knows Fiesko better than Fiesko knows himself, will reveal to Bourgognino how dangerous those ambitions are, and will warn him that Fiesko must be destroyed.

The scenic context of the second soliloquy contrasts sharply with the dark 'Vorzimmer' of the first. After a restless night tellingly interrupted by 'wilde Phantasien', Fiesko stands at dawn at a great French window and sees the sun rise, revealing the city of Genoa in its full glory at his feet. The good resolution, so easily made in the total absence of temptation, now fades and is forgotten as that temptation gleams, irresistible, before him; at the climactic moment of the sunrise the sun becomes for Fiesko the symbol of the regal splendour and power that could be his:

Diese majestätische Stadt! (*Mit offenen Armen dagegen eilend.*) Mein! — und drüber emporzuflammen gleich dem königlichen Tag — drüber zu brüten mit Monarchenkraft — ?

Fiesko's ensuing accompaniment of his rhapsody on absolute power 'mit erhabenem Spiel' and his assumption of a heroic posture at the end of the soliloquy again bring to the fore that incurable addiction to the histrionic which is repeatedly demonstrated in a whole variety of situations — the addiction that ultimately determines the manner of his death. For Verrina, the true republican, who alone has perceived the tragic truth about Fiesko, will lure him to the harbour by a ruse, knowing that he cannot resist the opportunity of being seen to make a grand gesture. Fiesko's tragedy is indissolubly linked with the tragedy of Genoa, the city-state endeavouring to rid itself of tyranny, in that the one man who *could* have set up the republic *would* not. And the link is compressed for us into that single visual image at the climax of the play: Fiesko's rapacious outstretching of his arms towards the Genoa that he alone could make free. Nor is this all. For as he moves eagerly towards the city, he is simultaneously moving towards something else, which is twice referred to in the accompanying stage-directions and then explicitly mentioned by him: Fiesko moves towards the sea, in which, as republican Genoa takes its revenge, he will ultimately meet his death. In retrospect we understand why the sea forms the background not only throughout Act v but also at this crucial moment in Act iii — precisely in the middle of the play — when the hero takes the decisive step towards his own annihilation. The water is his destiny: it is there, visible, waiting for him.

Even in a play which has been subjected to as much critical scrutiny as *Don Carlos*, due attention has not been given to the visual image which in this case not only provides the culminating link between the verbal imagery and the action of the play but also must affect our interpretation of the ending. A recent critic writes that 'at first impression *Don Carlos* appears to end in the extinction of hope and the blight of promise', but goes on to emphasize 'a feeling of harmony' which is 'the achievement of the movement of Schiller's verse'.[7] Now the same critic has perceptively drawn attention to the verbal imagery of nature, of plant, and of growth in *Don Carlos*, explicitly pointing out that these images are here prominent to an extent unparalleled in any of Schiller's earlier plays. And indeed the images recur in crucial passages in this play, which opens in a garden and ends in a dark enclosed space, in a manner that is striking and emphatic, as in the very section of Posa's appeal by which the King is first visibly moved:

> Und Sie hoffen,
> Zu endigen, was Sie begannen? hoffen,
> Der Christenheit gezeitigte Verwandlung,
> Den allgemeinen *Frühling* aufzuhalten,
> Der die Gestalt der Welt verjüngt? . . .

F

Sie werden nicht! Schon flohen Tausende
Aus Ihren Ländern froh und arm. Der Bürger,
Den Sie verloren für den Glauben, war
Ihr edelster. Mit offnen Mutterarmen
Empfängt die Fliehenden Elisabeth,
Und *fruchtbar blüht* durch Künste unsres Landes
Britannien. Verlassen von dem Fleiß
Der neuen Christen, liegt Granada *öde*,
Und jauchzend sieht Europa seinen Feind
An selbstgeschlagnen Wunden sich verbluten.

(*Der König ist bewegt; der Marquis bemerkt es und tritt einige Schritte näher*)

Sie wollen *pflanzen* für die Ewigkeit,
Und *säen* Tod?

(ll. 3160, 3180; my italics)

What the powers of darkness will actually attempt to plant, and
what nature means to them is finally brought home to us in the
horrifying exchange between Philipp and the Grand Inquisitor
which seals the fate of Carlos.

König: Kannst du mir einen neuen Glauben gründen,
Der eines Kindes blutgen Mord verteidigt?
Großinquisitor: Die ewige Gerechtigkeit zu sühnen,
Starb an dem Holze Gottes Sohn.
König: Du willst
Durch ganz Europa diese Meinung pflanzen?
Großinquisitor: So weit, als man das Kreuz verehrt.
König: Ich frevle
An der Natur — auch diese mächtge Stimme
Willst du zum Schweigen bringen?
Großinquisitor: Vor dem Glauben
Gilt keine Stimme der Natur.

(ll. 5265–5273)

Don Carlos does not quite end in the 'extinction of hope', for
the symbolic action before us tells us otherwise. The father,
already in his declining years, kills his son; the king destroys
his heir — not by accident or in a moment of uncontrollable
passion, but out of conviction, deliberately, characteristically.
The sterility and the inevitable self-destructiveness of the
repressive regime are amply signalled both in the concluding
lines and in the final dramatic image, as Philipp irrevocably

turns his back on Carlos ('*Er geht ab*'), leaving him to certain death at the hands of the terrifying figure of the Grand Inquisitor, who stands there aged and blind, waiting to act as the instrument of Philipp's latest, appalling 'selbstgeschlagne Wunde'. The final image thus itself includes the promise that Posa's hope of a better future must eventually be fulfilled.

But if we accept as a critical necessity the principle of giving full weight to the visual imagery of the drama, it is a principle which cannot be confined to the work of a particularly theatre-orientated playwright such as Schiller. Indeed much that is customarily dismissed as 'Lesedrama' or otherwise relegated to the theatre of the mind will be found on examination to contain an integrated visual component of no little significance. In a few cases, such as that of Goethe's *Torquato Tasso*, the visual elements have, hearteningly, received fairly full attention; in other cases they pass again and again unremarked in what might almost be a critical conspiracy of silence.

Of all the great dramas in the German language, perhaps none has fared worse in this respect than Lessing's *Nathan der Weise* — a work cursed by regular association with a trio of terms which seem calculated to reinforce the oft-stated opinion that it is not really a play at all. These terms are 'pulpit', 'parable', and 'dramatic poem'; and in employing them literary historians have frequently contrived to give the impression that Lessing, having been forbidden to publish further theological treatises, decided to use the stage as a pulpit, that is, to disguise a discourse or sermon in the semblance of a play — which in the event turned out not to be a play but a dramatic poem having as its climax, its key, and its *raison d'être* a parable where a play would have action. Certainly W. H. Bruford, in his excellent book on the German drama, summed up the views of many when in 1949 he wrote that *Nathan* was 'not so much a drama as a series of arguments and addresses . . .'.[8]

In fact the context of Lessing's notorious reference to the pulpit — in his letter to Elise Reimarus of 6 September 1778 — might well be taken to undermine rather than to strengthen the notion that he expected *Nathan* to be anything less of a play than his earlier dramatic works. The sentence 'Ich muß versuchen, ob man mich auf meiner *alten* Kanzel, auf dem Theater wenigstens, noch ungestört will predigen lassen' (my italics) suggests merely that the theatre is to be Lessing's pulpit *as before*;[9] and varied though interpretations of *Minna von Barnhelm* and *Emilia Galotti* may be, neither play is commonly found to lack some sort of 'message'. In the previous sentence, moreover, Lessing refers to his work as a 'Schauspiel'; while in a less often quoted letter to his brother Karl written six weeks later he expresses his conviction that *Nathan* 'wird ein so rührendes Stück, als ich nur immer gemacht habe —' (20 October 1778). It is this same term 'Stück' that Lessing consistently employs in his correspondence when referring to *Nathan*; furthermore, he devised for the work a special 'neue Interpunction für die Schauspieler' which he insisted the compositor should meticulously observe; while in a fragmentary essay or preface he ends with the words: 'Noch kenne ich keinen Ort in Deutschland, wo dieses Stück jetzt aufgeführt werden könnte. Aber Heil und Glück dem, wo es zuerst aufgeführt wird'. So far as the sub-title is concerned, the evidence suggests that the term 'ein dramatisches Gedicht' is here meant in much the same sense as in Number 79 of the *Hamburgische Dramaturgie*, where it is used to designate a serious play which is not a tragedy. After all, in 1779 the term 'Drama' might well have aroused expectations of a work similar in tone to the 'drame' of Diderot, while 'Schauspiel' might have suggested a piece akin to *Götz von Berlichingen, Der Wirrwarr*, or *Simsone Grisaldo*!

Yet the critics' determination to treat *Nathan* as less than a play dies hard. In his well-known recent study of the work, Peter Demetz comments unfavourably on the final tableau of 'allseitige Umarmungen', and suggests that Lessing might have done better to end with the prospect of a double wedding, as hinted at in the earlier 'Entwurf'.[10] Against this one might reasonably argue that the play in its justification of the workings of Providence positively required the final revelation that the characters, unknown to themselves, always *have* been related;

it is not enough that they *might* prove suitable partners for each other in marriage. But Demetz's objection that the tableau amounts to 'Statueskes, das mit dem Geist der funkelnd bewegten Dialektik, die das Stück durchwaltet, in Widerspruch gerät' — however persuasive it may seem at first sight — reveals a remarkable lack of sensitivity to the visual imagery of the play as a whole.

In fact the theme of separation and reunion is not only the subject of discussion in the opening lines of the play, as Nathan returns from his long journey: it then makes a striking re-entry in the opening lines of the second scene, in a passage manifestly superfluous both to exposition and to plot:

> So seid Ihr es doch ganz und gar, mein Vater?
> Ich glaubt', Ihr hättet Eure Stimme nur
> Vorausgeschickt. Wo bleibt Ihr? Was für Berge,
> Für Wüsten, was für Ströme trennen uns
> Denn noch? Ihr atmet Wand an Wand mit ihr,
> Und eilt nicht, Eure Recha zu umarmen?
>
> (ll. 169–174)

It seems remarkable that commentators should habitually ignore the force of these lines which clearly announce the important theme of the invisible barriers between human beings and the universal need to surmount these in the loving embrace. And the visual imagery of the play is overwhelmingly that of physical approach and contact, with a whole pattern of loving relationships expressed and established.

In Act II we see Saladin embrace Sittah on discovering that in her love she has for some time secretly maintained him and the whole court, while at the first crucial point in his enlightenment the Templar seizes Nathan's hand, recognizing in the Jew a human being more than worthy of his friendship. In Act III the climax is marked by Saladin's rushing up to Nathan at the end of the parable passage to grasp his hand, 'die er bis zu Ende nicht wieder fahren läßt'; and in Act IV, as Saladin and the Templar each recognize the integrity and the worth of the other, they immediately clasp hands. In the penultimate scene of Act V Saladin gently raises Recha to her

feet as he sees her innocence and her distress, while before
the final tableau we are witnesses to a whole series of embraces
as the true relationships of the characters are progressively
revealed. These gestures are, we observe, not sprinkled throughout the play in a haphazard manner: they are on the one hand
invariably responses to moments of recognition, and on the
other hand consistently restricted to members of the symbolic
family finally united before our very eyes. In fact Lessing's
Nathan is not a dry working-out in quasi-dramatic terms of the
ring-parable of Act III; for perfectly interwoven with the appeal
to the intellect made by the words is a carefully controlled
pattern of closely related visual images which lead us gradually
but inevitably to the final mime, as at the close of Act v all the
characters on stage embrace. And they do so without words,
for their emotion is beyond what words can express.

The essential connexion between climax and dénouement in
Nathan is not solely the result of the presence of related gestures;
nor does it depend merely on the forging in Act III of a link
essential to the plot — the link between two groups of characters. For if we are sensitive to the symbolic potential of drama,
we shall see something more. In Act III we hear — but only by
report in Nathan's parable — of the ring of precious metal
which has the wondrous power of making its owner beloved
of God and man, but which a judge presumes to be lost; in the
final tableau Lessing offers us the sight of a living ring of human
kinship, natural and spiritual: a circle of inter-relationship in
which the participants, having learnt to appreciate the inscrut-
able ways of Providence (and by contrast the potentially
catastrophic limitation of human vision) have surmounted and
come to count as naught the needless, artificial, and destructive
barriers that could forever have kept them apart. To the rings
described in the words of the parable scholars have devoted
hundreds of pages of background information and critical
debate; whereas the living ring of understanding and love so
carefully and finely forged in the visual imagery of the play and
ultimately presented *whole* before our eyes has merited scarcely a
mention. This is a case in which the relative fiction (the parable)

receives more attention than the relative reality (the play and its ending). But in a sense the parable is necessarily incomplete: unlike, say, the parable of the Good Samaritan, it does not go so far as to *show* the enlightened attitude embodied within it actually contributing to the welfare of mankind. This, however, Lessing's play richly does show, and in the manner of true drama — not in words alone but also (and in the end only) in the visual image. In a work which achieves an amazing — and delicious — balance between intellectual content and emotional impact, that image cannot be accounted out of place. The intermittent comedy, the penetration of the thought, and the jagged dialectic of the verse combine to save *Nathan der Weise* from lapsing into the downright sentimental; while the moving sight of the symbolic and gradual family reunion effected in the face of all odds — including those of statistical probability — preserves it from becoming a dry enlightenment essay. 'Das Werk lobt den Meister, und dies ist Manneswerk' wrote Herder of *Nathan*. He also had no hesitation in calling the work a play.

In his Preface to *Die Braut von Messina*, Schiller, already nearing the end of his lifetime as a playwright, found it necessary to point out, with admirable modesty and candour, that verbal text and play are not one and the same: 'Nur die Worte gibt der Dichter . . .'. But have we, after a century and three-quarters, really taken his warning to heart? It is surely futile to pay lip-service to the notion of drama by regularly substituting 'audience' for 'reader' throughout our criticism, while doggedly continuing to treat a play either as a defective novel or as a poem divided up into a series of speeches. To put it bluntly, we shall never achieve a balanced approach to the drama so long as we persist in mentally elevating the dialogue to the status of holy writ, while tacitly dismissing the theatre as an audio-visual aid for the mentally defective. Man does not live by words alone: if he did, he would never have invented drama.

REFERENCES

[1] R. Wellek and A. Warren, *Theory of Literature*, third edition (London, 1963), pp. 258–59.

[2] S. W. Dawson, *Drama and the Dramatic* (London, 1970), p. 84.

[3] W. H. Hudson, *An Introduction to the Study of Literature*, second edition (London, 1955), pp. 172–74.

[4] Wolfgang Clemen, *Shakespeare's Dramatic Art* (London, 1972), p. 210.

[5] K. Wölfel, 'Pathos und Problem. Ein Beitrag zur Stilanalyse von Schillers "Fiesko" ', *GRM*, 38 (1957), 240. For a critical scrutiny of adverse opinions on *Fiesko* and an interpretation of the whole play see my article 'Schiller's "Fiesko" Re-examined', *PEGS*, N.S., 40 (1970), 1–29.

[6] Schiller quotations are taken from Friedrich Schiller, *Sämtliche Werke*, edited by Gerhard Fricke and Herbert G. Göpfert, 5 vols (Munich, 1958), I and II. In the case of *Don Carlos*, the line-numbers cited are two lower than in other editions.

[7] H. B. Garland, *Schiller the Dramatic Writer* (Oxford, 1969), p. 137.

[8] W. H. Bruford, *Theatre, Drama and Audience in Goethe's Germany* (London, 1950), p. 168.

[9] Lessing quotations are taken from Gotthold Ephraim Lessing, *Gesammelte Werke*, edited by Paul Rilla, 10 vols (Berlin and Weimar, 1968), II and IX.

[10] *Nathan der Weise: Dichtung und Wirklichkeit*, edited by Peter Demetz (Frankfurt/Main and Berlin, 1966), p. 156.

The Coherence of Goethe's Political Outlook

By R. H. Stephenson

IN THIS article I shall draw on two aspects of Professor Wilkinson's work, separated by some twenty years, but none the less intimately connected. The one is her authoritative analysis, undertaken over twenty-five years ago, of Goethe's principle of *Steigerung* and its relation to his concepts of *Polarität* and *Specification*.[1] The other is her work, in collaboration with L. A. Willoughby, on the various uses to which Schiller — and Goethe[2] — put the concepts of subordination, co-ordination, and, most fascinating of all, the reciprocal relations (themselves subordinate or co-ordinate) between the two. In their Introduction to the *Aesthetic Letters*, Wilkinson and Willoughby have uncovered this principle of reciprocal subordination and co-ordination at work in Schiller's mode of thought, his strategy, his method, and in the detail of his language.[3] And in a more recent essay,[4] they have gone on to demonstrate how Schiller uses this same principle in order, not only to distinguish, but also to relate the two models of wholeness with which he is operating in the *Aesthetic Letters*, thus producing a third model again.

What I propose to do here is to show that these analyses can be used to illuminate what I shall suggest is a central text for anyone grappling with the subtle and often baffling complexities of Goethe's political thought. And, again, it is Wilkinson's work which encourages me to think that such an approach is on the right lines. In the first place, there are the clear hints, given in the *Steigerung* article, of the relevance of this concept to Goethe's political thinking (*Poet and Thinker*, pp. 198 and 200). In the second, there is the demonstration, in the Introduction to the *Aesthetic Letters* (*WW*, pp. xciii–xciv), of the similarities between Schiller's theory of the progressive refinement of the total personality and Goethe's theory of polarity and *Steigerung*.

It is one of the recurrent — and most tenacious — commonplaces of Goethe scholarship that Goethe, in the words of a recent commentator, 'never really came to terms with politics'.[5] The argument runs thus: Goethe, apparently sharing the Epicureans' view that a wise man will have as little to do with politics as possible, gave his support (perhaps reluctantly but certainly naively) to the status quo in the hope of finding that peace and order so essential to the development of personality.[6] And, certainly, scholars who have taken this view have had no trouble at all in selecting corroborative evidence. Did Goethe not tell Frau von Stein that he was 'essentially a private man' (letter of 17 September 1782)? And did he not also inform Knebel, a few weeks later, that his political and social life was quite separate from his 'moral and poetic life'? — 'ich habe mein politisches und gesellschaftliches Leben ganz von meinem moralischen und poetischen getrennt' (letter of 21 November 1782). However — and such tendentious treatment of primary evidence is typical of the literature on the subject — the most significant part of this letter is, to my knowledge, never quoted. After the passage cited above, Goethe adds, in parenthesis, the remark, 'only outwardly, of course' ('äußerlich versteht sich'), and goes on to discuss the *inward* unity of just those aspects of his activity which he had earlier separated: 'Nur im innersten meiner Plane und Vorsätze und Unternehmungen bleibe ich mir geheimnisvoll selbst getreu und knüpfe so wieder mein gesellschaftliches, politisches, moralisches und poetisches Leben in einen verborgenen Knoten zusammen.'

Clearly, whether Goethe was right or wrong in his assessment of himself as a *Privatmensch*, it hardly affects the case of his political awareness. For political life is, according to him, compatible with an inner, 'private', life. Indeed it is necessary, at the outset, if we are to obtain a clear picture of the available evidence, to distinguish between Goethe's reluctance to *speak* about politics, and the clear indications we have that he actually *thought* his political position through and was not simply clinging to the forms of the Ancien Régime out of loyalty to Karl August or from fear of disorder.[7] When we then bear in mind Klinger's remark that the Goethe of the early days in Weimar is 'immersed in political affairs'[8]; when we recall that an American visitor to Goethe a few years before his death reports his astonishment that 'in this interview with the chief of teachers, the wisest of the wise, . . . it was not Goethe who taught me, it was I who taught Goethe' — and that the topic was the American presidential elections;[9] and further that Goethe was able to converse with the Italian jurist, Filangieri, on the subject of Montesquieu and Beccaria,[10] we begin to suspect that his political interest went much deeper than has been supposed. If we add to this his statement to Eckermann, a few days before his death, that the modern world would do better to agree with Napoleon that 'politics is fate' than to operate with the Greek concept of fate,[11] we are more likely to believe him when he says that whenever he did speak about politics he spoke from deep conviction: 'In religiösen Dingen, in wissenschaftlichen *und politischen*, überall machte es mir zu schaffen, daß ich nicht heuchelte, und daß ich den Mut hatte mich auszusprechen, wie ich empfand.'[12]

The curious fact is that successive scholars have apparently not believed him. For whereas in the religious and scientific areas of Goethe's thought, scholars have been at pains to discover the inner logic of his attitudes, in the case of his political outlook they have, almost to a man, preferred to point out what they consider its inconsistencies and leave it at that.

The reason for this state of affairs is, I believe, not hard to find. The revival of interest in 'Goethe and Politics' which began in the 1960s has concentrated almost exclusively on his political activity within the context of Sachsen-Weimar;[13] and tacitly accepts the view that Goethe's political outlook is intellectually incoherent. But the persistence of the unfounded and almost universal assumption that Goethe did not really think about political matters coherently owes more, in my view, to the methodological malpractices of those who investigate his political attitudes than to those who choose to content themselves with factual accounts of his political behaviour. The most recent full-length study of the subject, Otto Badelt's *Das Rechts- und Staatsdenken Goethes* (Bonn, 1976) illustrates all of these defects only too well. There is, in the first place, the ham-fisted treatment of letters, diaries, and conversations, with little or no regard for the nuances of context, whether of personal relationship, place or time — and this despite the warning given by one of the earliest scholars in the field about the need for tact and discrimination in the handling of such material.[14] In the second place, there is the familiar reliance on scholarship long since superseded, without any effort on the author's part to come to terms with his predecessors,[15] a process which naturally favours the uncritical passing-on of general conclusions. And thirdly, there is the incredibly cavalier treatment of works of literature as 'sources' for Goethe's views. Badelt's handling of *Faust* as if it were an intellectual treatise (an 'Auseinandersetzung' he calls it!) (Badelt, p. 19) is only one instance of a methodological flaw pervasive throughout the scholarship on Goethe's political attitudes. It is therefore hardly surprising if Goethe's political thought emerges — even in Badelt, who is a notable exception in trying to argue *for* its coherence — as a tissue of vague, and often contradictory, generalities.

My aim in this paper is a limited but, I think, a precise one. It is to try to unsettle the widespread assumption about the muddled state of his political views by extrapolating the wholly coherent model of society Goethe offers his reader in a passage in *Dichtung und Wahrheit*,[16] the most relevant parts of which are quoted below:

Der beruhigte Zustand des deutschen Vaterlandes, in welchem sich auch meine Vaterstadt schon über hundert Jahre eingefügt sah, hatte sich trotz manchen Kriegen und Erschütterungen in seiner Gestalt vollkommen erhalten. Einem gewissen Behagen günstig war, daß von dem Höchsten bis zu dem Tiefsten, von dem Kaiser bis zu dem

Juden herunter die mannigfaltigste Abstufung alle Persönlichkeiten anstatt sie zu trennen, zu verbinden schien. Wenn dem Kaiser sich Könige subordinierten, so gab diesen ihr Wahlrecht und die dabei erworbenen und behaupteten Gerechtsame ein entschiedenes Gleichgewicht. Nun aber war der hohe Adel in die erste königliche Reihe verschränkt, so daß er, seiner bedeutenden Vorrechte gedenkend, sich ebenbürtig mit dem Höchsten achten konnte, ja im gewissen Sinne noch höher, indem ja die geistlichen Kurfürsten allen andern vorangingen und als Sprößlinge der Hierarchie einen unangefochtenen ehrwührdigen Raum behaupteten.

Gedenke man nun der außerordentlichen Vorteile, welche diese altgegründeten Familien zugleich und außerdem in Stiftern, Ritterorden, Ministerien, Vereinigungen und Verbrüderungen genossen haben, so wird man leicht denken können, daß diese große Masse von bedeutenden Menschen, welche sich zugleich als subordiniert und als koordiniert fühlten, in höchster Zufriedenheit und geregelter Welttätigkeit ihre Tage zubrachten . . .

Der Mittelstand hatte sich ungestört dem Handel und den Wissenschaften gewidmet und hatte freilich dadurch, sowie durch die nahverwandte Technik, sich zu einem bedeutenden Gegengewicht erhoben; ganz oder halb freie Städte begünstigten diese Tätigkeit, so wie die Menschen darin ein gewisses ruhiges Behagen empfanden. Wer seinen Reichtum vermehrt, seine geistige Tätigkeit besonders im juristischen und Staatsfache gesteigert sah, der konnte sich überall eines bedeutenden Einflusses erfreuen. Setze man doch bei den höchsten Reichsgerichten, und auch wohl sonst, der adligen Bank eine Gelehrtenbank gegenüber; die freiere Übersicht der einen mochte sich mit der tieferen Einsicht der andern gerne befreunden, und man hatte im Leben durchaus keine Spur von Rivalität; der Adel war sicher in seinen unerreichbaren durch die Zeit geheiligten Vorrechten, und der Bürger hielt es unter seiner Würde, durch eine seinem Namen vorgesetzte Partikel nach dem Schein derselben zu streben. Der Handelsmann, der Techniker hatte genug zu tun, um mit den schneller vorschreitenden Nationen einigermaßen zu wetteifern. Wenn man die gewöhnlichen Schwankungen des Tages nicht beachten will, so durfte man wohl sagen, es war im ganzen eine Zeit eines reinen Bestrebens, wie sie früher nicht erschienen, noch auch in der Folge wegen aüßerer und innerer Steigerungen sich lange erhalten konnte.

It is surely inept to point out, as Mommsen has done (Mommsen, p. 248), that Goethe has painted a falsely idealized picture, and that in fact the relationship between the middle classes and the nobility was a deeply problematic one during the period here evoked. Inept because such literal-mindedness overlooks the clear indications given that what Goethe is presenting, in this passage at least, is a *fiction*, a traditional device of the political theorist — a projection upon the past of ideal human relationships in society.[17] The use of the topos of an *enumeratio* of ranks and occupations,[18] and of the rhetorical formulaic with which Goethe ironically refers to the period under discussion (*jene schönen Tage*), clearly indicates as much. Moreover, even if we are blind to the rhetorical strategy employed, the widespread employment of such a method — 'of using historical modes of description for non-historical purposes'[19] — is enough to alert us to Goethe's true intention.

What we have here, then, is not a half-remembered and distorted historical sketch, but rather a conscious attempt to present a normative theory of society. It is therefore perfectly legitimate — indeed, by virtue of the vocabulary used, one might say required — to try to construe it in terms of those key-concepts of Goethe's which pervade all his thinking. But we shall go very wrong indeed if we interpret this passage in the light of the kind of simplistic view of Goethe's fundamental thinking which, for instance, Frederick S. Sethur brings to bear in his consideration of Goethe's political outlook. Goethe's acceptance of the principle of hierarchical subordination in political matters, Sethur argues, constitutes a betrayal of his own thought, a betrayal made necessary by his keen sense of self-preservation. For Goethe's basic notion of polarity, according to which all things in nature are in a constant state of flux, continuously alternating and never reaching stability — had he been true to it — would not have allowed him to embrace such a model of society.[20] This line of argument is, simply, quite untenable. And not only because in the passage quoted the law of polarity is in fact accommodated: Goethe refers to the merchant and artisan classes as in 'rivalry' with the same classes of other countries. But, far more importantly, because to speak of Goethe's thinking as being dominated by the law of polarity in this narrow sense is to caricature it out of all recognition. His fundamental thinking is infinitely more complex than that, and in order to come to terms with the question of whether Goethe's political outlook corresponded with other levels of his thought we need to take these complexities into account. Specifically, in order to construe aright the passages quoted we need to consider the principles of *Steigerung*, *Specification*, compensation, along with hierarchical subordination and co-ordination.

It is at this point that Professor Wilkinson's work on these concepts is so valuable. Let us take first the concept of *Steigerung*, which appears twice in the passages quoted. According to Wilkinson:

Any or all of [the following] complexity of thought may colour Goethe's use of *steigern* in other than scientific contexts, at least from 1790 onwards, and increasingly as time goes on: the idea that a qualitative change can result from a difference in degree, from the intensification of original characteristics, so that what is essentially the same may appear opposed in form and function; the idea that unusually fine forms of creation result from the synthesis of intensified opposites; the idea that the evolution of higher forms is characterized by increasing subordination of the parts in a definite hierarchy. (*Poet and Thinker*, p. 197)

Hierarchical subordination in Goethe's thinking is, then, the result of the different stages — or, rather, levels — to which different elements have managed to arrive through the ascending process of *Steigerung*. And that the social hierarchy in the Germany of his youth is 'seen' by Goethe as the result of such a process is supported by the fact that once we accept that Goethe is using this word in this way many foxing aspects of the passages quoted become clear. For example, the notion that a man's wealth entitles him to political influence hardly seems acceptable, unless, by the rhetorical device of synonymy, the word *vermehrt* takes on some of the colouring of *gesteigert*. For 'intensification' of wealth will involve not simply a difference in degree, but a 'qualitative change' to a 'higher' form of activity: that of public affairs and civic responsibility. Similarly it is at first sight puzzling that the very same term which has clearly positive connotations when applied to the wealth of citizens appears at the end of the passage quoted as denoting just those agencies which worked the undermining of this social structure. Puzzling that is until we recall that 'like everything else, functioning alone and unchecked, *Steigerung* becomes dangerous' (*Poet and Thinker*, p. 200). Goethe uses this term in two, distinguishable, senses: it denotes both the process of refinement itself *and* the interaction of this refining process with another natural tendency, that of taking, and persisting in, a form — a process that he called the *Specificationstrieb* (*Poet and Thinker*, pp. 195–96). To make sense of this apparent paradox, then, we have to assume that what is regretted here by Goethe is that the tendency to persist is not allowed to last long enough, and that what is achieved undergoes a precipitate metamorphosis, or *Steigerung*. Moreover, if we assume that Goethe is employing the concept of *Steigerung* with the same meaning as it has in his scientific writings, the apparently odd fact that in his account the nobility and the bourgeoisie do not enter into a polar relationship with one another can be explained. Once an organism has reached *Specification*, it does not again enter into polarity with other polarized organisms except at the cost of losing its achieved form. It is clear that these classes are 'specified': the nobility is secure in its time-honoured privileges; the *Bürger* has a highly-developed sense of his own dignity. And this is why Goethe can assert that the hierarchy he envisages is cohesive rather than divisive: man, as opposed to nature aware of his advantages, will tend to synthesis, for 'unusually fine forms of creation result from the synthesis of intensified opposites' (*Poet and Thinker*, p. 197).

However, if the assumption that *steigern* is being used by Goethe with the full force of the connotations it acquired for him in scientific contexts helps solve these puzzles in the passage, it also raises a crucial problem: how can the hierarchical structure outlined by Goethe accommodate the growth, the *Steigerung*, of the individual? But the problem is more apparent than real, for Goethe is not advocating a hierarchy of fixed subordination,[21] but a far more complex, and dynamic, model altogether. He says quite explicitly of the various ranks of the nobility that they felt 'at one and the same time both subordinate and co-ordinate' with one another. The sovereign princes, while subordinate to the Emperor, are also equal (they have a 'Gleichgewicht' in the form of privileges); the highest nobility, too, are equal ('ebenbürtig'). Similarly, the bourgeoisie are equal to the nobility, in that they sit as equals in the supreme courts of the empire and feel equal enough to regard the noble prefix of 'von' as beneath their dignity. In addition, each class is also superior 'in a certain sense': the highest nobility, as spiritual electors, take precedence over all others; the bourgeoisie have now a 'deeper insight', now a 'freer outlook' than the nobility.

Surely what is at work here is that reciprocal subordination and co-ordination which Wilkinson and Willoughby have shown to be at work in Schiller's thought. The relationships between the classes, and between the individuals within those classes (Goethe speaks of a 'highly varied gradation of personalities'), clearly change according to social function: it is the voting rights of the sovereign princes, the religious role of the electors, the juridical and administrative skills of the bourgeoisie which qualify each of these classes respectively to occupy a — temporarily — equal, or superior, position.

Equally clear is the connexion between this dynamic interplay of classes and the personal development — the Steigerung in its broader sense — of the individual. A static hierarchy could not conceivably accommodate the growth of the individual: he would be trapped within the fixed confines of his own class. In terms of Goethe's envisagement of a reciprocity of subordination and co-ordination, however, the individual who 'takes form' (Specification) within his class has every chance of rising socially to the extent that the form he has taken has a function which, at one time or another, becomes the dominant principle in the society. Of course, here again we must think in terms of reciprocity, this time between the environment (in general, society; specifically, a given social class) and the individual. For it is in the nature of Steigerung to take place 'in ever-renewed contact with the environment' (Poet and Thinker, p. 193). It thus follows that as the demands

G

made on the social structure change, so, too, the challenges posed for the different classes, and for their individual members, change. And it is the degree to which he is capable of meeting these challenges that determines both the personal development and the (periodically changing) social position of the individual member of society.

What I hope has emerged from this brief discussion is that the stereotype picture of Goethe's political thought, passed from one writer on the subject to the other, has little to recommend it. My argument has been that the uncritical acceptance of the conventional view has 'cramped' scholars' minds so that they both overlook and misread pertinent evidence. Moreover, it is at present a moot point whether the 'incoherence' of Goethe's political outlook, so much complained of, is in fact a feature of his thinking or merely the inevitable product of the methodological malpractices of his critics. In order to tilt the balance in the direction of a sympathetic response to Goethe's political thinking, I have re-presented a piece of evidence which I believe does not simply corroborate the view that Goethe compromised with the Absolutist climate of his day — the conventional view taken of the political significance of the passages quoted above — but rather, when read aright (i.e., in the light of some of Goethe's key concepts), presents us with a highly coherent, and original, political outlook.

If my interpretation and analysis of these passages proves acceptable, certain implications seem to arise. On the one hand, it can no longer be said with the assurance of unqualified generalization that Goethe's political outlook is 'simple',[22] incoherent, or based on a static, inflexible, caste-system. On the other, the model of society I have argued Goethe advocates may be useful in a methodological sense: as a working hypothesis which could serve as a regulative guide through the labyrinth of the pertinent evidence in the search for a more adequate account of his political thought. It might even serve as a theory in terms of which those works of literature in which Goethe dealt with political issues, so often merely ransacked by scholars

in search of quotable 'viewpoints' and long since discarded as
the failures of a mind grappling with subject-matter alien to it,
could be profitably approached.

REFERENCES

[1] In ' "Tasso — ein gesteigerter Werther" in the light of Goethe's Principle
of "Steigerung" ', *MLR*, 44 (1949), 305–28, reprinted in German in *Goethe:
Neue Folge des Jahrbuchs der Goethe-Gesellschaft*, 13 (1951), 28–58, and in *Goethe:
Poet and Thinker* (London, 1962), pp. 185–213. I shall refer to the 1962 version
throughout, as *Poet and Thinker*. The study remains authoritative despite Franz
Koch's *Goethes Gedankenform* (Berlin, 1967) of which the opening chapter, devoted
to 'Polarität und Steigerung', adds nothing to Wilkinson's account.
[2] On the reciprocal influence which each had on the other in this respect, see
Friedrich Schiller, *On the Aesthetic Education of Man*, edited and translated with
an introduction, commentary and glossary of terms by Elizabeth M. Wilkinson
and L. A. Willoughby (Oxford, 1967), p. lxxxiv, note 1, and p. xciv, note 1.
This edition is cited henceforward as *WW*. See, too, their article ' "The Whole
Man" in Schiller's Theory of Culture and Society: On the Virtue of a Plurality of
Models', in *Essays in German Language, Culture and Society*, edited by Siegbert S.
Prawer, R. Hinton Thomas and Leonard Forster (London, 1969), pp. 177–210
(p. 191). (Henceforward cited as 'The Whole Man'.)
[3] See particularly *WW*, pp. l, liv, lv, lxiv, lxx, lxxix, lxxx and lxxxiii.
[4] See 'The Whole Man', especially p. 195.
[5] F. J. Lamport, ' "Entfernten Weltgetöses Widerhall": Politics in Goethe's
plays', *PEGS*, N.S., 44 (1974), 41–62 (p. 41).
[6] See, for instance, G. P. Gooch, 'The Political Background of Goethe's Life',
PEGS, N.S., 3 (1926), 1–30 (p. 20); Frederick S. Sethur, 'Goethe und die
Politik', Parts 4–5, *PMLA*, 52 (1937), 160–94 (p. 182); and Wilhelm Mommsen,
Die politischen Anschauungen Goethes (Stuttgart, 1948), p. 10.
[7] This 'explanation' of Goethe's political position is offered by Sethur, 'Goethe
und die Politik', Parts 1–3, *PMLA*, 51 (1936), 1007–55 (p. 1014).
[8] 'Er steckt in politischen Geschäften . . .', to E. Schleiermacher, 12 June
1776, *Goethes Gespräche ohne die Gespräche mit Eckermann*, edited by F. von Biedermann (Wiesbaden, 1957), p. 71.
[9] Conversation with G. H. Calvert of 27 March 1825, *Goethes Gespräche*, edited by
Woldemar von Biedermann, 10 vols (Leipzig, 1889–96), v, 168–69.
[10] *Italienische Reise*, 5 March 1787.
[11] 'Anfangs März 1832', *Goethes Werke*, Gedenkausgabe, 24 vols (Zürich,
1948–63), XXIV, 508–09.
[12] To Eckermann, 4 January 1824. My italics.
[13] See, for example, Hans Tümmler, *Goethe in Staat und Politik: Gesammelte
Aufsätze*, Kölner Historische Abhandlungen, 9 (Köln and Graz, 1964).
[14] Ottokar Lorenz, *Goethes politische Lehrjahre* (Berlin, 1893), p. 18.
[15] See, for example, Badelt's re-exposition of Hippel: Badelt, pp. 77 ff. and
passim.
[16] Part 4, Book 17, *Goethes Werke*, Gedenkausgabe, X, 772–78.
[17] See, for example, Jean Blondel's discussion of the essentially hybrid nature
of utopias — part history, part theory — in his *Thinking Politically* (London,
1976), pp. 29–35.
[18] See Wilkinson and Willoughby's discussion of this widespread device in
'The Whole Man', pp. 185–86.

[19] *WW*, p. lxxvii, where Wilkinson and Willoughby argue that Schiller is using the same method, and point out that it was 'common in his day'.

[20] Sethur, 1936, p. 1034, and 1937, pp. 166 ff.

[21] Badelt's assumption (p. 329) that Goethe is simply advocating a fixed hierarchy in this passage lies at the centre of a dilemma which he never solves: how what he calls 'die höchste Aufgabe des menschlichen Daseins . . . die Ausbildung der Persönlichkeit' (p. 138) is to be squared with such a static social structure. But the dilemma is his, not Goethe's.

[22] G. P. Gooch, 'German Views of the State', in G. P. Gooch et al., *The German Mind and Outlook* (London, 1945), p. 12.

Der Dichtung Schleier[1]

From Theology with Love to Aesthetics

By WILLIAM LARRETT

Je finis par un vers allemand qui sera placé dans le Poeme que je cheris tant, parceque j'y pourrai parler de toi, de mon amour pour toi sous mille formes sans que personne l'entende que toi seule.   (WA, VI, 344)[2]

> In tausend Formen magst du dich verstecken,
> Doch, Allerliebste, gleich erkenn' ich dich;
> Du magst mit Zauberschleiern dich bedecken,
> Allgegenwärt'ge, gleich erkenn' ich dich.
>
> (JA, V, 94)

THE SECOND of these quotations (incidentally, it is not 'le vers allemand' referred to in the first) will be familiar enough, the first less so; it is taken from a letter Goethe wrote to Frau von Stein on 24 August 1784 whilst on a visit to the court at Brunswick. The two passages, separated in time by some thirty years, invite juxtaposition because they both speak of a kind of hide-and-seek between lovers, though the game is a little different in each case — note the different prepositions in the key phrases, '*sous* mille formes' and '*in* tausend Formen'. In his letter Goethe speaks of a secret oblique form of communication which he and Frau von Stein can enjoy, one to which — although it is in a public form, the poem will be published — the world at large will not be privy. The private message will lie 'beneath' the public utterance, visible only to the eye of the beloved. In the second quotation, taken from the last poem in the 'Buch Suleika' in the *Westöstlicher Divan*, delight is expressed in a game played between lovers, a game of playful loving teasing, in which the world is not involved (I am purposely dwelling here on the personal level, deliberately ignoring for

89

the time being the religious connotations of the language in which the 'game' is couched). Implicit in the letter, and explicit in the poem, is a reference to the veil and its twofold function of concealing and revealing, a function which lies at the heart of all literature, a function which is both result and cause of that subtle weave of experience and imagination, of intuition and insight.

When Goethe visited Brunswick in 1784, all the letters he wrote to Frau von Stein during his stay were in French. This was partly to practise his French, and partly it was the chameleon in him adapting to his surroundings and the French-speaking milieu. Nevertheless, one wonders why he should want to persevere in this, even in his most intimate correspondence, when he admits in his first letter (18 August, WA, VI, 338) that it is 'presque impossible de poursuivre ce jeu, ma plume n'obeit qu'a regret, et ce n'est qu'avec peine que je traduis, que je travestis les sentiments originaux de mon cœur'. Despite these reservations, mastery of an alien mode of expression is to be another 'talent' which he can offer Charlotte as a further sign of his love for her (his 'unique amie, chere confidente de touts mes sentiments', as he describes her in the letter of 22 August, WA, VI, 343). What is interesting is that these letters in French, in spite of Goethe's sense of travesty, seem very tender and loving. One might even go so far as to say that they *seem* almost *more* open and affectionate than those he writes in German. Might it be that he could say together with Thomas Mann's Madame Chauchat, being aware of the liberating effect of a foreign language, 'car pour moi, parler français, c'est parler sans parler, en quelque manière — sans responsabilité', words spoken as it happens in fancy dress at a carnival party.[3]

In his letters from Brunswick Goethe is very much concerned with the public mask and the private self, with the ease with which one can move 'incognito' through the world and society. For Goethe this is a source of both relief and regret, yet there remains the overriding consolation of being known truly by his beloved, of coming to know himself through her, and of attaining a sense of belonging: 'Je ne sens mon existence que par toi, tu m'as appris a aimer moimeme, tu m'as donné une patrie, une langue, un stile, et je finirois par t'ecrire des phrases' (18 August, WA, VI, 338). His use here of the word 'phrases' shows how these explicit statements of his love and indebtedness are felt to remain apparently but empty formulae, since they are cast in French; although direct, they paraphrase the original sentiments and the close correlation between language and feeling is fractured. It evinces the poet's awareness of the virtual impossibility of translating the language of feeling from one language into another, and — beyond this — those doubts about the poet's ability to translate feeling into any language. And it would seem to be precisely for this reason that when he wants to give his love for Charlotte more genuine expression, Goethe does not resort to his native prose, but prefers to leap from the mask of French to the veil 'd'un vers allemand', whereby one form of obliqueness gives way to another:

Gewiss, ich waere schon so ferne ferne
Soweit die Welt nur offen liegt gegangen
Bezwaengen mich nicht uebermaecht'ge Sterne
Die mein Geschick an deines angehangen
Dass ich in dir nun erst mich kennen lerne
Mein Dichten, Trachten, Hoffen und Verlangen
Allein nach dir und deinem Wesen draengt
Mein Leben nur an deinem Leben haengt.

(WA, VI, 344)

In the context of the *letter* this stanza by itself was an expression of the bonds that linked Goethe to Frau von Stein. It acknowledged the unique role she had played in his life and the debt he owed her. One can surmise that it was the product of his immediate situation, i.e. he was travelling and was apart from Charlotte; it repeats in the line 'Dass ich in dir nun erst mich kennen lerne' in condensed form what he had said a week earlier in French, 'Je ne sens mon existence que par toi, tu m'as appris a aimer moimeme'. But his separation from Frau von Stein was only part of his immediate situation, he was also working on an epic poem, and what we do not know unfortunately is how this stanza would have fitted into the intended *public* context of *Die Geheimnisse*, nor how differently it would have functioned once the 'ich' was no longer a personal 'I' but the personal pronoun of an epic character.

Frau von Stein had already received a copy of 'Zueignung' (it is, of course, 'Zueignung' that contains the famous line, 'Der Dichtung Schleier aus der Hand der Wahrheit') a few days before Goethe arrived in Brunswick. In referring to it in his letter of 11 August, Goethe again showed his pleasure in being able to express his love obliquely through the poem: 'Du hast nun ich hoffe den Anfang des Gedichtes ['Gedicht' here refers to the whole of the projected *Geheimnisse*, as does 'Poeme' in the later letter — 'Zueignung' was to form the introduction] . . . du wirst dir daraus nehmen, was für dich ist, es war mir gar angenehm dir auf diese Weise zu sagen wie lieb ich dich habe' (WA, VI, 334–35). With these words in mind, one can again 'read' 'Zueignung' simply in terms of Goethe and Frau von Stein: he is the young man and she the 'göttlich Weib'. It is easy to imagine the pleasure and satisfaction she would have felt when reading such lines as:

> Du gabst mir Ruh, wenn durch die jungen Glieder
> Die Leidenschaft sich rastlos durchgewühlt;
> Du hast mir wie mit himmlischem Gefieder
> Am heißen Tag die Stirne sanft gekühlt;
> Du schenktest mir der Erde beste Gaben,
> Und jedes Glück will ich durch dich nur haben!
>
> (JA, I, 4)

And she will have seen herself as the goddess of truth who hands the young man 'the veil of poetry'.

This is not the first time Goethe had given poetic voice to his love for Frau von Stein: all the 'Lida' poems were dedicated to her, but again the private message implicit in the public statement was only there for the initiated ear. Particularly relevant here, however, in the way that it anticipates 'Zueignung', is the short poem 'An Lida' (first published in 1789) which Goethe enclosed in his letter of 9 October 1781:

> Den Einzigen, Lida, welchen du lieben kannst,
> Forderst du ganz für dich, und mit Recht.
> Auch ist er einzig dein.

Denn seit ich von dir bin,
Scheint mir des schnellsten Lebens
Lärmende Bewegung
Nur ein leichter Flor, durch den ich deine Gestalt
Immerfort wie in Wolken erblicke:
Sie leuchtet mir freundlich und treu,
Wie durch des Nordlichts bewegliche Strahlen
Ewige Sterne schimmern.

(JA, II, 80)

Here the hurly-burly of life, the transient and the ephemeral, are but a slight veil through which the constant presence of the beloved radiates. The imagery is related both to 'Dauer' and 'Wechsel' and to illumination and enlightenment (note a certain similarity with 'Um Mitternacht'); however, the language of veiling and the reference to a divine presence wreathed in clouds is age-old. That Goethe, on one level, was expressing his love for Frau von Stein in the 'Lida' poems was not 'revealed' until the letters were published in 1848–51. For instance, in the letter of 9 October 1781 the Lida poem quoted above begins quite explicitly: 'Den einzigen Lotte welchen du lieben kannst' (WA, V, 201). Similarly, the direct involvement of Marianne von Willemer in the *Westöstlicher Divan* did not become known until much later — and this is part of the reason for linking the 1784 correspondence with the 'Buch Suleika' at the outset. In both the 'Lida' poems and the *Divan* Goethe could delight in giving public yet opaque expression to a love which was otherwise denied direct open expression by circumstance and convention.

One could perhaps contrast the different tone of those of Goethe's works which are associated with Christiane Vulpius. There is little time for the oblique and the veiled in, for example, 'Laß dich, Geliebte, nicht reun, daß du mir so schnell dich ergeben'. Love, as one of the *themes* of the *Römische Elegien*, is frank and open, though this says nothing about the veiling function of the elegiac form itself. Openness pertaining to the 'Stoff' is countered by discretion in the form. In the *Westöstlicher Divan* discretion, secrecy, delicacy, wit, all constitute part of the 'Stoff' as well as inhering in the form. The *Divan* abounds in codes and ciphers, both explicitly and implicitly, all contributing to that subtle and deft fabric, at once light-hearted (take, for instance, the 'rhyme': Morgenröte/Hatem) and profound.

The poem 'Zueignung' retained its importance for Goethe throughout his life — it was placed at the beginning of the first volume of the 1789 edition of his works and remained in this position, with one exception, in subsequent editions. In allegorical form it restores to poetry the divinely bestowed gift of mediating truth, boldly refuting the arguments in Book 10 of Plato's *Republic* where all claims to truth were denied to the poets. Between the *Republic* and 'Zueignung' there lies the long fundamental debate[4] about the relationship between religion, philosophy, poetry and truth. Put like that, it sounds as if 'Zueignung' had the last word, which would be nonsense. The debate continues, but Goethe's poem is a decisive statement in the debate, drawing on a long linguistic tradition, and forms part of that process of secularization which marks the eighteenth century.

One could quote many of Goethe's remarks about the nature of truth, but the most familiar all show an awareness of, and an acceptance of, man's limitations in his quest for truth. For example, from 'Aus Makariens Archiv' (first published in 1829), 'Das Wahre ist gottähnlich: es erscheint nicht unmittelbar, wir müssen es aus seinen Manifestationen erraten' (JA, IV, 234); and 'Das Wahre, mit dem Göttlichen identisch, läßt sich niemals von uns direkt erkennen: wir schauen es nur im Abglanz, im Beispiel, Symbol, in einzelnen und verwandten Erscheinungen' (*Versuch einer Witterungslehre*, first published in 1825, JA, XL, 55). The difference between 'gottähnlich' and 'mit dem Göttlichen identisch' reflects the old controversy which revolved around the 'Jota' of which Mephisto speaks,[5] but the words I want to stress are 'nicht unmittelbar', 'niemals direkt', 'Symbol' and 'schauen', and then to consider — bearing these late formulations in mind — an epigram thought to date from 1786:

> Jugendlich kommt sie vom Himmel, tritt vor den Priester
> und Weisen

Unbekleidet, die Göttin; still blickt sein Auge zur Erde.
Dann ergreift er das Rauchfaß und hüllt demütig verehrend
Sie in durchsichtigen Schleier, daß wir sie zu schauen
    ertragen.

(JA, I, 257)

Since absolute truth is not for man — it, like the sun, blinds
— it is only through the veil that man is permitted any vision of
truth at all. The church fathers wrestled with the just claims of
the human intellect in its approach to truth through analysis
and logic and with those self-evident truths which — beyond
dialectical proof — were granted to man only through revelation. Plato and Plotinus were acknowledged to be great
thinkers, who did the best they could *without* the benefit of
revelation, which is the foundation of the Christian religion.
The question of how to harmonize the insights of philosophy,
arrived at by applying the tools of logic, with knowledge
bestowed through revelation remained. It was the great
contribution of Saint Thomas Aquinas[6] that he offered an acceptable solution which did justice both to philosophy and to the
tenets of *doctrina sacra*. What Goethe does in 'Zueignung' is to
grant the poet a role analogous to that traditionally ascribed to
the priest as a mediator of truth as revealed to him through holy
scripture. *Die Geheimnisse* was to present in epic form the
'truths' of different religions and the search for ultimate truth.
In this context 'Zueignung' acts as the *apologia*, the justification
of the poet's right to embark upon such a presumptuous
venture. The title alone (*Die Geheimnisse*) states that inherent
challenge and contradiction: the theme is 'secrets', ones
essentially beyond the grasp of man, ones of which he can have
knowledge but which remain unfathomable and ineffable.

Underlying this is the concept of 'the open secret'. In the
Westöstlicher Divan it is the poet (in the poem 'Offenbar Geheimnis', JA, v, 22) who has pure intuitive knowledge,
knowledge which escapes 'die Wortgelehrten', whose wine is
'unlauter', whereas Hafis is 'mystisch rein'. 'Rein' is a word
which occurs again and again in this connexion and has the
meaning of both 'pure' and 'perfectly translucent', often stand-

ing as the opposite to 'trüb'. In 'Zueignung' it is the 'trüber Flor' of mist which in the hands of the goddess becomes 'der reinste Schleier', and is then given to the young man as 'Der Dichtung Schleier', a formulation in which the inverted genitive has the effect of a compound noun: 'Dichtung' *is* the veil of truth, and should not be regarded as an entity separate from the veil. In the *Divan* Hafis ('Der du, ohne fromm zu sein, selig bist') partakes of a vision normally reserved for the blessed in the life hereafter — 'Wir sehen jetzt durch einen Spiegel in einem dunklen Wort; dann aber von Angesicht zu Angesicht' (1 Corinthians 13. 12). Hafis is 'rein', not 'trüb' or 'dunkel', though the language of poets was traditionally regarded as 'dark'. For example there is a reference to the dark language of the poets in the *Republic*, Book 1: 'Simonides, then, *after the manner of poets*, would seem to have spoken *darkly* of the nature of justice' [my italics].[7] Here the word 'darkly' seems to allow some measure of significant mystery whilst denying adequate clarity, for Socrates continues, 'for what he really meant to say . . . '! Yet another instance is to be found in Paragraph 15 of Porphyry's *Life of Plotinus*, which is even more apposite to the present considerations; Porphyry relates:

At Plato's feast I read a poem, 'The Sacred Marriage'; and because much of it was expressed in the mysterious and veiled language of inspiration someone said, 'Porphyry is mad'. But Plotinus said, so as to be heard by all, 'You have shown yourself at once poet, philosopher, and expounder of sacred mysteries.'[8]

Praise indeed! Praise that Goethe would have found by no means exaggerated, for it is the poet who possesses that inspired combination of intuition, imagination, reflexion *and* the gift of articulate form, the gift of form being for the author of the *Westöstlicher Divan* in some way commensurate with the purity of the poet's vision: 'Schöpft des Dichters reine Hand, / Wasser wird sich ballen' (JA, v, 13). The couplet, with its crucial reflexive verb in the second line, suggests effortless ease, thereby emphasizing the inspired nature of the gift. In pure hands water will assume a form, an ancient image that Goethe used again later

— though not quite to the same purpose — in 'Paria', written in
1822:

> Seligem Herzen, frommen Händen
> Ballt sich die bewegte Welle
> Herrlich zu kristallner Kugel . . .
>
> (JA, II, 200)

Once purity is lost, however, silence results:

> Was ich denke, was ich fühle —
> Ein Geheimnis bleibe das.
>
> (JA, II, 204)

These are the Brahma's wife's last words.

The legend of the Brahma's wife is an oriental version of the
story of man's lost innocence; knowledge, even if it is derived
— as in this version — from a vision of sublime beauty, entails
a fall from grace and leaves man subject to that existential
confusion, caught between the conflicting pulls of heaven and
earth. He has gained knowledge through experience but has
lost total apprehension and the language of perfect understanding. As George Steiner puts it, paraphrasing the old
tradition: 'Our speech interposes itself between apprehension
and truth like a dusty pane or warped mirror. The tongue of
Eden was like a flawless glass; a light of total understanding
streamed through it'.[9] Yet in Goethe's view water, the fluid
element of language, will still take shape for the poet and the
gift of the purest veil compensates, in part at least, for what was
lost in Paradise. When Helena disappears from view after the
death of Euphorion, Faust is left holding her 'Kleid' and
'Schleier'. Mephisto, still in the guise of Phorkyas, warns
Faust to hold on tight to the garment as demons try to pull it
away:

> Die Göttin ist's nicht mehr, die du verlorst,
> Doch göttlich ist's. Bediene dich der hohen,
> Unschätzbarn Gunst und hebe dich empor:
> Es trägt dich über alles Gemeine rasch
> Am Äther hin, so lange du dauern kannst.
>
> (JA, XIV, 204–05)

The veil is a divine attribute and imparts knowledge of the
divine. According to Aquinas only the holy scriptures were to

be regarded as the veil of perfect truth,[10] since human reason
'cannot grasp divine things perfectly on account of their
superabundance of truth'.[11] Goethe ascribes to literature
(*Dichtung*) a similar virtue and defines the poet's role very much
in terms of the priest who is characterized by humility and
reverence, the indispensable prerequisites for any form of
insight (*schauen*) and both connotations of the veil. Reverence
and awe are central to Goethe's 'schauen', and to the imparting
and receiving of knowledge (see the end of 'Die Metamorphose
der Tiere' and any number of instances in *Wilhelm Meisters
Wanderjahre*). The respectful eye is the eye which is open to
truth and able to view with tact — to use a consciously mixed
metaphor!

Inherent, also, in the image of the veil, even the purest most
perfectly translucent, is a sense of separation. Something, no
matter how apparently imperceptible, lies between the viewer
and the object viewed. No matter how revealing, the veil must
always have a distancing function and with that we touch upon
the all-important 'aesthetic' aspect of this eloquent image.

Edward Bullough was the first to formulate the concept of
'psychical distance' and show how essential it was to any theory
of art.[12] Not surprisingly, perhaps, for one so steeped in artistic
and intellectual traditions, he too has recourse to the same
image (not surprising, either, of someone who had translated
Gilson's study of Aquinas into English![13]):

The point of importance here [he is discussing such antitheses as
idealism and realism] is that the whole sensual side of Art is purified,
spiritualised, 'filtered' as I expressed it earlier, by Distance. The
most sensual appeal becomes the translucent veil of an underlying
spirituality, once the grossly personal and practical elements have
been removed from it. And — a matter of special emphasis here —
this spiritual aspect of the appeal is the more penetrating, the more
personal and direct its sensual appeal would have been BUT FOR
THE PRESENCE OF DISTANCE.

Ungefähr sagt das der Goethe auch, nur mit ein bißchen
andern Worten!

> Das Wort ist ein Fächer! Zwischen den Stäben
> Blicken ein Paar schöne Augen hervor.

Der Fächer ist nur ein lieblicher Flor,
Er verdeckt mir zwar das Gesicht,
Aber das Mädchen verbirgt er nicht,
Weil das Schönste, was sie besitzt,
Das Auge, mir ins Auge blitzt.

(JA, v, 22–23)

The poet of the *Divan* knew all about that intricate and delicate interaction between the sensual and the spiritual in which the artist delights, and the notion of distance that the 'play' of art inevitably involves. To move, as Goethe invariably did, from the particular to the general is unthinkable without an accompanying notion of drawing back, and it is a drawing back into form; the distanced view remains in touch. It is born of truth and aspires to truth. Little wonder that Goethe should entitle his autobiography *Dichtung und Wahrheit* where the 'und' functions as a true conjunction. He justified the undertaking and his choice of title in a conversation with Eckermann, saying: 'Ich dächte, es steckten darin einige Symbole des Menschen-lebens. Ich nannte das Buch 'Wahrheit und Dichtung', weil es sich durch höhere Tendenzen aus der Region einer niedern Realität erhebt' (30 March 1831). The last clause recalls the power that Mephisto ascribes to Helena's veil in the lines already quoted above.

Goethe had earlier defined symbolism in terms which succinctly state both the concretion of the poetic mode and the inherent mystery of its content: 'Das ist die wahre Symbolik, wo das Besondere das Allgemeinere repräsentiert, nicht als Traum und Schatten, sondern als lebendig-augenblickliche Offenbarung des Unerforschlichen' (JA, xxxviii, 266). In discursive prose it restates most (though not *all*, since that by definition would be impossible) of what is expressed by the veil as the symbol of symbol; and aesthetics itself represents the attempt to elucidate in conceptual terms the many-stranded web of this image.

REFERENCES

[1] This 'article' pretends to be little more than a gloss on this celebrated metaphor, a gloss, however, which aims at reflecting something of Professor Wilkinson's main fields of interest — Goethe, the history of ideas, and aesthetics — and in so doing it acknowledges a personal debt to her teaching and stimulus which began in an undergraduate class in 1956. I am particularly indebted here to her edition of Edward Bullough's essays — Edward Bullough, *Aesthetics: Lectures and Essays*, edited with an introduction by Elizabeth M. Wilkinson (London, 1957) — and to two of her articles: 'The Theological Basis of Faust's *Credo*', *GLL*, N.S., 10 (1956–57), 229–39, and 'Goethe's *Faust*: Tragedy in the Diachronic Mode', *PEGS*, N.S., 42 (1972), 116–74.

[2] Texts of Goethe's letters are cited from *Goethes Werke*, Großherzogin-Sophie-Ausgabe (Weimar, 1887–1920), Abteilung IV, *Briefe*, as 'WA', volume and page number; texts of his works from *Goethes Sämtliche Werke*, Jubiläums-Ausgabe (Stuttgart and Berlin, [1902–07]), as 'JA', volume and page number.

[3] Thomas Mann, *Der Zauberberg*, Chapter 5, in the section 'Walpurgisnacht'.

[4] To attempt here to reproduce the detail of this fascinating debate would exceed both the scope of this article and my own competence. Two works which I have found particularly helpful and informative are: Etienne Gilson, *History of Christian Philosophy in the Middle Ages* (London, 1955), and F. C. Copleston, *A History of Medieval Philosophy* (London, 1972).

[5] See Wilkinson, 'Tragedy in the Diachronic Mode', pp. 152 f.

[6] See Etienne Gilson, 'Saint Thomas Aquinas', *Proceedings of the British Academy*, 21 (1935), 29–45.

[7] *The Dialogues of Plato*, translated by B. Jowett, third edition (Oxford, 1892), III, 7.

[8] *Plotinus*, translated by A. H. Armstrong, Loeb Classical Library (London and Cambridge, Massachusetts, 1966), p. 43.

[9] George Steiner, *After Babel: Aspects of Language and Translation* (New York and London, 1975), p. 59.

[10] For a fuller account of Aquinas's distinction between the uses of metaphor in holy scripture and those in poetry, see Oskar Walzel, 'Der Dichtung Schleier aus der Hand der Wahrheit', *Euphorion*, 33 (1932), 83–105.

[11] Saint Thomas Aquinas, *Summa Theologia*, edited by T. Gilby et al. (London, 1963—), XXIX (1969), pp. 119 f. (Prima Secundae, CI, Art. 2, ad. 2).

[12] See his essay '"Psychical Distance" as a Factor in Art and an Aesthetic Principle', in his *Aesthetics*, pp. 91–130.

[13] *The Philosophy of St Thomas Aquinas*, translated by Edward Bullough from the French of E. Gilson (Cambridge, 1929).

Goethe and Embarrassment

By Sylvia P. Jenkins

> When you've dressed for a party
> And are going downstairs, with everything about you
> Arranged to support you in the role you have chosen,
> Then sometimes, when you come to the bottom step
> There is one step more than your feet expected
> And you come down with a jolt.[1]

EMBARRASSMENT, Professor C. Ricks has suggested, may be a 'narrowly English' sentiment. 'There is indeed something very English about the importance accorded to embarrassment.'[2] Of all experiences and sentiments, embarrassment is not one that one would immediately think of as central in Goethe's thought or poetry, and a study of blushing would hardly uncover the sensitivity and depth of concern that have here been so admirably revealed in Keats. But there is one particular type of embarrassment which Goethe understood profoundly and depicted with sensitivity, according it an important place in several of his literary works.

I refer to the social indiscretion, and the ensuing sensation which is so vividly and aptly described by T. S. Eliot in the lines quoted above: aptly, because whatever one does or says when causing or suffering this kind of embarrassment, the sensation is that of falling — 'there is one step more than your feet expected' — and we reflect this when we call the indiscretion a *faux pas* or speak of 'putting one's foot in it'. It occurs when in a context of normal, accepted behaviour something is said or done which is out of tune and suddenly disrupts the ordered social pattern: something breaks ('the ground opens up beneath one's feet', 'the bottom falls out of one's world'); there is an awkward pause or silence which interrupts the flow of conversation or the natural movement of people, and embarrassment may be

H

experienced by the agent/speaker or by the spectator/listener or
by both. What is actually done may be quite trivial: a slight
breach of etiquette, an accidental slip of the tongue, for instance.
The effect, like that of a physical fall, is often out of all proportion, rationally viewed, to the cause, for the sudden shock of
realization may lift the lid of a Pandora's box and act as a catalyst
in bringing buried experiences and half-understood fears and
emotions to light. There may be a sense of shock and horror, of
shame and guilt, of humiliation, or simply of confusion. In the
same moment one's picture of the outside world is changed, and
one may also experience uncertainty about one's own identity
or even loss of identity.

> There's a loss of personality;
> Or rather, you've lost touch with the person
> You thought you were.[3]

The effect will depend to some extent on the friendliness or
hostility of surrounding relationships, but principally on the
temperament and degree of maturity of the individual concerned. One may rage against one's humiliation, run away from
it, wallow in it or rationalize it; or one may face all its implications, come to terms with it and achieve deeper self-knowledge
in the process. The ultimate effect may be destructive, or it may
be healing and growth-producing, or it may simply be
superficial and ephemeral.

It is proposed here to study three instances of the use Goethe
makes of this experience of embarrassment in his drama and
prose fiction: Werther visits the Graf von C. and outstays his
welcome; Tasso embraces the Prinzessin; and the Engländer
introduces conversational topics of disturbing relevance in *Die
Wahlverwandtschaften*.[4]

The episode in *Werther* occurs at a crucial point in the novel,
near the beginning of Book II. Werther now has a position with
the Ambassador. For the first time he has work to do, a pattern
to fit into and a functional relationship with the world outside,
all of which could help him turn away from his melancholy
brooding. If he loses this opportunity, there may well be no hope

for him. He has already exhibited many of the traits that make a *faux pas* likely to occur: he is self-absorbed, given to violent swings of emotion from elation to despair, incapable of any realistic, objective appraisal of the world outside, seeing it only as a reflection of his own changing moods, prone in his melancholy to see it as unsympathetic or even hostile to him. Constantly critical of the Ambassador, he depends disproportionately on his good relations with the Graf von C. and with Fräulein von B. as his only source of gratification, and, aware of the prevailing social code, he is flattered as a bourgeois by their attentions and therefore all the more likely to forget himself in their company. As his mood darkens, letter by letter some new sadness or unpleasantness appears; he rages against the world at large, against society and its conventions and particularly against the Ambassador. Reproved by the Minister for his insubordinate behaviour, he is on the point of asking to be released when a mild and reassuring letter restores his self-confidence. Then comes the news that Lotte and Albert are married.

Thus the scene is set. What happens? He is invited to a meal by the Graf, outstays his welcome and is still there when the nobility begin to arrive. He fails to see their whispered disapproval and to take a hint from the unexpected coolness of Fräulein von B. and eventually the Graf has to ask him to leave. He tells the tale in an apparently calm and unemotional way, 'plan und nett, wie ein Chronikenschreiber das aufzeichnen würde'. This is sadly contradicted by the opening tone of the letter (15 March): 'Ich knirsche mit den Zähnen!', by the fury with which he blames others for ever persuading him to accept this position, and by the scathing and malicious terms in which he describes the nobility as they arrive. His 'plan und nett' account is clearly an attempt to hide the extreme violence of his feelings. When asked to leave he does so with extreme graciousness. He apologizes: 'Ihro Exzellenz, fiel ich ein, ich bitte tausendmal um Verzeihung; ich hätte eher dran denken sollen, und ich weiß, Sie vergeben mir diese Inkonsequenz; ich wollte schon vorhin mich empfehlen, ein böser Genius hat mich zurückgehalten, setzte ich lächelnd hinzu, indem ich mich neigte.' Apparently master of the situation, he behaves impeccably: even at this moment he sees himself as the perfect guest. His immediate reaction is to take a carriage and remove himself some distance. He watches the sunset and reads about Ulysses in Homer. 'Das war alles gut.'

But was it? He has not only removed himself from the scene of his discomfiture and characteristically turned to a passage of classical serenity in a poet of a remote age; he has in fact run away from facing his own humiliation and living through it in his own depths. But if he tries to flee from it, others will not let him. He makes light of it when first questioned: 'Du hast Verdruß gehabt? — Ich? sagt' ich. Der Graf hat dich aus der Gesellschaft gewiesen. — Hol' sie der Teufel! sagt' ich, mir war's lieb, daß ich in die freie Luft kam.' But he is infuriated when he hears that news of his disgrace has spread. He hates the pity of well-wishers and the triumph and mockery of those who envy him: 'da möchte man sich ein Messer ins Herz bohren'.

What is he running away from? The first-personal letter-form of the novel provides only an illusory closeness between the reader and the hero, and Goethe's art lies in the subtle irony with which he reveals to the reader what Werther is hiding from himself. This is particularly evident in the episode under consideration. For Werther's experience is not presented directly as in a drama; he has had time to think, to distort the facts and to apportion blame. His character, temperament and attitude to other people lead one to expect that a humiliation of this kind will have a devastating effect on him. When it apparently does not, it is clear that there is something missing, something that is essential to his development if he is to grow beyond it. Nowhere does he admit to any wrong-doing. His apology to the Graf is fulsome and perfunctory. Yet it is all too obvious that he has offended against the social code, and not as unwittingly as he would have us, and himself, believe. Whether the particular code of his day was just or not is irrelevant: it is part of the givenness of his environment with which he has to come to terms. And his failure to admit his own fault is also a failure to accept his embarrassment. For this kind of indiscretion, though rarely connected with anything profoundly evil, always implies some sort of wrong-doing, however superficial: a *faux pas* is a 'wrong' step. In failing to accept the sensation of falling, of going down into the depths of his humiliation, he fails to lose and hence to find himself, to understand himself better, to change and so to grow. For such an exploration can lead

> To finding out
> What you really are. What you really feel.
> What you really are among other people.[5]

But for Werther the hurt would be too great if he were fully to face himself and his guilt. He takes refuge in anger, anger against the world outside in whatever form it appears. When he next meets Fräulein von B., oblivious of her distress, he sets out, 'ihr . . . meine Empfindlichkeit über ihr neuliches Betragen zu zeigen'. He acts as though he were in the superior position and she were to blame; he fails to respond to her kindness and compassion and chafes against her pity. For the less he faces his own degree of involvement and guilt, the less able he is to see others as they are. His resistance to accepting his disgrace is revealed in the intense physical reaction when she forces the realization upon him:

alles, was Adelin mir ehgestern gesagt hatte, lief mir wie siedend Wasser durch die Adern in diesem Augenblicke . . . Man erzählt von einer edlen Art Pferde, die, wenn sie schrecklich erhitzt und aufgejagt sind, sich selbst aus Instinkt eine Ader aufbeißen, um sich zum Atem zu helfen. So ist mir's oft, ich möchte mir eine Ader öffnen, die mir die ewige Freiheit schaffte.

The greater his resistance, the more the tension increases. From now on there is no real movement or change in him, only an intensification of his rage and despair. It is as though in failing to go through and beyond his humiliation, he closes himself up and becomes petrified in his present mood. For the feelings described later towards the end of the year (12 December) remain substantially the same: 'es ist ein inneres

unbekanntes Toben, das meine Brust zu zerreißen droht, das
mir die Gurgel zupreßt!'.

Werther's appointment with the Ambassador is his last real
link with a positive, active kind of life which might have led
him to look outside himself, in a context where, despite his
criticism of the Ambassador, those around him care about his
welfare and do all they can to assist him. Factually the 'Verdruß'
episode is vital in the development of the theme of the novel.
For as soon as it happens he determines to leave: 'Ich hab'
einen Verdruß gehabt, der mich von hier wegtreiben wird'.
(The date, 15 March, the Ides of March, is significant.) Shortly
after, he asks to be released. Later, when the Editor takes over
the tale, it is this episode which is particularly mentioned (before
the letter of 12 December) as contributing to his increasing
inability to face life: 'Alles was ihm Unangenehmes jemals in
seinem wirksamen Leben begegnet war, der Verdruß bei der
Gesandtschaft, alles, was ihm sonst mißlungen war, was ihn je
gekränkt hatte, ging in seiner Seele auf und nieder . . ., und
so rückte er endlich . . . immer einem traurigen Ende näher.'

It is significant too that his embarrassment at the Graf's is
connected with leave-taking.[6] For it provides an ironical
anticipation of the conclusion of the novel, which is also a
leave-taking. As Werther here fails to take his leave at the
appropriate time and so has it forced upon him, so later he
engineers his own leave-taking as though in a desperate attempt
to be master of his own destiny. He chooses his own death,
physically and literally, because he cannot accept the little deaths
that come inevitably in daily living, in a society which by its very
nature, regardless of the age or the prevailing social and moral
code, must sometimes be cramping and condemnatory to the
individual. Slowly and carefully he works out the stages that
will lead to his death: unable as he has been to create anything
in life, he now, like an artist biding his time for the right moment
of inspiration, finally creates his own death. Just as at the Graf's
he had been kept from leaving, so he felt, by some evil genius —
'. . . wollt' ich mich eben empfehlen, und wartete nur, . . . blieb
ich eben, . . . wollte gehn, und doch blieb ich . . .' — and is

finally forced to leave by pressure from the Graf, so now he accords himself the freedom he had spoken of earlier, 'das süße Gefühl der Freiheit, und daß er diesen Kerker verlassen kann, wann er will' (Book 1, 22 May).

If Werther's indiscretion, occupying a central position in the novel, foreshadows the final tragedy, a similar parallel can be seen in *Torquato Tasso*, but in the reverse order. For Tasso's indiscretion when he embraces the Prinzessin (Act v, Scene 4) is anticipated by his offer of friendship to Antonio in Act II, his rejection and consequent drawing of the sword; and the same emotional imbalance, self-absorption, undue expectation of the approval of others and dependence on it (all traits equally to be found in Werther) lie behind both his ill-fated actions. The first four acts provide a kind of slow-motion version of the last two scenes of the play, though without the final solution. Goethe has slowly unfolded a detailed picture of Tasso, his search for his true self and for true relationships with others, using the drawing of the sword as a focal point, and then, with the problem still unresolved, he leads up to Tasso's attempt to embrace the Prinzessin and his subsequent reaction, in which all that has gone before is repeated, telescoped and speeded up, and out of which a solution rapidly emerges. Psychologically, it would be impossible for Tasso at this juncture to react in such depth and with such flexibility and immediacy, had he not lived through the experiences of the earlier acts; aesthetically, without the earlier anticipation, the audience would find the two final scenes neither intelligible nor convincing.

In this crucial scene, Tasso, still in a state of depression and confusion after his disgrace with Antonio and feeling rejected by everyone, suddenly becomes aware again of the Prinzessin's real regard and compassion for him. He mistakes it for an avowal of love, fails to heed her warnings, and carried away completely by his feelings he casts himself upon her, only to be thrust away immediately with the one word, 'Hinweg!'.

Tasso's 'fall' is greater than Werther's, for it is a moral as well as a social offence, and more seriously it is a personal offence against the Prinzessin, in so far as he has misinterpreted her so completely. At first he is almost speechless: 'O Gott!', and can reply to Antonio at the beginning of the next scene only 'nach einer langen Pause'. Unlike Werther, Tasso makes no attempt to gloss over his misdemeanour, to behave with propriety; he absorbs the full horror of it in silence. But the first shock is succeeded by rage and hatred as he lashes out against Antonio, whom he sees as a hangman, the Prinzessin, a siren, and Leonore, 'die verschmitzte kleine Mittlerin', and by self-pity as he feels himself the victim of a conspiracy, a beggar, deprived of his poem, his only possession. Antonio, though used to Tasso's swings of emotion, is appalled at the extreme form of his reaction and counsels: 'Besinne dich! Gebiete dieser Wut!'. He fails to see that Tasso must both endure and articulate the violence of his feeling, that this is the only way in which he can be healed. Rage against others may be a perversion; but it is also 'das dumpfe Glück' — 'dumpf' as the product of dark, confused feelings, yet also 'Glück' because momentarily rage helps preserve the contour of his own personality.

But Tasso is shattered and he now recognizes it:

> Ich fühle mir das innerste Gebein
> Zerschmettert, und ich leb', um es zu fühlen.

He has 'fallen', every bone is broken; despair, rage, the torment of hell, annihilation, all threaten him, but he lets himself suffer the experience of falling, he does what Werther cannot face doing, and goes down into the depths of his own suffering, his humiliation, his rage, even his destruction. Because of his misdemeanour something is broken not only in him but in his relationships with others, and the parting that he pictures symbolizes this. But the image of parting also suggests to him an escape, a flight into the future, or else an attempt to recapture the past. But there is no recovery this way.

> Ich will ja gehn! Laßt mich nur Abschied nehmen,
> Nur Abschied nehmen! Gebt, o gebt mir nur
> Auf einen Augenblick die Gegenwart
> Zurück! Vielleicht genes' ich wieder. Nein,
> Ich bin verstoßen, bin verbannt, ich habe

> Mich selbst verbannt, ich werde diese Stimme
> Nicht mehr vernehmen, diesem Blicke nicht,
> Nicht mehr begegnen —

At last he sees the situation as it really is in all its misery and bleakness. He accepts his own responsibility for what has happened — 'ich habe / Mich selbst verbannt' — and he faces the utter emptiness he has brought upon himself.

On this level of experience, Antonio's promptings are once more wide of the mark. 'Du bist so elend nicht, als wie du glaubst.' But it is essential for Tasso to probe the depths of his misery. 'Ermanne dich! Du gibst zu viel dir nach.' It is equally essential for him to let go, to take all the experience and hence all the suffering that comes, in a feminine, receptive, non-cerebral way. And this not just because of the poet in him who must be open to experience, but for ordinary human reasons too. For without this self-surrender, regardless of cost, his personality will become dwarfed and distorted. This is not yet the time for control and closing in; he has to face even the annihilation, the loss of identity which he knows and fears:[7]

> Ist alle Kraft erloschen, die sich sonst
> In meinem Busen regte? Bin ich Nichts,
> Ganz Nichts geworden?
> Nein, es ist alles da, und ich bin nichts;
> Ich bin mir selbst entwandt, sie ist es mir!

When Antonio counsels: 'Vergleiche dich! Erkenne, was du bist!', the first part of his advice proves unfruitful, for Tasso can find no point of comparison to alleviate his suffering. He is indeed out in uncharted territory. As for 'Erkenne, was du bist!', he still does not know. He can only respond as his anguish makes him: he can weep, he can cry out in pain and he can tell how he suffers:

> Nur eines bleibt:
> Die Träne hat uns die Natur verliehen,
> Den Schrei des Schmerzens, wenn der Mann zuletzt
> Es nicht mehr trägt — Und mir noch über alles —
> Sie ließ im Schmerz mir Melodie und Rede,
> Die tiefste Fülle meiner Not zu klagen:
> Und wenn der Mensch in seiner Qual verstummt,
> Gab mir ein Gott, zu sagen, wie ich leide.

There is no doubt at all that these lines refer primarily to Tasso's gift of poetic expression. But seen in the context of the embarrassment situation and at this point in his recovery, they have also a meaning on another plane. For he has not only the ability to live through and consciously accept all the painful emotions that come to him; that is only part of the experience. He has also the power to articulate them to himself. It is as much a 'gift', though of a lower and more common order, as that of poetic talent, and recognition of it begins to bring healing and liberation.

This conscious and willing acceptance of experience, even when all is confusion and the direction it is taking him is not known, demands courage of a quite different kind from that shown by a man of action, and it demands flexibility. Both are revealed in the pattern of images in the concluding monologue. For here again, though the central and overriding impression is that of Tasso the poet, we are given also a vivid and condensed description of Tasso's personality, his relationships, his experiences and his response to them, which have been slowly unfolded in the first four acts of the play and more sharply crystallized in the indiscretion scene with the Prinzessin and Tasso's reactions afterwards.

For Tasso, a storm-tossed wave in his emotional turbulence in comparison with the solidity of Antonio, has also the 'Beweglichkeit der Welle', the openness to experience, the ability to change his shape, to be moulded by the world outside. For the wave exists only as part of the sea. He has the open and intimate contact with nature which enables him to accept its storms; and the repose and tenderness which make him receptive to the images it projects upon him, reflecting them in his life as well as in his poetry. But this gift of 'Beweglichkeit' exposes him to danger as well as to the heights of experience — the danger of being overwhelmed, of complete loss of self — and the image yields to the direct first-personal cry:

> Verschwunden ist der Glanz, entflohn die Ruhe.
> Ich kenne mich in der Gefahr nicht mehr,
> Und schäme mich nicht mehr, es zu bekennen.

The shame he felt formerly in this loss of identity has gone because he recognizes it as the price he pays for his 'gift' of responding freely to experience and articulating it. The metaphor changes from the wave to the ship: the rudder is broken, the ship crashes apart, the ground opens up beneath his feet: an extreme description of the sensation of falling inherent in the embarrassment experience. Once again the image which had recapitulated the sensations of the earlier part of the scene gives way to the first person: 'Ich fasse dich mit beiden Armen an!' and thence to the sailor saved on the very rock on which he was to founder.

Embarrassment cannot be claimed as the key to the solution in *Tasso*, any more than Werther's indiscretion, though an important turning-point, can provide the chief motive force behind the tragedy.[8] For the sake of clarity other factors have necessarily had to receive scant treatment in this brief study. But I would contend that to single out this particular thread in a work of so finely woven a texture neither distorts the meaning of the play nor necessarily disproves other interpretations.[9] For the characters are conceived and created in the round and there is more than one way of approaching them. The dramatic form ensures that we understand them through their own utterances in a way that was not possible, except with Werther himself, in the epistolary novel. It also ensures that we see Tasso's indiscretion, embarrassment and recovery within a whole pattern of relationships, and concentration on this one theme illuminates aspects of the other characters which may not always be much in prominence.

Antonio is the 'rock', the dependable man of affairs, rational, capable and genuinely concerned about the welfare of Tasso. But is there not also in him something of the hostility that Tasso senses and unduly exaggerates? He has indeed been envious of Tasso, sarcastic about the laurel wreath, grudging him his success while still so young, above all rigid and un-self-giving. As we follow the stages of Tasso's recovery in the last scene of the play, Antonio's counsel appears singularly obtuse and runs counter to all that Tasso needs, so that Tasso's self-discovery emerges rather in spite of it than otherwise. Antonio serves largely as a sounding-board, and it matters little that he cannot understand Tasso, who can come nearer the truth about himself in his presence than when alone. At the conclusion of the play Tasso is in the ascendant, triumphantly accepting the dangers and the richness of his personality, while Antonio is the passive onlooker. Tasso is saved by the rock on which he might have perished — disappearing as he had felt himself before, 'Ein Widerhall, ein Nichts' (l. 800) — because he has seen Antonio as he really is, with his limitations as well as his capability, and now he has the courage to accept his own opposing personality. When he says: 'Ich fasse dich mit beiden Armen an!' it is as though the physical embrace included the element of comprehension also implicit in the word 'fassen'.

When Tasso accuses the Prinzessin of tempting him 'so zart, / So himmlisch', like a siren, again there is some truth in his exaggeration. Just as she was part responsible for Tasso's disastrous approach to Antonio in Act II, so now she is not without blame for arousing expectations in him which she cannot or will not fulfil. Nor does she show any command of the situation or any understanding once Tasso's misdemeanour has occurred: with the one word, 'Hinweg' she casts him off and rushes away (hardly a satisfying or dignified exit for the unfortunate actress in this role). Neither loving him fully nor content to let him go, in her detachment and lack of involvement she shows a rigidity and helplessness not unlike that of Antonio in Act II.

If one visualized the play in choreographic terms, it might begin with a contrast between the well-defined, harmonious classical movements of Antonio and the Prinzessin and the writhings and contortions of Tasso. But the contrast at the end would be between the statuesque rigidity of the others and the free-flowing expressiveness of the whole body on the part of Tasso. The future may be uncertain: lacking a kind of protective skin that others have, he will always be vulnerable, incautious, likely to be suspicious, or to misplace his trust and take risks in

self-giving, and he will suffer for it, but he will be alive in a way
that the others are not.

An embarrassment of a different order is portrayed in the
episode in *Die Wahlverwandtschaften* now to be considered.[10]
Not only are the characters different, but the fictional technique
here, the conventional third-person narration, enables their
experiences to be described, analysed and reflected upon. The
Englishman is a man of mature years, urbane and sophisticated.
He has already shown considerable insight and intelligence in
his appreciation of the development of the estate and has proved
an entertaining companion for Charlotte and Ottilie. Yet his
unfortunate generalizations about the futility of building for the
next generation and his descriptions of his own rootless, noma-
dic existence are painfully applicable to the absent Eduard.
Charlotte is sufficiently accustomed to 'eine solche zufällige
Verletzung' not to be unduly discountenanced by it. Ottilie,
however, with the inexperience of her years, is deeply disturbed.
Yet characteristically (and perhaps as a presage of the saintliness
revealed in her at the end of the novel) the Englishman's words
cause her little embarrassment, which always pre-supposes some
degree of self-concern, but cut right through to her anxiety
about Eduard and serve only to intensify her suffering on his
behalf, to the extent that she vows to do everything in her
power to reconcile Eduard and Charlotte. Yet there is no
thought of blame or guilt in Goethe's depiction of this painful
situation: he reveals plainly the inevitability with which such
an embarrassment can be caused, even by the most discerning
and well-intentioned person, and awareness of this prevents
the Englishman from feeling any embarrassment himself. 'Dem
Lord tat es leid, ohne daß er darüber verlegen gewesen wäre.
Man müßte ganz in Gesellschaft schweigen, wenn man nicht
manchmal in den Fall kommen sollte: denn nicht allein bedeutende Bemerkungen, sondern die trivialsten Äußerungen
können auf eine so mißklingende Weise mit dem Interesse der
Gegenwärtigen zusammentreffen. Wir wollen es heute Abend
wieder gut machen, sagte der Lord'. But as though Werther's

'böser Genius' were abroad, their attempt to make amends proves even more disastrous, for the Englishman's companion tells the story of *Die wunderlichen Nachbarskinder*, which unknown to him had its origins in a youthful experience of the Hauptmann's. Charlotte can no longer maintain her composure and has to leave the company to hide her distress.

Causing embarrassment is not confined to the socially awkward; suffering it is not necessarily the sign of an immature or neurotic personality.[11] By some it can be mastered to the point of extinction, and then, as in the case of the English Lord, nothing is suffered and nothing is gained. For more sensitive souls who are willing to suffer it and its accompanying losses, the reward may be a deeper self-knowledge and richer experience. It is an inevitable, indeed essential strand in the fabric of human relationships, but one that receives little attention, perhaps because of its very ordinariness, perhaps because it belongs among the sensations that are often repressed or else deliberately masked. The kind of indiscretion here considered is indeed a gift to the creative writer, providing with advantageous economy a kind of mustard-seed from which all manner of growth can develop. It is a mark of the genius of Goethe that he could create such depth and range of human experience out of incidents in themselves so commonplace, so unimpressive and even so uncomfortable.

REFERENCES

[1] T. S. Eliot, *The Cocktail Party*, Act I, Scene I.
[2] C. Ricks, *Keats and Embarrassment* (Oxford, 1974), p. 5.
[3] *The Cocktail Party*, loc. cit.
[4] Texts are cited from *Goethes Sämtliche Werke, Jubiläums-Ausgabe* (Stuttgart and Berlin [1902–7]): *Die Leiden des jungen Werthers*, XVI, 1–145; *Torquato Tasso*, XII, 89–220; *Die Wahlverwandtschaften*, XXI, 1–302.
[5] *The Cocktail Party*, loc. cit.
[6] For the frequent association of embarrassment with leave-taking, see Ricks, Chapter X.
[7] See Act II, Scene I, and Act IV, Scenes I and 2 in particular.

⁸ Goethe had treated its consequences in greater detail in the original version of the novel and deliberately lessened its importance in the final form.

⁹ See especially E. M. Wilkinson, 'Goethe's *Tasso*: The Tragedy of a Creative Artist', *PEGS*, N.S., 15 (1946), to which this study owes much. I would only suggest that the pattern of images in the final speech both describes the experience of the man and witnesses to the activity of the poet; that we see here the simultaneous operation of the *two* gifts of 'telling' how he suffers.

¹⁰ Part II, Chapter 10. Embarrassment, inherent in the central situation, plays an extensive if unobtrusive role in this novel, and the relation of this one relatively self-contained episode to other instances and to kindred themes of falling, stumbling, shock and sudden self-illumination would be a study in itself.

¹¹ Anthony Storr, in his review of Ricks (*Sunday Times*, 31 March 1974), criticizes psychoanalysts for tending to regard embarrassment as wholly neurotic. 'But to do so surely postulates a false ideal — a perfectly controlled individual invulnerable to spontaneity, and insensitive both to the feelings of others and also to conflict within himself. Although the inexperienced and the adolescent may show and feel embarrassment more readily than the mature adult, it would be inhuman *never* to feel it.'

The Vexed Question of Egmont's Political Judgement

By JOHN M. ELLIS

CRITICS have loved to find fault with Goethe's *Egmont*[1] ever since Schiller did so in his celebrated review of the play.[2] And it is largely Schiller's major criticism that they have repeated and elaborated: Egmont does not earn our sympathy as the tragic hero of the play because he neglects political duties and realities, and irresponsibly turns his attention to private enjoyment. Schiller's own prestige has naturally enough helped to gain acceptance for his view of the play, but taken by itself the quality of his argument is so weak that it ought to have cancelled out that advantage. At every turn, it is obvious that Schiller concerns himself only with the play's effectiveness at a superficial level, and not at all with its meaning. For example, he criticizes the absence of the historical Egmont's wife and children because it deprives the audience of 'das rührende Bild eines Vaters'; and when he compliments Goethe on the Egmont–Ferdinand scene he enthuses 'was kann rührender sein'. He does not speak of the thematic point in either case, just as in approving Margarete's being 'veredelt', he does not begin to approach her thematic importance in the play as a personality contrasted with Egmont — that she is ennobled is enough for Schiller. Again, in praising the crowd scenes as accurate and lively representation of historical fact, he lets pass by him their considerable thematic content. Schiller had his own concerns, and they were not Goethe's. He wanted the inspiring spectacles, great figures and moving events of dramatized history; Goethe was using and adapting a historical situation to write a thematic study. The two conceptions are so far apart that Schiller's review is virtually irrelevant to Goethe's

play. Where Schiller criticizes Goethe's deviation from historical fact as a weakening of 'das Interesse seines Gegenstandes'
(i.e., a historical situation), any critic interested in Goethe's
meaning might have used this deviation as a way into that
meaning, since it evidently required such a deviation. And yet,
though Schiller is so evidently wrapped up in his own concerns,
and so thoroughly remote from what Goethe is writing about,
his view of the play has continued to be influential.[3]

A second major source of negative judgements of *Egmont* has
been the genesis of the play. It was written over a long period
of time, and during this period Goethe's writing and way of
life changed a good deal. That has led many to suppose that the
text must lack internal consistency; specifically, *Egmont* is often
thought to be a play which started out as a presentation of a
grand Sturm-und-Drang hero, and degenerated into the more
reflective and less vigorous style of Goethe's classical period.[4]
But, as before, scepticism is in order here too. For those who
are impressed by this kind of inference from biography ought
also to have taken seriously Goethe's own pronouncements on
Egmont. For example: 'Das Stück ist so oft durchdacht, daß man
es auch wohl öfters wird lesen können'; or 'Kein Stück hab' ich
mit mehr Freiheit des Gemüts und mit mehr Gewissenhaftigkeit
vollbracht als dieses'.[5] I must confess that I have always found it
very implausible to suppose that a great writer would come
back to an unfinished manuscript and either go on without
re-reading what he had already written, or, when re-reading,
fail to understand the point of his earlier conception.[6] (But
then, I also find it inherently implausible that Goethe could
have thought that his play would make sense if its hero and
central figure were politically irresponsible or naive — or that
having made him so he would not have understood what he
had done there too.) Could Goethe really not have *noticed* that
his conception was altering? Only a professorial critic, blue
pencil in hand, eager to condescend to and scold Germany's
greatest poet as lazy and inattentive, could easily believe that.
But Goethe's statements that he *had* thought it all through again
carefully[7] greatly increase the inherent implausibility of this idea.

I

For those who take biographical pointers (whatever their direction) with some scepticism, there is always Goethe's text, and it very soon establishes a stance that makes both of the streams of criticism which I have mentioned look wrong at the outset. Goethe very quickly impresses on his readers, in a variety of ways, that judging *Egmont* is an exceedingly complex matter, that they should be very careful not to make any quick and superficial judgements, and that the whole structure of the play will need to be carefully considered before a final judgement is made. Though the title of the play makes Egmont its central figure, Goethe does not allow him to appear at all in its first act; instead, we hear opinions of him in three different contexts (the streets of Brussels, the Court, Klärchen's house), and even within the given context those opinions differ markedly. Margarete von Parma finds Egmont frivolous and irresponsible; Machiavell thinks he acts conscientiously. Margarete's view is one among many others, and so part of a developing picture of Egmont that moves in the direction of greater complexity; to take that view as a final one, as so many critics have done, would be to ignore the movement of the play's structure — what could the rest of the play be for, if we have the truth so early?

The character of Egmont's eventual entry in Act II emphasizes even more strongly how complex a matter it is to judge him. What we have heard of him so far is already somewhat contradictory, but the circumstances of his appearances in Act II seem dominated by paradoxes and surprises, and seem in fact to be almost calculated to clash with what we have already heard. Throughout Act I, for example, we have heard much about Egmont's being identified with and admired by the Netherlanders. This seems to be summed up in Zimmermann's comment 'Ein gnäd'ger Herr! der echte Niederländer! gar so nichts Spanisches'. But Egmont's first entry, as Jetter notices, is in clothing 'nach der neuesten Art, nach spanischem Schnitt'. The point is emphasized when Egmont visits Klärchen, in magnificent clothing: 'Ich versprach dir, einmal spanisch zu kommen.'[8] This is obviously paradoxical, and there is much more like it. The Egmont of Act I seems predominantly free and easy, a ruler who lives and lets live, who has instinctive rapport and sympathy with his people. But his first two entrances in the play cast him somewhat obtrusively as a representative of authority and order. In the first scene of Act II, he puts down an incipient riot with the words 'Ein ordentlicher Bürger, der sich ehrlich und fleißig nährt, hat überall so viel Freiheit, als er braucht'. And in the next scene, with his secretary, his first actions shown are decisions as to how law-breakers are to be punished. The decisions are humane, to be sure, but the decision to give priority once more to Egmont's exercising governmental authority makes these two entries seem designed to contrast with the impression we had had until now. The emphasis is no longer on light-hearted enjoyment, but on the responsibilities of citizens, the limits of freedom, and punishment of those who do not respect those limits. Though no death sentences are meted out, we may well be jolted by the mention of hangings — an indication that Egmont knows how much depends on maintaining the equilibrium of so politically charged a situation, and that he has on some occasions felt obliged to take severe action to do so.[9] The contrast is, then, something for the spectator to ponder; Goethe began with one image of Egmont in what was said about him, but surprises us when we see Egmont for ourselves.

Yet another clash of views, on a smaller scale, is seen in his secretary's grumblings that Egmont is late again: 'wenn er strenge wäre und ließ' einen auch wieder zur bestimmten Zeit.' That sounds like the familiar notion of the irresponsible Egmont again. But we know what it is that has made Egmont late — his attending to his duty to keep public order. The point seems clear: what seems irresponsible from one perspective can seem like conscientious attention to an unexpected duty from another.

What all these paradoxes and clashes of image amount to is that Goethe gives us plenty of warning not to assess Egmont in a hasty or superficial manner. And, if we had not got that message by now, there is at the end of the third act the still more surprising self-portrayal of Egmont as two people, one of whom we scarcely recognize: 'Jener Egmont ist ein verdrieß-licher, steifer, kalter Egmont. Der an sich halten, bald dieses, bald jenes Gesicht machen muß, geplagt, verkannt, verwickelt ist, wenn ihn die Leute für froh und fröhlich halten.' Again the text warns us: be careful that you understand the whole complex before you decide what Egmont is, and what he stands for. But its warnings have been largely in vain.

In 1949, E. M. Wilkinson published a remarkable essay on the play.[10] In one of the most brilliant and sophisticated pieces of criticism ever written — on Goethe or any other figure — she showed that the texture of the play is thematically carefully organized and complex, and that, for example, Egmont's freedom from care is to be distinguished from mere careless-ness. Had her subtle argument been fully appreciated the history of *Egmont* criticism in the last quarter century would have been very different. These days there is much discussion of the state and plight of *Germanistik* as a discipline; I wonder if there is anything that so dramatically points to its real limitations, and the source of its depressed condition, as this failure to learn from so distinguished a piece of criticism. For both Schiller's super-ficial criticisms, and the notion that the play's gestation over a long period indicates radical textual inconsistencies, have continued regardless, and a series of recent articles has even stepped up the attack on Egmont as a 'naive and irresponsible man'.[11] This is basically Margarete von Parma's view, taken as authoritative in spite of its being textually circumscribed as limited, but made even harsher. Egmont now is seen as a man who refuses to plan or calculate, has an exaggerated and even arrogant confidence in himself and his own fate, suffers from hubris, is foolhardy, self-deceived and irrational, is out of touch with political reality, is too naive to understand that injustice is a fact of life, and refuses to heed sensible warnings.[12]

There is no doubt that the circumstances surrounding the play's outcome, and Egmont's death, provide the main impetus for this view: Egmont appears to have misjudged Alba's intent, is surprised by his arrest, has rejected a warning from Oranien, and is evidently not reconciled to his death after his arrest. A correct understanding of these circumstances is indeed the crucial factor in interpreting *Egmont*. But earlier parts of the play already do not seem to be consistent with the standard interpretation. Egmont's discussion with Oranien seems to show both seriousness and judgement on his part. In that scene Egmont presents a well thought out rationale for his action, and in so doing shows more *fundamental* political realism and responsibility than anyone else in the play, including Alba and Oranien. Egmont clearly sees, first of all, that a refusal to see Alba is an act of war. This is a fundamental political insight, and Oranien shows no comparable grasp of the situation. Egmont questions him about the consequences; Oranien thinks they can get by with excuses. *That* is naive. Egmont says that they must at the outset take seriously their responsibility for starting a devastating war which will destroy thousands. Oranien does not argue that this is an acceptable loss which is in the long term interest of the people, but on the contrary that as princes they have a right to save themselves at the expense of the people. *That* is arrogance and irresponsibility. Oranien, not Egmont, acts out of personal considerations.[13]

Egmont doubts that the Spanish will act as Oranien thinks, and here he is wrong. But he is wrong not because he trusts their integrity, but because he sees a fundamental political reality that he assumes will be obvious to them — and it is not. Egmont sees that it is not in the interests of the Spanish to act as Oranien fears. He says that it would be 'eine Torheit, die ich ihm [Philipp] und seinen Räten nicht zutraue'. He sees that such an action would unite the people and 'Haß und ewige Trennung vom spanischen Namen würde sich gewaltsam erklären'. Egmont is correct; that is just what happens.[14] Alba the politician, and the Spanish, are the great political losers in what happens, and Egmont foresees it. Can this really be a man out of touch with political reality? Alba is the one who turns out to have been politically naive. Egmont did not have an exaggerated trust in Alba's goodness as some critics would have us believe; he assumed that Alba would have a little more sense of

what was politically intelligent for the Spanish, and refused to
risk starting a war on the assumption that Alba had as little
grasp of the politics of the situation as turns out to be the case.
It is true that Egmont also disbelieves the possibility of Philipp's
being capable of an act of 'Niedrigkeit'. But a base act that is
self-defeating is harder to believe in than a base act that has
advantages; and the *main* thrust of Egmont's argument lies in
the two points, first, that the Spanish action which Oranien
envisages would quickly lead to the loss of the Netherlands, and
second, that the act which Oranien proposes would certainly
lead to a devastating and possibly avoidable war. In this scene,
then, Egmont grasps political reality better than anyone, accepts
personal risk having weighed it against the risks to others, and
errs only in underestimating Alba's total lack of political
understanding.

One other early scene has attracted criticisms of Egmont,
namely that with his secretary, where, it has been argued,[15]
Egmont's distaste for administration and irresponsible neglect
of it is shown, especially in his haste to be finished with it. This
too represents a misreading of the emphases of Goethe's text.
The point of Egmont's admittedly brisk style lies in the contrast
with the parallel scene between Margarete and her secretary.
Unlike Egmont, she urges Machiavell to be 'ausführlich und
umständlich', but as she listens to the resulting letter to the
King, she exclaims: 'Ach, wie ergreift mich aufs neue der
Schmerz bei deiner Wiederholung!' Length here is equated
with agonizing, with that lack of freedom from care that
characterizes Margarete, with fruitless and pointless worry.
Machiavell's advice to her pointedly cuts through detail:
'Ein Wort für tausend . . .' Egmont likewise cuts through detail
to get a clearer view of the *essentials* of a situation. Goethe surely
means us to be impressed not by irresponsible haste here, but by
the swiftness and sureness with which Egmont makes accurate
and appropriate judgements. Egmont does brush aside the
details of the iconoclasts' activities — but only after satisfying
himself that this would be more of the same thing that he has
heard already.[16] And there are in any case plenty of textual

details which militate against any notion of unseemly haste here; Egmont is unavoidably late, the 'Boten' are waiting, and his secretary has an assignation that is important both to him *and* to Egmont. All of this would in any case justify Egmont's 'Sag' an! Das Nötigste . . . nur geschwind!'.

It is difficult to find any sign in Goethe's text of Egmont's alleged arrogant disregard for danger, or exaggerated confidence in his own fate. His conversation with Oranien, for example, clearly has him weighing one danger against a greater one; e.g., 'Bei so großer Gefahr kommt die leichteste Hoffnung in Anschlag.' And a fearful obsession with danger would clearly be an inconsistency of character. The source of this notion that Egmont is foolhardy in his disregard for danger seems to me to lie largely in a misinterpretation of the key image of the horse and charioteer. The image is striking: 'Wie von unsichtbaren Geistern gepeitscht, gehen die Sonnenpferde der Zeit mit unsers Schicksals leichtem Wagen durch; und uns bleibt nichts, als mutig gefaßt die Zügel festzuhalten und bald rechts bald links, vom Steine hier vom Sturze da, die Räder wegzulenken.'

This is not about boundless self-*confidence*, but about self-*acceptance*; it is not about human calculation 'counting for little', but about calculation counting for *something*; it does not signify 'no control of direction', but instead real control within limits.[17] Courage and skill are both necessary and effective in guiding the chariot round the obstacles in its path; but they cannot change its basic direction. Thought and planning are important but they must work within and respect the limits set by unalterable personality. But the full meaning of the image can only be grasped through an appreciation of its place in the play's structure. Egmont, Alba, Oranien and Margarete all have their own images of fate, and of the limits of thought and action, and it is the contrasts among the four that most determine their meaning. Margarete sees herself on a wave that 'treibt uns auf und nieder, hin und her'; Alba's view of human action is gloomy in a different way: 'Wie in einen Lostopf greifst du in die dunkle Zukunft'; Oranien's image is that of the chessboard at which he sits, studying the significance of each move of his opponent. Margarete and Alba are much more fatalistic than Egmont. Margarete sees no possibility of control, no reins to manipulate adroitly; she is pushed wherever the wave takes her. Alba tries to control everything, and because he cannot do so, is reduced to complaining that fate is not kind to meticulous planners: 'Das Glück ist eigensinnig, oft das Gemeine, das Nichtswürdige zu adeln und wohlüberlegte Taten mit einem gemeinen Ausgang zu entehren.' The paradox is startling; because Alba cannot accept any limits to controlling people or events, he is condemned to the conclusion that fortune does what it wants to do *regardless* of the planner's skills. His whole plan is an instructive failure; he will not accept the fact that the character of the Netherlanders imposes limits on his actions, and the results of those actions (failure to capture Oranien, loss of the Netherlands) will therefore be completely unpredictable to him, and experienced only as fate's unfairness. Oranien, like Alba, seeks total control of the chessboard which for him represents life, but he can only do so by treating all the rest of humanity as pawns, dead wood to be sacrificed. Even so, he is only a move-by-move tactician, not a strategist, as his replies to Egmont's questions make clear. He looks at the opponent's every move, but allows his actions to be determined as tactical responses to those moves without having a plan of his own, or a larger view of the situation. Only in Egmont's case does the image allow for control (unlike Margarete) but respect the limits of control (unlike Alba) and retain a sense of humanness, individual identity and general goals and directions (unlike Oranien).

Quite how important the horse and charioteer image becomes is shown by its many extensions and transformations. Egmont's main use of it is as a metaphor for the relationship of the conscious mind to the individual's unalterable personality. An important parallel use refers it to the relationship of ruler to people; Egmont says to Alba that a shepherd can easily drive a herd of sheep before him, but 'dem edlen Pferde, das du reiten willst, mußt du seine Gedanken ablernen . . .'. Just as Egmont knows that his actions cannot ignore his own individuality, he also knows that a ruler's actions cannot ignore the individuality of his people; otherwise, he would destroy 'den innern Kern ihrer Eigenheit'. In neither case does the rider have unlimited freedom (the King, complains Egmont, 'will sich allein frei machen'); but in both a rider is indispensable if the chariot is not to be quickly smashed. Here is the point of what Egmont says to the citizens of Brussels on the limits of their freedom, and of his awareness that by itself the people 'nicht weiß, was es will'. Egmont's concept of personal and political freedom is a balance of the need for control and respect for what is controlled; both are indispensable.[18]

Margarete's first appearance shows the pervasiveness and intricacy of the play's dominant image. She appears 'in Jagdkleidern', but immediately says: 'Ihr stellt das Jagen ab, ich werde heut' nicht reiten.' She is so much a prisoner of her own worrisome nature that she wants nothing more than to get off the horse; incapable of being 'mutig gefaßt', she is too oppressed by dangers which beset its course. Soon she speaks of abdication; again, rather dismount than face the anxieties of guiding the chariot. Abdication and refusing to ride are, then, parallel expressions of her anxiety about life; this contrast with Egmont's use of the image further determines its meaning.

There remain what have always seemed the most plausible reasons for criticism of Egmont's judgement and his lack of seriousness: his apparent misjudgement of Alba's intent, his surprise on being arrested, and his passive death. But rightly understood, these circumstances do not give support to that view; on the contrary, attention to the entire context and textual detail of the final act leads to a very different interpretation.

Throughout the play, an important characteristic of Egmont is his freedom from anxiety ('Sorge'), not to be confused with carelessness or carefreeness in their usual senses in English. This is an essential part of Egmont's freedom; Margarete is the slave of her anxieties, but Egmont is not at the mercy of his. This fact has a crucial bearing on how we should assess Egmont's surprise at his arrest. For once Egmont has weighed a situation and made a decision, he is able to accept his own decision without further agonizing. This means that he does not obsessively go through the same reasoning over and over again, fruitlessly remaking the decision (this is the point, again, of the contrast between his brevity and Margarete's 'Ausführlichkeit'). It also means, even more importantly, that having weighed the dangers of various courses of action, and having decided that the dangers of one course must be accepted, he does not then allow himself to be dominated by visions of those dangers, to *visualize* them constantly. It would not be in his nature to imagine and tremble at the thought of arrest and execution, even though his conversation with Oranien shows that he knows and accepts that this is a danger in the situation. To visualize that danger constantly would be to incapacitate himself. His surprise, then, is the reaction of a man who has accepted danger in advance, but has refused to let himself be dominated by visions of the actual effects of that danger. Egmont's freedom from anxiety allows him to do what has to be done; it even allows him to speak out with great frankness in his conversation with Alba, to utter truths which must be uttered even though they carry risks independent of the inherent risk in Egmont's being there at all.

This is surely the import of the 'Nachtwandler' image, too often misinterpreted as indicative of Egmont's failure to heed warnings.[19] Egmont's utterance has clearly a different focus, and one relevant to his later actions: 'Und wenn ich ein Nachtwandler wäre, und auf dem gefährlichen Gipfel eines Hauses spazierte, ist es freundschaftlich, mich beim Namen zu rufen und mich zu warnen, zu wecken und zu töten?' The point of the image is that the sleepwalker is *already committed* to the dangerous situation he is in, and to wake him is to incapacitate him by making him focus on and become horrified by that danger. He will become dizzy, and fall. It is not a friendly act, he says, to try to instil in him an obsession with dangers which he is committed to by his actions. That *general* awareness has no need to be translated into *specific* mental pictures, concrete visualizations of particular horrendous possibilities — all that this can achieve is to increase anxiety to the point where the individual cannot function as he thinks he must. In his prison, Egmont makes part of this explicit: 'Doch es ziemt dem Menschen nicht mehr zu grübeln, wo er nicht mehr wirken soll.'[20] Again, thinking and rethinking is pointless unless it relates to action; where it does not, it is destructive.

It is within this general framework that Egmont's apparent surprise ('Das war die Absicht?') at his arrest, and his despair at his death, must be understood. He had reckoned with this outcome as a possibility, but had not visualized its actual shape, and had not lived its pain in advance. Thus, he must face that pain now, for the first time, and his distress is as real as that of any other human being. Egmont had not wasted time, or peace of mind, by trying to calculate more precisely whether Alba would or would not arrest him, since he had decided that it was necessary to go — that too would have been fruitless 'grübeln', unnecessary and possibly incapacitating. The proverbial coward dies a thousand deaths, through obsessive visualizing of future dangers; Egmont is free of this, but he must still face the pain of the one death that is real.

Ultimately, however, we must read the passivity of Egmont's death in the light of a tone which is established throughout the last act, and which brings it into the orbit (and gives it part of the meaning) of the most celebrated of all passive deaths: that of Jesus Christ. This crucial fact has been ignored by the play's critics. There are obvious broad structural parallels between the deaths of Christ and Egmont which would on their face allow a comparison, but without requiring it and making it a necessary part of the play's meaning. For example, we first see the crowd's adulation of Egmont, and even hear of how, when Egmont rides into the city ('Er kommt von Gent') everyone stops to look; but then following his arrest they shy away, and do not wish even to acknowledge his name ('Nennt den Namen nicht'). So far, this seems generally parallel to the contrast between Christ's enthusiastic reception as he rode into the city, and the people's deserting him following his arrest. But some details of the language force the parallel to be made; Klärchen tells the people how they are betraying and denying him: 'Und so wechseln wir Worte! sind müßig, verraten ihn ... Ihr verbergt euch, da es Not ist, verleugnet ihn'. And there are countless other such pointers. Brackenburg reports that at the place of execution a crucifix is 'an der einen Seite hoch aufgesteckt'; Klärchen declares to the people that 'Seine Wunden flossen und heilten nur für euch'. Ferdinand's expression of his loss in Egmont's death adds another dimension to Egmont's death by using the language of St John: 'Bei der Freude des Mahls hab' ich mein Licht ... verloren.' Brackenburg attempts to persuade Klärchen that 'Noch ist nicht jedes Licht verloschen', yet the lamp that she asks him to extinguish after her death finally goes out in spite of his forgetting to do it. The emphasis here is on the meaning of Egmont's way of life as a light to others, as Christ's was.[21] Here, then, is a major aspect of the meaning of the passive quality of Egmont's death. When we see this biblical language, and its import, we can no longer be tempted to see Egmont's death as a witless, pointless failure to avoid an obvious trap. Christ knew of his arrest in advance, and did nothing to avoid it. Egmont's case falls short of such clear knowledge (and so he has to tell himself, not tell someone else, to put up his sword!) but the language of the final act spells out the fact that his death is to be seen in the light of Christ's — the passive acceptance of a martyrdom which is the inevitable outcome of an uncompromising insistence on his way of life, itself a 'light' and inspiration to others. This is what finally justifies Egmont's saying 'Ich sterbe für die Freiheit, für die ich lebte und focht, und der ich mich jetzt leidend opfre'. Egmont's despair, too, must be seen in this context: Christ also despaired in a human way when faced with the reality of death, though he had reckoned with it in advance.

Egmont's death, like Christ's, has sufficient moral force to resurrect after his death the ideal that he stood for, and that is the meaning of his final vision.[22] The refusal of the people to rally round Egmont after his *arrest* does not defeat Egmont's prediction that the people will rally to his ideal after his *death*;[23] it only cements further the analogy with Christ's arrest and death, for Christ too was deserted by everyone immediately after his arrest.

Christ's acceptance of a martyr's death was probably the most politically effective action in human history. This action might not have seemed well calculated either, and it might even have seemed passive and weak. But the moral force of Christ's insistence on his way of life proved more powerful than any more conventionally political action. The devastating answer to the view that Egmont was a questionable politician is that Goethe went to some pains to link him with the most politically effective figure of all time.

REFERENCES

[1] I cite the text of the play from *Goethes Sämtliche Werke*, Jubiläums-Ausgabe (Stuttgart and Berlin [1902–7]), XI, 235–336.

[2] 'Über *Egmont*, Trauerspiel von Goethe' which can be found in *Schillers Werke*, Nationalausgabe, XXII (Weimar, 1958), 199–209. For example: 'Nein, guter Graf Egmont! . . . Wenn es euch zu beschwerlich ist, Euch Eurer Rettung anzunehmen, so mögt Ihr's haben, wenn sich die Schlinge über Euch zusammenzieht.'

[3] See, for example, R. Peacock, *Goethe's Major Plays* (Manchester, 1959), p. 42: Schiller 'puts his finger on the two great weaknesses in Goethe's presentation of Egmont'; and H. Hatfield, *Goethe: A Critical Introduction* (Cambridge, Massachusetts, 1964): Schiller was 'the most incisive critic of Egmont . . . Basically, however, he was in the right' (p. 49).

[4] For example, H. G. Haile, 'Goethe's Political Thinking and *Egmont*', *GR*, 40 (1967), 96–107; and H. M. Waidson in his edition of the play (Oxford, 1960).

[5] Letter to Frau von Stein, 16 November 1788; and *Italienische Reise*, 10 November 1787.

[6] There are of course many more logical reasons to suspect this kind of inference; cf. Chapter 5 of my *The Theory of Literary Criticism: A Logical Analysis* (Berkeley and Los Angeles, 1974).

[7] J. L. Sammons, 'On the Structure of Goethe's *Egmont*', *Journal of English and Germanic Philology*, 62 (1963), 241–45, thinks that Goethe took almost 'pedantic care' over external details, but makes the usual criticisms of the play's structural inconsistencies. The notion of Goethe's devoting so much care to the play's surface, but none to its basic conception, is to me a strange one.

[8] Haile (p. 99) sees the clash, but concludes, oddly, that what is stressed here is Egmont's not being Spanish; Hatfield (p. 48) sees 'a certain narcissism' in Egmont's dress. Again, the urge to carp allows an important structural contrast to become lost.

[9] Sammons is moved to indignation by Egmont's behaviour here: 'His dispensation of justice is cursory and arbitrary, and his generosity barbaric' (p. 250); and he also complains that Egmont will not take the iconoclasts seriously. Yet the alleged 'barbarism' (can a reading which is appropriately historical make such a charge?) is evidence that Egmont *does* take them seriously.

[10] 'The Relation of Form and Meaning in Goethe's *Egmont*', *PEGS*, N.S., 18 (1949), 149–82.

[11] Principally those by Sammons; G. A.Wells, 'Egmont and "das Dämonische"',
GLL, N.S., 24 (1970–71), 53–67; M. W. Swales, 'A Questionable Politician:
A Discussion of the Ending to Goethe's *Egmont*', *MLR*, 66 (1971), 832–40;
S. Burkhardt, '*Egmont* and *Prinz Friedrich von Homburg*: Expostulation and
Reply', *GQ*, 36 (1963), 113–19. See also Liselotte Dieckmann's recent book
Johann Wolfgang Goethe (New York, 1974) for a comparable view.

[12] Examples are: Burkhardt, p. 114 ('refuses to plan, to calculate'); Dieckmann,
p. 94 ('arrogant trust in his own fate, a hubris . . .'); Wells, p. 64 ('is greater
naivety possible? . . . unconscious of the villainy in others'); Waidson, p. xxiii
('subjective, irrational') and p. xxvii ('politically ineffectual'); Swales, pp. 835–37
('politically naive . . . irrational . . . inconsistency and irresponsibility'). Swales
also approves the interpretation of E. M. Wilkinson: that surely outdoes even
his Egmont for inconsistency.

[13] Swales says that Egmont is 'impelled by purely personal motives'; that his
criteria for rejecting a course of action are 'exclusively personal' and that Egmont
wants only to be true to himself without considering the demand that 'he be
true to other people' (p. 835). That reverses Goethe's text in the Egmont/Oranien
discussion. Compare I. Hobson, 'Oranien and Alba: The Two Political Dialogues
in *Egmont*', *GR*, 48 (1975), 260–74; Hobson points to further inaccuracy in Swales's
quotation from Goethe, and also concludes that his interpretation 'arises from
a misreading of the text' (p. 260).

[14] The initial behaviour of the people in Act v, following Egmont's arrest, is
not an objection to this assertion; I argue this point below, pp. 127–29.

[15] Wells, p. 62; Swales, p. 836; Sammons, pp. 249–50.

[16] Contrast Sammons, above, n. 9. Wells's criticism ('Hardly statesmanlike!',
p. 61) of Egmont's reply to Oranien, who had asked him whether he heard what
Margarete said at their last meeting ('Nicht alles; ich dachte unterdessen an was
anders') also misses the larger context. Egmont knows the basis of her views too
well to need to listen to every needlessly elaborated detail, every repetitious
point.

[17] Waidson, p. xxx; Swales, p. 836. Peacock (p. 41) thinks that it signifies
yielding to 'impulse and instinct'. E. M. Wilkinson's comments on this image are
particularly accurate.

[18] By contrast Sammons, p. 250, says that Egmont is interested only in 'the
freedom of Egmont', not that of the Netherlands; and Swales (p. 837) echoes
Sammons: 'Egmont is very much the aristocrat who is largely concerned with his
own personal freedom of action'. These judgements miss the complexity of the
idea of freedom, personal and political, in the play.

[19] For example, Swales, p. 836, who sees it only as part of Egmont's rejection
of prudence.

[20] M.-L. Waldeck notes that this is the spirit that allows Egmont to visit
Klärchen in a political crisis; this is surely a completely adequate rejoinder to
Schiller's criticism, and to critics who have repeated it ('Klärchen: An examination
of her role in Goethe's *Egmont*', *PEGS*, N.S., 35 (1965), 68–91).

[21] John 12, 35–36 and 46: 'Es ist das Licht noch eine kleine Zeit bei euch . . .
Glaubet an das Licht, dieweil ihr's habt . . . Ich bin gekommen in die Welt ein
Licht . . .'.

[22] Waidson, pp. xviii–xix: the 'execution, which was intended to cow the
populace into submission to Alba's will, had the opposite effect . . . After
Egmont's death the revolt of the Netherlands . . . became a force with which
Alba was unable effectively to contend'.

[23] Wells, for example (p. 63), says that 'the view Egmont here expresses is
wrong', missing the point of the language of 'verraten' and 'verleugnen' in
Act v.

'Geeinte Zwienatur'?

On the Structure of Goethe's *Urfaust*

By ILSE GRAHAM

I

IT IS CUSTOMARY to regard Goethe's *Urfaust* as falling into
two halves which are but tenuously connected: the 'Gelehrtentragödie' and the 'Liebestragödie'. For instance, L. A.
Willoughby writes: 'The *Urfaust* makes no attempt to fuse the
theme of the despairing scholar with that of love's betrayal.
The first meeting between Faust and Gretchen reads like the
beginning of a new play, and its libertine hero bears but little
resemblance to the earnest young professor in his study.'[1]
Erich Trunz comes to a similar conclusion. In his view, too,
the *Urfaust* falls into 'zwei große Szenengruppen, die Gelehrtentragödie und die Gretchentragödie'.[2] It would seem that
Faust's own later 'Zwei Seelen wohnen, ach! in meiner Brust'
retroactively puts the seal of Goethe's approval on this view.
But is Faust's voice necessarily that of his maker? Are we
really constrained to accept a reading which suggests that in this
drama there are two heroes, or one that is schizoid? Is there
no evidence to show that Faust's rational and passional sides
cohere, that his whole self is involved in those seemingly
disparate sequences and the different quests enacted in them?
Could it not be that the *fortissimo* on which the play begins and
ends, in what curiously enough are two *Kerkerszenen* — 'Weh!
steck ich in dem Kerker noch?' Faust laments in his study —
argues a Faust who is each time fully motivated and the same
except that the signs are, as it were, reversed? That in the
opening scene we are introduced to a Faust who is engaged on
a spiritual quest backed, however, by the full force of his

libidinal drives, whilst the finale shows us a Faust in the grip of a passion that takes its resonance and magnitude from the fact that his spiritual resources are wholly aroused? Which is, maybe, why the impact of both is so reverberating?

I would suggest that wholeness is the hallmark of beginning and end alike, and that the intervening sequences serve to break down that initial wholeness into its component parts by a technique I shall presently indicate, and thence proceed to build it up again, by a similar technique, in reverse fashion; the point of intersection and reversal being the scene 'Straße' in which Faust first sets eyes on Gretchen and commissions Mephistopheles to procure her for him. To show continuity through reversal and to indicate something of the marvellously sinewy energy of a poetic organization as lean and keen as a young race-horse, yet full of growing-points for future filling in, is the purpose of these observations.

I have, on another occasion, argued Faust's wholeness of motivation in the opening scene 'Nacht'. Then I leaned heavily on the imagery that springs to the hero's lips, oral imagery that is sensual *per se* and, moreover, interlaces with such images as will later on be used by and of him in contexts that are patently erotic. Such link-imagery I largely found to be images of fluid; and understandably so, since *Faust* is a drama about creativity, and water, for Goethe, at all times was the symbol *par excellence* of the creative mode.[3]

Here I propose to alter my slant and demonstrate Faust's wholeness in 'Nacht' by concentrating on what I should like to call 'the beat' underlying his soliloquy. A close look at the first four paragraphs of this monologue will demonstrate my point. Although it is only the first portion which is strictly speaking written in *Knittelvers*, the general impression is that sections one and three belong together, by reason of their metrical harshness as much as their content, whilst sections two and four make an altogether different impact on mind and ear. Let us start at the beginning and run through these four interlaced sections.

The feel of the *Knittelvers* — uneven, angular and gnarled — lends itself perfectly to the matter Faust is in this first section putting before us, in his angry exposition of an academic's predicament. It is a tormented mind that circles around a plight which he reiterates with a monotonous obsessiveness in a series of breathless variations on the same theme. He darts from angle to angle to assault his wretchedness — the utter futility of a scholar's life — in ever renewed thrusts. As though he were beating his head against a brick wall, he bombards his own despair again and yet again. The impression made by part and whole alike is passionate, yet curiously jagged and brittle. There is really no logical beginning and end to what is of its essence a protracted tantrum. Only towards its conclusion does relaxation seem to set in, as at long last Faust pronounces the words — very physical words indeed — which effect a release precisely because they give utterance to the — quite unacademic — depth of his need. These words are *Würkungskraft* and *Samen*. They serve magically to quieten the uproar that has preceded them. Their mere mention effects a transition to an altogether different strain: flowing, lyrical, breathing.

The lines of the following section are made up of four stresses that regularly alternate with unstressed syllables. No one would be surprised to find them slipped into a collection of Goethe's lyrics. As metre and rhythm flow, so does thought. Effortlessly it glides from one association to the next, from Faust's desk to his window and thence to the pacified scene outdoors. Each association is evocative because it is nourished by a unified mood; and together they go to articulate an encompassing mood that is similarly rounded. Allowed free rein, Faust's associations become ever more flowing and physical. For what does this 'Auf Wiesen in deinem Dämmer weben' tell us? Here the first verse of the later lyric 'An den Mond' comes to mind. In those exquisite lines as here, in the *Urfaust*, the poet evokes the blurring and dissolving of all separate contours in space and, with it, the communion, with its own depths as well as with its surroundings, of a soul that was, as it were, in a stranglehold. It is important to realize both, the reverberations in depth as well as the outward radiations set up by this event: both will continually recur, and always they appear inseparably interlaced.

K

The *Nebelglanz* in the later lyric and the *Dämmer* here form the continuous yet semi-pellucid medium in which all that was separate — the bitty mind, the discontinuous vision — now gently blends together.

The force of this image is further enhanced by the one that follows:

> ... Von all dem Wissensqualm entladen
> In deinem Tau gesund mich baden!

Bathing means the washing away of all alien matter that obstructs the skin; it means the gradual equalization of different temperatures as the pores of the body open to let the moisture in, an acclimatization which issues in a final sense of the self fluidly extending into its environment, and in the very act of surrender — a characteristically Goethean dialectic! — being revitalized and confirmed. It means a person being wholly sensitized to the self as well as to the 'other', the encompassing element. No wonder these lines breathe a sense of wholeness and enlargement; no wonder, indeed, that they breathe!

The third eruption takes us back to the temper and tone of the first; but it is spat out in yet more frustrated strains. Claustrophobic to the point of distraction is perhaps the right way to describe this renewed assault. With an obsessiveness that borders on the maniacal it evokes a scene cluttered with objects all of which are separate and dead: an assemblage of disparate artifacts tightly jammed together to make up a stifling and supremely inorganic conglomerate. The very pores of these objects — the dusty books, the sooty papers — are occluded. This sense of constriction is supported by metre and rhythm. Regular if harsh at first, it gradually obtrudes itself as it becomes more restive. The last two lines, with their embittered realization of the sort of world Faust calls his own, obstreperously syncopate, the accented syllable at the beginning straining against the metrical leash. The last one, when properly spoken, should consist of nothing but stressed syllables crowding each other out as indeed do the warring objects that cram Faust's monastic cell chock-a-block.

In the following section, the fourth — which mirrors the second as, once again, speech flows outward in a soft urgency — the realization is borne in on us that this roomful of dead junk — 'Das ist deine Welt, das heißt eine Welt!' — is indeed Faust's own world in the precise sense that it is the outward reflection of an inert body encasing, and choking, sense and soul. The claustrophobia that was earlier associated with his abode is now explicitly referred to his own self, to his heart which 'sich inn in deinem Busen klemmt' — a marvellously graphic rendering of being jammed, this 'inn in', considerably toned down by the 'bang' in the final version — and to some unexplained pain which 'Dir alle Lebensregung hemmt'. It is his own bony cage which haunts him as 'Tiergeripp' and 'Totenbein' meet his eye all around. This intimation will be confirmed time and again, not least in the illumination that follows Faust's vision of the Macrocosm: 'Dein Sinn ist zu, dein Herz ist tot . . .' he reminds himself, and the accent is, as the context demands that it should be, squarely on the 'Dein'.

I do not propose to trace the alternating rhythm set up by these four sections further into the scene with which we are concerned, from the expansion engendered first by the sign of the Macrocosm, then by the Erdgeist, to the abrupt contraction alternating with both, or indeed through the drama as a whole, in its first and final forms. To do so would be easy and tempting. Here all I am concerned to show is that the young author has, in these opening lines of his first drama, set up a 'beat' which will carry him right through it, much as Bach in his compositions set up a steady beat in his ground bass, enough to sustain any number of actualizations and their development. It is precisely this unflagging beat indeed, which Jacques Loussier so brilliantly utilizes in his improvisations on Bachian themes, which permits of an almost indefinite number of controlled variations. I would suggest that the young Goethe has employed a similarly modern and exciting technique here, in the continuous pulse he set up at the beginning of a long life's work. This is, fundamentally, the pulse of *Verselbstung* and *Entselbstigung* of which he will speak at the conclusion of the

'Cosmogenic Myth', the home-spun credo of his youth of which he tells us in *Dichtung und Wahrheit*.[4] It is a beat on which he now bases and will continue to base a great many controlled improvisations and variations: the polarity of inflation and deflation (so shrewdly utilized by the devil), elation and depression, *groß* and *klein*, *der große Hans* and *der kleine Hans*, *Gott* and *Wurm*, *Wanderer* and *Hütte*, and *fern* and *nah* — actualizations sufficient to nourish and weave together the two-part drama in its final form, sixty years hence. Here they are operative *in nuce*, as it were, at the sheer physiological level of an alternation between expansion and contraction, the systole and diastole of the pumping heart. And what is of special interest in the present enquiry is this: a being that discharges its tensions, however much these may on a first reading seem to stem from the intellectual top drawer of the mind, in a pulse that is itself organic, like the beating of a heart, is one that has from the very outset been envisaged as organic and whole. Yet this wholeness is envisaged dynamically, by way of a rhythmic oscillation from any one pole to its opposite. It is the sense of psychosomatic wholeness, engendered by the mere *form* of Faust's soliloquizing rather than by *what* he bemoans, which endows his words with their resonance and his figure with that stature and force of assault which linger in the memory long after that opening sequence is past and makes us measure what follows as our eyes measure the force of an atom bomb by the spreading umbrella of its mushroom cloud, long after the detonation itself is spent.

II

The three scenes that follow and conclude the 'Gelehrtentragödie' — the conversation with Wagner, Mephistopheles's initiation of the freshman and the episode at Auerbach's tavern — all serve a double purpose. They act as a prism refracting the spectrum of Faust's being into its constituent colours, that is to say, they break down his psychic wholeness into its several components; and, in doing so, keep us alive to the fact that the whole we have encountered, a resoundingly organic one if any, is incomparably greater than the sum of its parts.

To begin with, then, the confrontation with Wagner. Wagner who, as the later Goethe explicated, represents 'Helles, kaltes wissenschaftliches Streben',[5] obviously is the externalization of those very intellectual drives which have failed to bring Faust satisfaction. The scene is a tragicomical exercise in non-communication, again extremely modern in conception, foreshadowing not only Kleist's dialogues which are covert monologues, but techniques explored by contemporary writers such as Edward Albee and Harold Pinter. Faust's study, an intolerable *Kerker* to him, is a cosy if somewhat remote *Museum* to Wagner; the *Quellen*, to Faust the very breasts of Nature, to Wagner denote the Otfrids and Tatians of the philological seminar. The word 'erkennen', for him, has all the cheerful overtones of the unquestioning humanist. Faust, at its mention, shudders as he looks into the darkest human abysses, those of the martyrs of the Cross and, beyond it, to Socrates, Sophocles, and Genesis. Not only is this encounter a bitter parody of human relations — the gulf between the two speakers is so vast that one of them, Wagner, does not even suspect its existence; it scenically enacts Faust's disgust at 'rummaging in words', words being the level of awareness he craves to leave behind. Yet words are all that Wagner, with his *deklamieren* and *profitieren* and his managerial *besprechen*, has to offer; more precisely, words about words. The intellectual element of Faust's totality has been excised from its organic context; and how shallow and ineffectual it seems, compared with his huge brooding presence.

In the figure of the young student, conversely, Goethe has exteriorized Faust's creature drives, his 'dumpfes, warmes wissenschaftliches Streben'[6] as he calls it, and challenges us once again to measure the part against the totality we witnessed at the start. It is Mephistopheles who bares these unacknowledged motive springs, as it is his function to do with Faust. And here it is illuminating to compare the first and final versions of the scene. Much material that figures large in the

Urfaust will be left out in the scene as it appears in its final form: above all, the devil's long rigmarole on students' lodgings and, flanking it at either end, the freshman's description of the desiccation of the academic scene (l. 263 f.) and his sadly receding vision of the university as 'ein Tempe voll frischer Quellen' (l. 332). The mature Goethe could dispense with such detail, replacing it by Mephisto's solitary sardonic reference to 'the breasts of Wisdom' (l. 1892) which, at one bold stroke, forges a formal and highly economical link between the student's creature-self and Faust's. But the broader space given over to this material in the early version does show that, even at this stage, the young author was concerned to bring to the fore, in a separate figure, the 'dumpf, warm', libidinal aspect of Faust's striving. This intention is fully implemented at the end, through Mephisto's snide allusion to the joys of medicine and the young innocent's eager response to it: 'Das sieht schon besser aus als die Philosophie!'

Yet once again, how puny such creature urges seem in their separate embodiment, in isolation from Faust's own vehement spirituality. This lack of passionate involvement Goethe was to realize with one brilliant stroke when, in the final version, he altered the student's initial *fassen* (*Urfaust*, l. 338) to the neutered *erfassen* (*Faust I*, l. 1900), thus leaving the bodily intensity of Faust's assault on nature and the harmless mediocrity of the freshman's quest to speak for themselves.

But these two comparative figures have done more than to break down the psychosomatic totality of Faust's being into its static components: they have exteriorized a secret movement that is at work within him. The figure of the freshman follows upon that of Wagner. It must be so; for this order reflects the shift from distant contemplation to the immediacy of physical participation in Faust himself, which has already found expression in his turning from the sign of the Macrocosm to the actual spirit of the Erdgeist. The distant and vast phenomenon gives way to one that is smaller and nearer at hand, blueprint to presence, cosmic spectacle to organic process, simultaneity of meditation to polarity in participation. This is Faust's consistent trend; and his gradual movement towards physical involvement comes to its climax — or nadir — in the scene at Auerbach's tavern, the last of the reflectors built into the 'Gelehrten-tragödie' to mirror the emergence of Faust's libidinal drives and the temporary eclipse of his spiritual ones. That this is the function of the scene is abundantly clear. It shows little more than human animals at play — Faust among them, which is psychologically cruder but more stringent structurally than his impassivity in the final version — and as such leads on seam-lessly to 'Straße', the opening scene of the 'Liebestragödie' which shows a Faust now denuded of all but naked libido discharging itself in promiscuous sexual desire. With one exception. Interspersed between these two rock-bottom scenes we come upon that sharp little vignette 'Landstraße' which was regrettably omitted in the final version and shows the devil hurrying past a crucifix. In the distance, a peasant abode is to be seen. This glimpse marks the exact inner centre of the tragedy, the point of transition from the study to the world. It is the pointer on the scales showing which aspect of Faust is about to win the day. For as, 'warm und dumpf', he now enters the world of Gretchen, herself 'mit kindlich dumpfen Sinnen / Im Hüttchen auf dem kleinen Alpenfeld . . .', he enters the real and, with it, the jurisdiction of the real polarity: ecstasy and agony, desire and remorse, involvement and guilt which are the alternative poles of participation. This indeed is what the Cross signifies. For: 'If it had not been for the law, I should not have known sin', as St Paul has it.

III

'Straße' is a racy evocation of animal lusting, what with Faust's 'appetite' being too voracious to brook even pleasurable procrastination and the devil's promise that, alone and un-observed in Gretchen's room, he will be able to 'pasture' to the point of satiety in her atmosphere, her 'Dunstkreis'. Not to speak of Faust's excited question at the prospect of being led to her room: 'Und soll sie sehn? Sie haben?' How crude and physical it all is, and how young! Here again is one of those growing points I have alluded to: for this 'sie haben', in its simplicity, foreshadows from afar the esoteric mode of 'having' through distance and renunciation which the mature Faust will formulate in the words: 'Am farbigen Abglanz haben wir das Leben'; beyond that, it foreshadows, first, 'Fauste's' possessive grab at Helena — 'So fern sie war, wie kann sie näher sein!' (II, l. 6556) — then his brief symbolic union with her and, finally, the colossal regression of the centenarian enunciated in the name and figure of his helpmate Habebald. And again, the word *Dunstkreis* — Gretchen's physical aura — points forward to the ultimate sublimation of 'Der früh Geliebte, / Nicht mehr Getrübte' sixty years hence.

But even here, in the very next scene of the *Urfaust*, the young Goethe will let his fetishistic lecher speak in very different strains. Despite himself, almost, his spiritual potential which had loomed so large in the beginning, of which we had virtually lost sight since he set foot in the real world, is re-activated here, through the deep orderliness of Gretchen's world. And it is reawakened in a characteristically Goethean way, through the ultra-sensitive receptivity this vehement lover shows here, of all moments and places, by Gretchen's fourposter bed in which he had insisted that he must enjoy her that very night. This receptivity it is which now makes him perceive Gretchen's life spread out before his mind's eye with a *Gegenständlichkeit* and disinterestedness that is wholly tender and reverent. The precious product of Nature's own 'heilig reines Weben' which he here ponders reflects that organic process at the 'Webstuhl der Zeit' of which the Erdgeist had spoken to him; but equally it adumbrates Faust's mature marvelling at Nature's mysteries in 'Wald und Höhle' and, beyond that, his wonder at the phenomenon of the rainbow and, later still, at Helena. Growing-points everywhere, stretching out their tendrils as far as the late essay 'Bedeutende Fördernis durch ein einziges geistreiches Wort'! Even the *Dunstkreis* of the preceding scene has been cleansed of its physical ingredients and re-emerges as a *Zauberduft* so finely pervasive as to make Faust's intention 'so grade zu genießen' dismally collapse and his knees turn to jelly.

Almost imperceptibly, the process of building up has begun. Before our eyes as it were, the libidinal drives that have been set free metamorphose, through arousal crossed by incipient tenderness, into a towering passion, and through passion to an all-embracing committed love, backed by all the spiritual resources at Faust's bidding. To project this growing momentum Goethe had first and foremost the figure of Gretchen to help him. The moment of her entry into the drama marks, as it were, the confluence of two streams, and the curve of Faust's growth can no longer be traced in isolation. The lovers move in a sensitive inner concord even when they are not outwardly together; and Gretchen's giddy rate of growth parallels and augments that of her lover. Moreover, Goethe once more adopted the technique he so ingeniously employed in the first portion of the tragedy: once again he makes use of a number of comparative figures eminently static in character, and representing the norm, 'Hilfskonstruktionen' — to use Fontane's favourite term — which enable him to drive home the irresistible *accelerando* of the lovers' growth, both severally and jointly.

First, then, Gretchen, that lovely single strand from which the melodic thread to the rich symphonic weave of Faust's being is spun (the spinning wheel is Gretchen's symbol as the loom is Faust's). We only need to follow her lyrics to trace the swift and steep curve of her growth. At either end the two folk-songs, repositories of those collective and largely unconscious values in which she is embedded and to which she will return, after her brief and tragic emancipation to a fully articulate individual stature. In the middle, two lyrics and one lyrical drama reflecting that growing humanity in increasing measure. In 'Meine Ruh ist hin' first arousal finds for itself verses of a marvellous erotic intelligence, the monotony of the strophic form and the recurrent refrain reflecting the pounding of the blood against the veins — so insinuatingly rendered by the piano part of Schubert's song — and the two enjambments between separate stanzas enacting the brimming over of desire driving towards union. Gretchen's growing articulateness — spiritual as well as emotional — is next expressed in the highly personal idiom of 'Zwinger', with its free rhythms, its Faustian rhyme of *fühlet* and *wühlet* and, last but not least, the sheer melodic daring of the line 'Ich wein, ich wein, ich weine!'. The lyrical drama of 'Dom' is really a three-part song scored for one voice, a tripling of consciousness that heralds its final disintegration. Gretchen's nostalgic evocation of her childhood faith is terrifying in its knowingness and its almost Rilkean exploration of bewitching verbal registers.

Interestingly, these two last and most highly individualistic lyrics are flanked by the poet's interpolation of two eminently conventional and emotionally static figures: Lieschen before 'Zwinger' and Valentin after 'Dom'. They are an index of the rapidity of Gretchen's growth and the uprootedness from her milieu and its mores to which this development has inevitably led.

Swelled by Gretchen's melodic intensity, the accelerating momentum of Faust's passion is similarly offset against figures that represent the norm. As with Wagner and the freshman, so here: Frau Marthe and Mephistopheles are deployed as part-aspects, this time of the man-woman game; and their calculated shoddiness by contrast magnifies the heedless blaze of Faust's and Gretchen's all-consuming passion.

Such is the function of the scene 'Nachbarin Haus', a rollicking satire on institutionalized love viewed as an insurance policy. Goethe achieves his effects by hilarious rhymes such as between *Pein* — with its associations of purgatory — and *Totenschein* with its shrewd pragmatism. Or by the down-to-earth ruthlessness of Frau Marthe's insistence that she must *see* her man dead —

> Ich bin von je der Ordnung Freund gewesen,
> Möcht ihn auch tot im Wochenblättchen lesen

—which sets her at liberty to look ahead as she will presently do in the scene 'Garten'.

This scene may well rank as the most technically accomplished in the whole play. To appreciate it, let me quote Humboldt's comment on it. Goethe, Humboldt complains, spoilt the first meeting of the lovers by interpolating the *rohe* and *undelikate* episodes of Mephisto's toying with Frau Marthe. 'Goethe hätte sie nicht sollen einander begegnend spazieren lassen. Denn so oft ich nun lese, was Grete sagt, seh ich schon im Geiste immer wieder die unausstehliche Marthe auf sie zukommen.'[7] But precisely this juxtaposition of the alternating couples is Goethe's stroke of genius! For by this ploy he succeeded, with the utmost dramatic economy and in the shortest space of time, in scenically enacting the uncanny momentum of the lovers' relation, a dynamism which is doubled by the inner stationariness and cynicism of the other couple. Where Frau Marthe and Mephistopheles engage in a time-honoured dance in which each calculated step forward leads to one taken backward, and the choreography of each of their subsequent appearances remains rooted to the spot, Faust and Gretchen move onward in a *pas de deux* executed with a swift grace and an ardour that take the breath away, sweeping them from her 'Mein Herr' and 'Ihr' to her final 'Er liebt mich' and to Faust's answering 'Ewig!'. Barker Fairley's observation that the devil's cynicism is the secret undertow of Faust's lyricism, in that what this starry-eyed lover wants is nothing less than to seduce Gretchen, is correct to a point, but only to a point.[8] For just as Wagner's intellectualism and the freshman's creature-drives are distortions of Faust's totality, precisely because they represent part-aspects of it seen in isolation from the whole, so here: Faust's sensuality — admittedly a motivating force — is part and parcel of an encompassing response, including tenderness and care, which is total and resounding and for that reason towers above Mephisto's libertinism. Once again, the whole is greater than the sum of its parts.

Indeed, it is almost at once that the deepening of passion, together with the growth of spiritual involvement this brings, is borne in on us, in the 'catechization-scene'. And however much Faust's credo may be a trumped-up rationalization of his desire, the fact must not be overlooked that Mephisto will immediately after this conversation speak the crucial words of this tragedy which directly point forward to the 'geeinte Zwienatur' of the second part, as he calls Faust 'Du übersinnlicher, sinnlicher Freier!'. The man that is thus dubbed — and complimented — is a whole man who moves at once.

It is in the scene which, like the opening scene of the drama, is called 'Nacht', that Faust's development begins to come full circle. He now experiences in brutal earnest what 'Landstraße' had visually prefigured: his undermining of the beloved's true little world 'Im Hüttchen auf dem kleinen Alpenfeld'. And he experiences what the Cross, past which the devil had hurried, had heralded: the ineluctable polarity of life lived out in reality. Ecstasy has turned into anguish — *Seelennot* — desire into stinging remorse, involvement into guilt. His passion has become a bitter Passion ablaze with spiritual suffering. All the registers of his soul are sounded. He is a fully realized human being in an existential predicament that shakes body and soul. The word 'durcherschüttern' (which was dropped in the final version) articulates his condition perfectly.

This *fortissimo* is sustained throughout the scene that follows and the whole of the 'Kerker' scene; in the despair that Gretchen's agony should not suffice to redeem 'die Schuld aller übrigen', an implied demand that will be met sixty years later in the mediating function assigned to 'UNA POENITENTIUM, sonst Gretchen genannt'; and in the magnificent alternation, in the 'Kerker' scene, of inarticulate gusts of passion and the deepest spiritual anguish on the beloved's behalf, a pulse that is reminiscent of the opening scene. In both, Gretchen is his match. For her violent assaults on her lover incongruously, yet with compelling force, give way to piercing insights into her spiritual condition, to the illumination — which answers Faust's outcry — that her suffering is indeed representative,[9] and finally, to her submission to the divine judgement. Both lovers, one half crazed, the other wholly so, rise to their fullest human stature in a 'durcherschütternde' end which matches the intensity of the beginning and, if anything, surpasses it.

Spiritual anguish, instinct with all the passion of an organic being craving for participation in life in one *Kerker*, at the beginning, and passion which has become a purgatory at the close, in another *Kerker* into which life and involvement have led two lovers: does not this pattern spell unity rather than dichotomy, wholeness of total conception on the young Goethe's part and the promise of 'geeinte Zwienatur' for Faust himself? Of course it does. This early improvisation of pure genius is the first instance in Goethe's life of 'Geprägte Form, die lebend sich entwickelt'.

REFERENCES

[1] *Goethe's Urfaust and Faust, ein Fragment*, edited by L. A. Willoughby (Oxford, 1943), p. xix.
[2] *Goethes Werke, Hamburger Ausgabe* (Hamburg, [1948–60]), III, 468. (This edition is henceforth referred to as *HA*.)
[3] Ilse Graham, *Goethe and Lessing: The Wellsprings of Creation* (London, 1973), Chapter II.
[4] Part II, Book 8: *HA*, IX, 351 ff.
[5] 'Schema zu *Faust*' (circa 1797–1800), *HA*, III, 427.
[6] Ibid.
[7] To Caroline von Dacheröden, 24 May 1790.
[8] Barker Fairley, *Goethe's Faust: Six Essays*, second edition (Oxford, 1965), pp. 48 ff.
[9] See E. M. Wilkinson and L. A. Willoughby, *Goethe: Poet and Thinker* (London, 1962), p. 101.

Free Indirect Speech ('erlebte Rede') as a Narrative Mode in *Die Wahlverwandtschaften*

By ROY PASCAL

Die Goetheschen Romane laufen innerhalb der
Kategorien des Erzählers ab.

GEORG SIMMEL

I MIGHT perhaps have used only the familiar German term, 'erlebte Rede', in my title and elsewhere in this essay, and omitted 'free indirect speech', the English equivalent of 'le style indirect libre', the term that Charles Bally invented for the linguistic phenomenon he was the first to analyse. But, as I have explained in my study *The Dual Voice*,[1] the French term seems more apt than the German, and above all offers the practical advantage of greater ease of identification. As a form of indirect speech it will be expected to occur as a means of rendering the words or thoughts of a character (in the widest sense, the perspective of a character), and we shall expect therefore the pronouns (third person) and the tenses characteristic of normal indirect speech.

Goethe's *Die Wahlverwandtschaften* is an amalgam of old and modern stylistic features. Its theme and its symbol pattern are extremely 'modern', while the narrative structure and descriptive methods often hark back to the eighteenth century. The extensive and brilliant use of free indirect speech makes it a landmark in the history of the European novel, yet even in this region there are older features. In *The Dual Voice* I linked the full efflorescence of free indirect speech with the emergence of the non-personal, so-called omniscient narrator, who has the right of entry to the most secret places in the minds of his characters; and in *Die Wahlverwandtschaften* we find the narrator making full use of this right. But also, the narrator claims and acquires the lineaments of a person; Paul Stöcklein, followed in this by H. G. Barnes, gives a persuasive portrait of him — an elderly, urbane, rationalistic but tolerant man of the world and elegant stylist, writing about persons he has known, to whom he is bound with affection.[2] At times it is difficult to reconcile these two aspects or roles of the narrator, and serious problems of interpretation may arise — for instance, we can ascribe the inaccessibility of Ottilie's inner life at the end of the novel to the spiritual limitations of this particular narrator, or we can read into it some more profound insufficiency on the part of the most 'omniscient' intelligence itself. But here I refer to this duality in the narratorial function for a different and more practical reason.

Though free indirect speech has no specific and distinct grammatical form of its own, it often reveals its presence through various indicators, all of which suggest that the statement in question embodies the view (words or thoughts or angle of vision) of a character, and not that of the narrator; embodies, that is, a subjective view and not an objective, authoritative one. Notable among these pointers are the exclamation and exclamatory question, ejaculations like 'alas', 'yes', or 'so' ('so kind'), and particles and verbs that indicate an inner argument, like 'yet', 'after all', 'surely', and verbs like 'must' or 'ought'. These do not inevitably place the reader within a subjective perspective, but may do so, and there are very many examples in *Die Wahlverwandtschaften* which signal the presence of free indirect speech, as we shall see. But the narrator in his personal role sometimes uses these indicators himself, to communicate his own feelings about persons and events, perhaps to address the reader directly, too. He can express doubt, surprise, regret, can enliven his account with rhetorical questions, qualify statements with an 'alas' and so forth. Examples given below will show the presence of this intrusive author. This means that even the most distinctive signs of free indirect speech are not its exclusive property. This confusion does not occur only in *Die Wahlverwandtschaften*, for it is to be found in Thackeray and many other nineteenth-century novelists; it can be called confusing only because these signs of a personal narrator occur in texts where they are also used for free indirect speech. That the presence of free indirect speech in Goethe's novel has been overlooked by many critics, even though Oskar Walzel had shown it to be there, is perhaps due to the intrusions of the personal author.[3] To identify it we shall have to consider not only every linguistic feature of grammar, syntax, and style, but above all the actual content; on quite a few occasions we shall not be able to be certain, though we may be able to find different meanings in a given statement according to whether it is understood as subjective or objective.

I do not need here to demonstrate the frequency of the incidence of free indirect speech in *Die Wahlverwandtschaften*; this has been established by Professor L. W. Kahn and my own analysis in *The Dual Voice*. My purpose is to indicate, through a few examples, how its impact differs from that of direct speech or normal indirect speech, and how recognition of its presence affects our understanding of the whole work.

The specific narrative function of free indirect speech

After Charlotte has forced Eduard to face up to the implications of his love for Ottilie, he tells her in a letter that he is leaving the mansion, on condition that Ottilie remains there, and concludes with the promise that he will not resist a 'cure' of his passion, should absence provide the chance. Then he contemplates what he has written (1, 16, 119):[4]

Diese letzte Wendung floß ihm aus der Feder, nicht aus dem Herzen. Ja, wie er sie auf dem Papier sah, fing er bitterlich zu weinen an. Er sollte auf irgend eine Weise dem Glück, ja dem Unglück, Ottilien zu lieben, entsagen! Jetzt erst fühlte er was er tat. Er entfernte sich, ohne zu wissen, was daraus entstehen konnte. Er sollte sie wenigstens jetzt nicht wiedersehen; ob er sie je wiedersähe, welche Sicherheit konnte er sich darüber versprechen?

The first two sentences are straightforward statements of the narrator; the exclamatory 'Ja' is a personal note of his, a note of intensified concern. The following sentence transplants us from the narrator's perspective to that of Eduard. It is free indirect speech, a typical exclamatory expression of Eduard's sudden awareness of the implications of his letter. 'Sollte' gives his feeling of obligation, of compulsion; 'auf irgend eine Weise' betrays his general, vague resentment ('one way or another they'll force me . . . '); 'ja' this time is *his* word, as he realizes that love is more than happiness. The next short sentence, 'Jetzt erst fühlte er was er tat', might be narratorial or subjective, for 'jetzt', like 'now', can mean either 'at this moment' (the present) or 'at that moment' (the past). But the next sentence is strikingly subjective. For 'entfernte sich' does not mean the objective 'he went away' but the subjective 'he was (would be) going away', i.e. the thought in his mind (this is a rare case where English falls in with the French habit of using the imperfect, 'l'imparfait', for free indirect speech, when the main narrative is conducted in the preterite; in German preterite and imperfect use the same form). Similarly, in the following sentence, 'sollte' establishes Eduard's feeling of the obligation he has brought on himself, and the closing exclamatory question, one typical of free indirect speech, is not asked in order to elicit an answer, but to express Eduard's resentfully despairing mood.

Suppose this passage were put in direct speech or simple indirect speech, what differences would be made? Direct speech would preserve the expressive elements, Eduard's vocabulary and his tone, including the exclamations, but it would necessarily be more diffuse, broken, rambling. To speak to himself so logically and forcefully as here would suggest an inappropriate mastery of his situation. So we see that, in comparison with direct speech, free indirect speech preserves some of the expressive elements of the character's self-expression, but can 'edit' his speech or thoughts in the sense of ordering them, condensing them, giving their gist, without thereby suggesting that these thoughts were thought in this order or with this finality. That is, free indirect speech bears witness to the guiding hand of the narrator, it is a narrative mode that merges

L

the character's self-expression with the forward movement of the narrative.

Normal indirect speech also performs this ordering function, and the sentences quoted could be written in the form 'Eduard believed he was forced . . . He realized that he was leaving . . . He wondered whether . . . '. But this form is not only clumsy, with the repetitions of introductory verbs and conjunctions; it also transforms the language of Eduard into that of the narrator and loses all the lively expressive features, all ejaculations, particles like 'ja' and the verbs that express his inner arguments, in short his whole tone. This form belongs entirely to the narrator, who forces all events into his own mould. There is of course in German another form of reported speech, the indirect with the subjunctive, which preserves the normal order of the clause. This does allow for more liveliness of expression, but the continued use of the subjunctive introduces a troublesome note of uncertainty or hypothesis, even though it is not meant to do so. Also, this form usually suggests that the actual words, spoken or written, of a character are being reported, as opposed to thoughts (this is why it is so useful to scholars when reporting the printed opinions of others).

Free indirect speech, to sum up, has a distinctive function. Very strangely, it fuses the expressive features of a character's speech and thought with the narrator's narrative purpose. This is one of the chief reasons why the term 'free indirect speech' is preferable to 'erlebte Rede', for the latter singles out our response to only the subjective element in this form.

We have seen that, in free indirect speech, the third person replaces the first, and the verbal tense corresponds to that of the narrative (the past). There are, in *Die Wahlverwandtschaften*, passages where the narrative is conducted in the present tense, and here the reported speech is also in the present. The following passage belongs to one of the chapters narrated in the present; it gives Eduard's thoughts on receiving the business document that Ottilie has copied from the original in his hand, where he notices that her handwriting grows more and more like his own (I, 13, 100):

O daß es ein andres Dokument wäre! sagt er sich im stillen; und
doch ist es ihm auch so schon die schönste Versicherung, daß sein
höchster Wunsch erfüllt sei. Bleibt es ja doch in seinen Händen, und
wird er es nicht immerfort an sein Herz drücken, obgleich entstellt
durch die Unterschrift eines Dritten!

The first sentence gives Eduard's thought in direct speech.
The next might be objective-narratorial or subjective, though
the curious subjunctive 'sei' would seem to express Eduard's
own tremulous hope, and the particles 'auch so schon' seem to
indicate an inward effort to comfort himself, so that it reads
more probably as free indirect speech. The rest, exclamatory, is
indubitably free indirect speech, a curious combination of an
exclamatory statement and exclamatory question. 'Ja doch'
administers consolation to himself, and the phrases 'immerfort
an sein Herz drücken' and 'entstellt durch die Unterschrift
eines Dritten' are evidently a lover's hyperbole and excessive
sensitivity. The syntactical complexity of this sentence brilliantly
evokes the whirl of excitement in Eduard's head, while the
simple feeling of the earlier, opening sentence easily finds the
words of direct speech. For the rush of elation the narrator does
not only rely on Eduard's own words and stresses, but invents
a complex sentence form which communicates it indirectly,
through the form. The detachment of the last clause, 'obgleich
entstellt . . . ', slightly accentuates the absurdity of his resentment over the presence of the signature of his business partner,
and thus intensifies the irony that is so typically present in
this passage of free indirect speech. Here the irony is gentle,
elsewhere it can be sharp, just as the narrator may also introduce a sympathetic note through this medium. If the passage
were entirely in direct speech, the irony, i.e. the narratorial
modulation, would be lost; if it were in simple indirect speech,
the character would not appear so immediately and vividly.[5]
It will have been observed that sentences or phrases in the
form of free indirect speech can freely alternate with those in
other forms; the narrator slips in and out of his roles with
great ease. The indicators are often of the slightest. A series of
encouraging truisms at the beginning of Chapter 10 (Part 2)

can be recognized as emanating from Charlotte only because most are given exclamation marks (II, 10, 208–09); the irony attaching to them emerges only when circumstances prove them to have been false. On page 209 there is a proof of Goethe's subtle awareness of the peculiarity of free indirect speech. The narrator is describing the advantages of the new building to which the ladies are to withdraw with the child during Eduard's absence:

Das Haus selbst war nahezu bewohnbar; die Aussicht [. . .] höchst mannigfaltig. Je länger man sich umsah, desto mehr Schönes entdeckte man. Was mußten nicht hier die verschiedenen Tageszeiten, was Mond und Sonne für Wirkungen hervorbringen!

The opening two sentences are straightforward narrative. The exclamatory last one is Charlotte's wishful thought, and we know this not only because of the exclamation mark (which on occasions is used for the narrator's own comments), but particularly through the use of the past indicative 'mußten'. If it belonged to the narrator, it would almost certainly be the subjunctive 'müßten'; as Charlotte's reported speech, it expresses her resolute will to believe in a salutary change of heart, engaging here the processes of nature to confirm the promise of a good outcome that her earlier thoughts had held out.

Goethe handles this as yet rarely used form, free indirect speech, with astonishing ease and skill in this novel, just as Jane Austen did in these very same years. Like Jane Austen, Goethe would almost certainly not have been able to give any grammatical definition of the device, though intuitively he was aware of using it. The question arises, do readers and critics need to understand the form, to be conscious of it? It can easily be discovered that critics are often aware of the fact that certain statements give the view and perspective of a character, even though their grammatical form would seem, as often with free indirect speech, to attribute them to the narrator. Thus H. G. Barnes, who shows no sign of being acquainted with free indirect speech as a stylistic form, frequently shows that he intuitively apprehends the difference between narratorial (objective) statements and the subjective opinions expressed through free indirect speech. But there still is the danger of misunderstanding a particular passage; and perhaps a larger danger still, of failing to recognize the general and accumulative bearing of a stylistic habit which, in this novel, is so pervasive. We must now turn to these two questions.

Free indirect speech and the interpretation of the novel

When Ottilie is about to leave the mansion and take up work at her boarding school, the travel plans have to be reconsidered because her companion, Nanny, is not able to travel. There were many reasons not to postpone the journey. We read (II, 15, 253):

Man wollte die Reise nicht aufschieben; Ottilie drang selbst darauf: sie hatte den Weg schon gemacht, sie kannte die Wirtsleute, bei denen sie einkehren sollte, der Kutscher vom Schlosse führte sie; es war nichts zu besorgen.
    Charlotte widersetzte sich nicht; auch sie eilte schon in Gedanken aus diesen Umgebungen weg.

Barnes comments on this passage: 'When the narrator concludes his account of Ottilie's departure with the reassuring words: "es war nichts zu besorgen", the irony is obvious' (p. 59). In view of the disastrous outcome of this journey, the irony is clear enough; but are the statements the narrator's? Kahn (p. 274) has pointed out that, though the last sentences of the paragraph might from a formal point of view be narratorial, the likelihood is that they give Ottilie's arguments. There are grounds, which Kahn does not advance, to turn this 'likelihood' into a certainty. For the colon that precedes 'sie hatte den Weg schon gemacht' is very often used to introduce the direct and indirect speech of a character; and the opening of the following paragraph, 'Charlotte widersetzte sich nicht', clearly shows that we are hearing a discussion between the two women. So the statements must be Ottilie's. As a consequence the irony is directed against her; she, like all the other characters at different times, nurses false hopes which are to be cruelly deceived.

The point has more than an immediate importance. If Ottilie deceives herself here, we are more prepared to believe she can deceive herself elsewhere. In that last letter, in which she informs her friends of her 'strenges Ordensgelübde' of silence and begs them to help her 'durch Nachsicht und Geduld' to keep her vow, when she adds: 'Ich bin jung, die Jugend stellt sich unversehens wieder her', we do not need to suspect, as do some critics, that she is deliberately misleading the others with this consoling thought. Like the others, she is fallible, willing to hope for some resolution of their troubles, ready even to qualify the absoluteness of her vow by her reminder that it is valid only while her heart requires it, 'so lange mir das Herz gebietet'. The responsibility for the final catastrophe is thus thrown more fully on accident — the blunder of Mittler — which shatters the delicate equilibrium that might have ensured a happy outcome. But, more importantly, it means too that Ottilie's dedication, her 'saintliness', is much less absolute than has often been thought (for instance, by Barnes), much more subject to contingencies both external and internal. Again, a recognition of free indirect speech will enable us to understand how some of this misapprehension could arise.

There is a particular form of free indirect speech which affects the general interpretation of the novel, and which may easily be overlooked. It may occur without any of the indicators mentioned above, especially since it may be without a verb; it involves the insertion into the narrative of a phrase or a word characteristic of the character concerned, a flash of mimicry. Graham Hough noticed this practice in Jane Austen's style, and gave it the name of 'coloured narrative'.[6] It is more frequent in Die Wahlverwandtschaften than might be expected from the generally rather staid style.

The narrator describes how imagination cheats reality the night that Eduard spends with his wife, and how in the morning actuality claimed 'ihr ungeheures Recht' (I, 11, 94):
er [Eduard] schlich sich leise von ihrer Seite, und sie fand sich, seltsam genug, allein, als sie erwachte.
Whose is this 'seltsam genug'? It cannot be the narrator's or

reader's thought, because we have already been informed that Eduard has left Charlotte. It must be Charlotte's thought, embedded in the narratorial account. In the preceding paragraph there is an apparently similar ejaculation, 'wundersam genug', but this directly conveys the narrator's reflection.

A more striking case occurs when Eduard is searching through old ledgers to find the date when he had planted the plane trees (1, 14, 108):

Er durchblättert einige Bände; der Umstand findet sich: aber wie erstaunt, wie erfreut ist Eduard, als er das wunderbarste Zusammentreffen bemerkt. Der Tag, das Jahr jener Baumpflanzung ist zugleich der Tag, das Jahr von Ottiliens Geburt.

'Das wunderbarste Zusammentreffen' must be Eduard's astonished and delighted thought, not the narrator's, for the latter has several times pointed out with irony Eduard's weakness for finding signs and portents of future happiness. Here again there is no indicator of free indirect speech, though the following sentence has the exclamatory character we can often associate with free indirect speech; closing the chapter with a flourish, it bears the marks of Eduard's excitable and credulous personality.

A special interest attaches to endearments that the narrator sometimes introduces into his narrative, particularly those that are used for Ottilie — 'das gute Kind', 'das liebe Kind', and towards the end 'das himmlische Kind' and even 'die Heilige'. Most are normally attributed to the narrator, and therefore are understood to be objective and authoritative, conveying indeed the evaluations of the author himself. Once however we understand that the narrator may momentarily adopt the idiom of a character, we may have to interpret them differently. Professor Kahn (p. 274) has alerted us to one prominent case, when Eduard is out walking with the Baronesse and somewhat discourteously presses on to meet Ottilie, whom he has spied in the distance. The whole paragraph is apparently straightforward, objective narrative, but in its course the following sentences occur (1, 10, 88):

Eduard versprach, nötigte sie [die Baronesse] aber Ottilien entgegen
geschwinder zu gehen, und eilte ihr endlich, dem lieben Kinde
zu, mehrere Schritte voran. Eine herzliche Freude drückte sich in
seinem ganzen Wesen aus. Er küßte ihr die Hand [. . .] Die Baronesse
fühlte sich bei diesem Anblick in ihrem Innern fast erbittert. Denn
wenn sie auch das, was an dieser Neigung strafbar sein möchte,
nicht billigen durfte, so konnte sie das, was daran liebenswürdig
und angenehm war, jenem unbedeutenden Neuling von Mädchen
keineswegs gönnen.

It is clear that 'jenem unbedeutenden Neuling von Mädchen'
is a phrase formed in the spiteful mind of the Baronesse, a
quotation, as it were. But if so, what about 'dem lieben Kinde'
higher up? Is this not Eduard's thought and phrase? No proof
is possible, but it is likely that, as a judgement, it does not here
carry the narrator's authority.

There are, however, occasions when the narrator does
express his affection for Ottilie, particularly during and after
the painful events following the drowning of Charlotte's child.
But this more frequent use of affectionate and admiring epithets
applied to 'das Kind' may be less an indication of the narrator's
feeling than a reflection of what the others feel and hope. When,
after overhearing the discussion between Charlotte and the
Major, in which Charlotte takes all the blame on herself,
Ottilie reveals her 'laws' and solemnly renounces marriage
with Eduard, her speech is introduced thus: 'Zum zweitenmal
— so begann das herrliche Kind mit einem unüberwindlichen
anmutigen Ernst — zum zweitenmal widerfährt mir dasselbige'.
The admiring sympathy of the narrator is not concealed, but is
he not, at the same time, and more importantly, conveying the
hearer's, Charlotte's, response? We cannot actually separate
him from the characters when he writes in his personal role, he
belongs to the same social group and shares their evaluations;
but when he speaks in this personal way, do his judgements not
lack the authoritativeness of a non-personal narrator? In
particular, we surely cannot attribute his views to the author,
to Goethe. As far as the author is concerned, we flounder much
deeper in ambiguity and irony than suits most critics.

We can fathom the depth of this irony by following the

terms that build up the idea of Ottilie's saintliness. It is Ottilie herself who introduces this concept. When Charlotte warns her that she may, on returning to the Pension, attract the attentions of the Gehülfe, Ottilie answers confidently that he will respect her as 'eine geweihte Person' dedicated to 'dem Heiligen'. This confidence is not put to the test, since she does not return to the Pension, but it is shown to be unreliable in respect of Eduard, when he breaches her inviolability at the inn. It surely betrays the same sort of youthful self-confidence as leads her to make the ill-fated journey, and later to impose her will on the others when she threatens to drown herself if they proceed with the divorce plans. There is of course no doubt attaching to the purity of her resolve to renounce and atone, but *how* this resolve can be put into practice, and how it will fare in changing circumstances, are problems that Ottilie herself cannot solve. She gives up her plan of work at the Pension, returns to the mansion, and there establishes that strange 'reines Zusammensein' which she admits can only be provisional. How can we reconcile the failures to fulfil her resolve with a narratorial statement, made at the point just preceding her decision to go to the Pension, which seems to suggest the resolution of all conflicts within her (II, 15, 247):

Durch ihre [Ottiliens] Reue, durch ihren Entschluß fühlte sie sich auch befreit von der Last jenes Vergehens, jenes Mißgeschicks [her love for Eduard and the death of the child]. Sie bedurfte keiner Gewalt mehr über sich selbst; sie hatte sich in der Tiefe ihres Herzens nur unter der Bedingung des völligen Entsagens verziehen, und diese Bedingung war für alle Zukunft unerläßlich.

How can the objective narrator write this, when he knows that at the inn she will find herself unable to carry out 'völliges Entsagen', and will succumb to the pangs of conscience when she overhears Mittler's diatribe? It must be that we have here not the narrator's view, but Ottilie's. After the narratorial statement 'sie fühlte sich befreit', which explicitly tells us this confidence is a 'feeling', the rest is to be read as free indirect speech, also conveying Ottilie's conviction, so tragically to be refuted by events.

It is at this same point, when Charlotte and Ottilie are alone after the death of the child, that Ottilie is referred to as 'das himmlische Kind' — 'Sie [Charlotte] wußte, wie sehr das himmlische Kind Eduarden liebte'. Now, it would be a very curious term for the narrator to use at this juncture, and I would suggest it has meaning, and a full meaning, only if it is Charlotte's term. She alone has the right to call the girl who loves her husband 'heavenly'. But this sophisticated woman uses the term in a non-religious sense, to pay tribute to the purity of Ottilie's resolve, the depth of her suffering, the entanglement of her feelings and life, all of which Charlotte can think of as characteristic of the pains, struggles, errors of youth, now that, as we are explicitly told, her protective care is invoked and, at the same time, she is still secretly hoping that the union of Eduard and Ottilie will become possible.

In the same sense, after Ottilie's collapse over Mittler's untimely moralizing, she is described sitting in a corner of the sofa as 'das bleiche himmlische Kind' (II, 18, 268). The adjective expresses all the tenderness, love, admiration of the adults present, but nothing religious. The use of 'himmlisch' as Ottilie's body is borne in its coffin out of the mansion — 'die aufgehende Sonne rötete nochmals das himmlische Gesicht' (p. 270) — has perhaps a more religious note, appropriate to the funeral and the crowd of onlookers, though only a conventional and superficial one; the expression used a little later for the corpse, 'der unter seiner Glasdecke gar liebenswürdig dalag', is even trivial. While all onlookers are moved, it is only in relation to Nanny's 'miracle' that a deeper note occurs, explicitly in connexion with Nanny's feelings — 'Überirdisch, wie auf Wolken oder Wogen getragen, schien sie [Ottilie] ihrer Dienerin zu winken' — and there follow Nanny's fall, her extraordinary escape from injury, and her vision of the dead girl's blessing.

Now the narrator, admitting the marvel of Nanny's escape and the sober good sense with which she later describes her vision, yet makes clear the factors that would encourage scepticism — Nanny's nervous exaltation at the time of her fall, the failure of bystanders to witness any miracle, the scepticism of most people. And when he comes to describe the rumoured miracles at Ottilie's tomb, he warns us from the outset: 'Jedes Bedürfnis, dessen wirkliche Befriedigung versagt wird, nötigt zum Glauben'. The form of the description that follows ironizes the simplistic logic that brings anxious mothers to visit the grave (II, 18, 273):

Die vor den Augen aller Welt zerschmetterte Nanny war durch Berührung des frommen Körpers wieder gesund geworden: warum sollte nicht auch ein ähnliches Glück hier andern bereitet werden?

There can be no doubt that this exclamatory question is free indirect speech, and not a question asked by the narrator. In addition to the gentle irony attaching to it, there is also irony entailed in the assumption that Nanny's limbs had been broken; in the earlier description of the accident we read: 'es [Nanny] *schien* an allen Gliedern zerschmettert'. Similarly, after testifying to the popular wish to believe in a miracle, the narrator commits himself no further than to say that the afflicted pilgrims to the tomb '*glaubten* eine plötzliche Besserung zu spüren', so that many in great need flocked to the church, until the authorities prevented access.

These rumours prosper among the common people, especially those in distress. There is no indication that such beliefs are shared by the educated, the gentry. If Eduard, more and more withdrawn into his memories of Ottilie, thinks of her as a martyr, as one who in renunciation found 'Seligkeit', it is only in this sense that she becomes a saint in his eyes. And when, after his death, Ottilie is spoken of as a saint, it is in this sense of the term (II, 18, 275):

Und so lag denn auch dieses vor kurzem zu unendlicher Bewegung aufgeregte Herz in unstörbarer Ruhe; und wie er in Gedanken an die Heilige eingeschlafen war, so konnte man ihn wohl selig nennen.

After the sceptical remarks about the cult of the 'saint', it would be surprising to find the narrator using this term; but here, once again, we find him adopting the term appropriate to the character, to Eduard. The last sentence is indeed cradled in mental reservations, as if to make the use of 'saint' more palatable.

The recognition of the pervasive frequency of free indirect speech in *Die Wahlverwandtschaften* does, then, affect our interpretation of the whole novel. The fallibility of many of the apparently explicit judgements or insights of the narrator has often been commented on. But the recognition of the use of free indirect speech unmasks what seem to be authoritative opinions and judgements of the narrator as subjective views of the characters, modified in many cases by an irony that itself often evades positive commitments. Thus we very largely lack an objective moral criterion that would rank the characters and actions and motives in an order of value — unless it be the principle of sympathy and tolerance. The story itself, its shape and ending, counters this uncertainty by providing a hierarchy of interest, since Ottilie moves more and more into the centre, and her resolve and fate constitute the climax. But she is not, I believe, exemplary like the more usual heroine; it is rather that of all characters she is the most absolute, the most vulnerable, the most touching in her youth. All are victims of the conflict between moral feeling and the natural 'affinities', and she, no more than the others, can arrive at a stable condition in which the contending values are secured; but in her both sides of the conflict, love and renunciation, take the purest and most unconditional form of selfless, religious dedication, and she is the least capable of adaptation or compromise. She wins the narrator's deepest sympathy, as she does ours; but she does not provide a standard by which the others might be judged. Eduard, whom she draws into the centre of attention at the end, attracts the narrator's irony more than the others. Critics have tended to find in Ottilie or Charlotte a sort of ideal. But I do not believe the narrator commits himself to the one or the other. If one were to argue in terms of the concept of 'elective affinities', one would have to say that it would be as wrong and absurd to complain that the chemical elements were different from one another, and unequally unstable, as to require that one person, one age, one profession should have the qualities of another.

This reserved, non-committal narrator of *Die Wahlverwandt-schaften* does not betray what was the author's, Goethe's, interpretation; the limitations of his understanding, the reservations he imposes on himself, seem to invite us, the readers, to look beyond him, without giving us a clue except his tolerant sympathy. That is, Goethe throws the whole thing open to us, to wrestle with as we may, much more than in any other of his works. This itself is an extraordinarily modern conception of a novel, and for this purpose this narrator, and the use of free indirect speech, seem ideally suited.

REFERENCES

[1] Roy Pascal, *The Dual Voice: Free Indirect Speech and its Functioning in the Nineteenth-century European Novel* (Manchester, 1977). I have here given, pp. 37–45, a systematic analysis of Goethe's use of free indirect speech in *Die Wahlverwandt-schaften*.

[2] Paul Stöcklein, 'Einführung', in *Goethes Werke*, Gedenkausgabe, Volume IX, *Die Wahlverwandtschaften* (Zürich, 1949), and H. G. Barnes, *Goethe's Die Wahl-verwandtschaften* (Oxford, 1967).

[3] Oskar Walzel, *Das Wortkunstwerk* (Leipzig, 1926). The first extended analysis of free indirect speech in Goethe's novel is L. W. Kahn's article 'Erlebte Rede in Goethe, *Die Wahlverwandtschaften*', *PMLA*, 89 (1974), 268–77. Kahn rightly rejects the frequently held view that, in passages of 'erlebte Rede', the narrator or author disappears from sight behind the character; but he does not consider the problem of the combination in this novel of the intrusive, personalized narrator and free indirect speech. This combination caused Flaubert such difficulties in *Madame Bovary* that, after establishing a personal narrator in the first chapter, he then finally and absolutely dropped him, replacing him by a non-personal narrator, whose insight into the secret thoughts of the characters, often expressed through free indirect speech, provoked none of the scruples attaching to a personal narrator.

[4] Quotations from *Die Wahlverwandtschaften* refer to the text in *Goethes Werke*, Gedenkausgabe, Volume IX (Zürich, 1949). The roman numeral indicates 'Part', the second figures the chapter, the final figures the page.

[5] In his perceptive discussion of this and other passages, Professor Kahn concludes that the distinctive function of 'erlebte Rede' is the ironic tinge, through which the narrator's voice merges with and modifies the voice of the character. It is perhaps carelessly that he adds (p. 270): 'Zur bloßen Wiedergabe der inneren Gedanken stünden ... auch andere Mittel zur Verfügung', by which he means direct speech or other forms of indirect speech etc. Such a view fails to take into account the distinctive character of free indirect speech as a mode of reporting thoughts or words, different in its effect from other forms of reporting or describing.

[6] Graham Hough, 'Narrative and Dialogue in Jane Austen', *Critical Quarterly*, 12 (1970), 201–29. I have analysed a typical passage of this kind from *Mansfield Park* in *The Dual Voice*, pp. 55–56.

Stifter's *Letzte Mappe* and the Idea of Wholeness

By ALEXANDER STILLMARK

> Das Merkmal eines Kunstwerkes aber ist einzig
> das, daß es im Leser jede Stimmung aufhebt,
> und seine hervorbringt.   STIFTER

> Schön ist was durch die Vollkommenheit in
> seiner Art die Idee der Vollkommenheit im
> allgemeinen erweckt.   GRILLPARZER

IT IS GENERALLY acknowledged that Stifter's narrative art passes through several distinctive phases before it reaches maturity in the major novels and late stories. The last phase of Stifter's stylistic development, which culminates in the fourth and unfinished version of *Die Mappe meines Urgroßvaters*,[1] has proved something of a stumbling-block for critics; it still attracts much too little attention and has at times been dismissed as the ageing writer's decline into sterile formalism or the like.[2] It is not generally recognized that the strange rigidities of Stifter's late style, this austere linguistic asceticism, this wilful reductiveness of the verbal material, are in fact the products of new experimentation with form. Far from being the badge of spent energies, these severities of a mature style are properly seen as proof of bold imaginative creativity, of a sovereign artistic will ever resistant to convention, remaining resolute and consistent with itself. The *Letzte Mappe* is the very embodiment of that consistency, for this 'Lieblingskind', as Stifter called it, represents an abiding vision of the pathway to perfection.

It is all the more difficult to place the late Stifter in the context of contemporary European prose, since from at least *Der Nach-*

sommer onwards he writes in defiant opposition to contemporary literary trends. In resuming work on the *Letzte Mappe* he writes to his publisher Heckenast: 'Gegen so viel naturloses Zeug unserer Tage könnte das Ding fast wie eine Perle werden, wenn Gott seinen Segen gibt.'[3] He belittles the successful novelists who court success by pandering to popular taste as one who has set himself a higher task: 'wäre ich ein bloßer Büchermacher, so wäre ich auch vielleicht ein reicher Mann',[4] and he roundly condemns the general level of taste and dearth of literary sensibilities in what he calls 'unsere dichtungsarme, prahlende und leere Zeit'.[5] To his friend, the painter Bürkel, he writes in similar vein of the rarity of genuine art in an age which desires diversion by what is purely decorative, ornamental and ostentatious: 'Es tut so innig wohl, in unserer Zeit prahlerischer Arbeiten wieder einmal ein echtes Kunstwerk zu sehen, das, jeden Firlefanz verschmähend, nur in seiner eigenen Tiefe, Würde und Lieblichkeit ruht.'[6]

Stifter's last attempt to reconcile the high idealism which was a legacy of Weimar classicism with the prosaic concerns of the nineteenth-century realist tradition, despite the latent antinomies, in fact produced a harmonious work of astonishing originality. Though left uncompleted at his death, it is an achieved entity. In paying respect to the classical ideal of formal clarity, simplicity and beauty, he evolved a highly economic style full of discrimination, tactful allusiveness and high-minded restraint. The ethical purity of content, which was always his avowed aim, consists foremostly in the gentle humanity made manifest in the three central figures; what Stifter elsewhere called 'die sittliche Tiefe (Majestät der sittlichen Menschheit)'.[7] At the same time the finer psychological traits, the development of human relationships, the diversification of the social image, the lavish treatment of local customs and institutions, the intense interest in locality (the novel is set in the landscape of Stifter's birthplace and carries many auto-biographical accents), and the all-embracing presence of nature, neither conflict with nor dwindle beside this strong ethical accentuation. Indeed, it must be said in passing, that the work offers more diverse historical realism in many of its pages than any fiction he had written to date; in the portrait of the Jewish pawnbroker for instance, of the Prague seamstress Cäcilia, or in details of early medical practice among an ignorant peasantry in the 1730s. Not since he had written those colourful Dickensian sketches, collected in the volume *Aus dem alten Wien* (1844), had he produced such closely observed pictures of social life.

For all that, the work does not draw its meaning and force from such elements of realism as are here mentioned, but rather from the power and consistency of an ideal of wholeness which permeates every feature of the work, and which finds expression in the design and proportions of the whole as well as in individual motifs and symbolic features. In the following I will attempt to define more fully the meaning Stifter attributes to the idea of wholeness, to examine the precise ways in which it finds expression in the work and show how it helps us to discover an inner unity in the novel.

Essentially the *Letzte Mappe* is, in its narrative form, a doctor's personal diary, the record of his life and practice in the early eighteenth century. More significantly, this intimate record is the revelation of his inner growth to fuller humanity. It is written in regular instalments on bound parchment which is then tied with ribbons and sealed. The narrator, a descendant of the doctor, describes the book in the framework to the narrative with a circumstantial piety which suggests a possession more precious than a mere heirloom. Details of its shape, measurements, binding, fastenings and script are all meticulously noted. The impression increases that this diary with its many seals and strange, almost indecipherable handwriting, is a recondite book of wisdom which has to be read worthily. The narrator remarks: 'ich sah bald, daß ich das Lesen dieses Buches erst lernen müße' (p. 17). Stifter's presence may be discerned within these words which seem to contain a veiled reference to the inward manner adopted by him in unfolding his subject. This treasured account of a life is entitled *Calcaria Augustiniana* (*calcaria* meaning 'spurs', both literally and metaphorically), and this adds weight to the idea of an instructive or enlightening document. Already in the *Urmappe* one finds the idea of a spur to moral growth appropriate to the book: 'So. Und dann schreibe fleißig ins Lederbuch, das Mittel ist gut, und lies es erst in drei Jahren wie der Obrist tat, ob du dich dann auch vorwärts gehend findest.'[8] The sense of aspiring and advancing towards a clearly envisaged goal of perfection is to be taken up again in a resonant passage, which we shall encounter later, concluding Book 1 of the *Letzte Mappe*.

The two volumes of this diary are more than just the record of a life, for the writing of the record has itself helped to shape that life. The process of constant self-reflection is seen to lead to self-improvement. Augustinus solemnly calls it 'der Eckstein meiner Zukunft' (p. 29) and therewith touches on the motif of building which figures prominently in the narrative and which comes to suggest moral growth and progress. The Goethean idea of 'offenbares Geheimnis' is also applied in a subtle way to express the fruitful relationship between this testimony and the life it has helped to fulfil: 'Einige meinten, da müssen Geheimnisse sein. Andere sagten, dann müßten in beiden Büchern Geheimnisse gewesen sein, die dann offenbar geworden sind' (p. 23). Indeed, the inwardness of the diarist's concern is outwardly manifested in the transformation of personality.

The act of making conscious the process of living, of rendering account for each stage of life, serves to give that life point and wholeness. The diary is the chief instrument which directs the mind towards that goal of self-perfection which Augustinus sets himself. At the same time, the writing of it helps to heal the deep wound which his jealous impetuosity had inflicted on his love. The Obrist's experience as chronicler of his own life is also most significant, for he recalls that as he matured the individual parts of the diary became more and more similar: 'Ich schrieb sehr fleißig an meinen Päcken, sie wurden immer gleichartiger, bis jetzt die, welche ich in meinem Alter öffne, einer wie der andere sind' (p. 221). Such similitude, resulting from self-mastery and increase in self-knowledge, is a mark of perfection. But an important difference exists between

M

the balanced similitude, hard-gained by lifelong self-discipline and conscious effort, and the dull regularity of fruitless repetition which Augustinus fears in examining his conscience: 'Ich bin gewesen wie ein Handwerker, der seine Beschäftigung wie ein Wasserrad stets gleichmäßig betreibt' (p. 246). To be the victim of senseless routine is precisely the opposite of having mastered the forms that give meaning to life until at last harmonious regularity is achieved. It is precisely this quality which Risach points to in Der Nachsommer when he speaks of that rare state of mind when sameness of experience fills and transports the mind in sublime stasis: 'ein Einerlei, welches so erhaben ist, daß es als Fülle die ganze Seele ergreift' (VII, 243). This 'Einerlei' is not a term of indifference or monotony. It implies a deeply contemplative manner of perceiving which attains a perfect balance in the mind; it is the resolution of all relativity. Such euphoric fulfilment in the mind signifies the experience of perfection and borders on the mystical. Fullness of humanity in Stifter's sense, as an achieved harmony in which the passions have no part and the moral sense predominates, comes to mean a capacity for serene sameness in the quality of experience. The problem of tedium, which has often engaged Stifter criticism, seems to me to find another answer in such a view as this.[9]

Many features of the work which suggest the perfection of wholeness are related to this notion of sameness. Several of the figures in the novel reflect something of that wholeness. That is why they appear to resemble each other. Thus Augustinus is astonished at the likeness between Margarita and Christine.[10] Margarita also is a living reminder of her mother, while Eustachius is described as resembling Innozens. This is not to say that Stifter's characterization is deprived of all individuation but that he repeatedly allows a single, potent, idealized image of humanity to shine through the individual features. Stifter derives his idea of a human model from the Christian idea of imitatio. In this sense Augustinus models his life on the Obrist's, whose mild nature and goodness impress him as exemplary. The idea of perfect humanity is represented in the imagery of roundness which implies fulfilment. Thus Augustinus speaks of his friend's moral personality as 'die sanfte gleiche Rundung seines Innern' (p. 337).

The supreme economy of Stifter's late style derives in part from associated motifs of roundness and wholeness which give the work a somewhat abstract quality. Thus the detailed description of the Prince's 'Lustgarten' produces image after image of perfection. It is compared to a work of art and to other examples of beauty. It is neither pure artefact nor wild nature, but represents a harmonious blend of both. At first it cannot be recognized as a garden, yet it later converts the eye into seeing nature as a garden. There is a delicate parallelism between these examples and the ideas of self-perfection in the lives of Augustinus and the Obrist. The symbolism of the garden in *Die Wahlverwandtschaften* may possibly be Stifter's model, though he had himself given pride of place to the 'Rosengarten' in *Der Nachsommer* as concrete symbol of human refinement.[11] But instead of the *hortus inclusus*, the sanctuary of culture, the *Letzte Mappe* offers us the open pleasure garden. It is open to the forests and hills, beautifying the earth with which it merges, and is governed only by the law that nothing in it should be destroyed. It is the image of a paradise regained.

It will be seen in the following that the idea of wholeness, which figures so prominently in this work, is not so much indebted to the preceding tradition of classical Weimar, but in much larger measure derives its inspiration from that ancient religious source, the biblical allegory of Eden. The decided moral purport of Stifter's art naturally gives his treatment a highly individual accentuation. If one refers to Schiller's ideas on human wholeness, as the most notable immediate historical antecedent, one will find a significant contrast between his conception and that of Stifter. Of course, one must make due allowance for the important difference of mode — as between theory and imaginative literature — recognizing also that Stifter inevitably modified and simplified Schiller's thought. Schiller's intricate model of wholeness in man is not so plainly founded on a moral premise as Stifter's is; it is sustained by scientific and practical observation, it implies a highly involved, dynamic process of growth, a bringing into play of the divers faculties (which can, but need not, include the moral, according to circumstances), but always involves the regulating principles of co-ordination and subordination.[12] For Schiller, the education of man is not based on any ideas of fallibility and redress, of making reparation for guilt; it rests chiefly on the positive understanding of human perfectibility. In no sense can his theory be said to be conceived as a corrective to man's fallen state.

By contrast, Stifter is profoundly concerned with the recovery of a state of perfection both within humanity itself and in man's relationship to the world. The model which remains deeply impressed on his imagination from youth to age is that of a lost paradise. Likewise, the image of life consistently presented by him, if reduced to fundamentals, is that of a fall from grace; it is the condition of man expelled from the perfect state by reason of his sin. The paradigmatic situation is that of guilt brought about by the passions or the will. This constitutes the fatal flaw which disrupts the perfect plan of creation and which has to be expiated. Within this scheme, the notion of innocence carries particular weight. The terms 'unschuldig' and 'schuld-los', which abound in his prose, carry equivalent meaning; what is stressed is freedom from guilt rather than the positive idea of innocence. Nature serves as a perpetual reminder of a paradise that was lost. Already in *Feldblumen* he writes of 'die Natur, das einzig Unschuldige' (I, 137) and of 'Gottes urewige, schuldlose Berge' (I, 133). In *Der Hochwald* we are offered an image of nature as the very pattern of moral purity from which man can learn: 'Unschuld lernen von der Unschuld des Waldes' (I, 296). In *Brigitta* only nature is free from the stigma of the passions: 'in dem ersten Zusammenleben mit der Natur, die leidenschaftlos ist, grenzt sie zunächst an die Sage von dem Paradiese' (III, 216), and in the *Studienmappe* (the second published version) the Obrist speaks lovingly of his plants, 'weil sie unschuldig den Willen Gottes tun' (II, 173). It is only through wholesome activity and interaction with nature that many of Stifter's

characters come to work out their own salvation. Nature
serves as a flawless model not merely by virtue of the moral
attributes tradition has ascribed to it, but through the complex
sources of a creative imagination which is inspired by personal
belief. In the same way, the well-known lines by Wordsworth,
which agree so closely with Stifter's view, convey a conception
of nature's moral influence which has the force of an act of faith:

> One impulse from a vernal wood
> May teach you more of man,
> Of moral evil and of good,
> Than all the sages can.[13]

Stifter's *Letzte Mappe* takes up this theme of the loss of that
perfect state of innocence, of what might have been but for
original sin, which we find enacted again and again in his
writings. As in *Der Nachsommer* it concerns the breaking of
faith, the severance of a bond of absolute trust.[14] The love
binding Augustinus and Margarita founders on the inability to
keep faith. The fateful exchange in which he expresses his doubt
as to the truth of her pledge of love to him, produces a profound
look of astonishment in her eyes which reveals the depth of the
hurt:

'Ich habe zu euch gesagt, daß ich euch nach meinem Vater unter
allen Menschen am meisten liebe', antwortete sie.
'Ja, das habt Ihr gesagt, liebe Margarita, ob es aber auch wahr
ist', entgegnete ich.
Sie sagte auf diese meine Rede kein Wort, sondern sah mich mit
ihren großen Augen an. Ihre Augen erschienen mir fast noch größer,
als sie mich so anblickte. Dann füllten sie sich mit Wasser.
Sie wendete sich ab. (p. 186)

The terse reticence of this style no more than intimates the
momentousness of the incident. It is noteworthy that the precise
circumstances of this break in the relationship, its psychological
aspects, the intensity of feelings, the nature of inner thoughts,
are in no way enquired into. What receives stress is the breaking
of faith itself and the outward signs of grief. This loss of faith
is like the intrusion of original sin. Something humanly precious
and whole has been betrayed and rent apart. Augustinus later
uses the revealing phrase, 'als das Band zwischen mir und

Margarita zerrissen war' (p. 287). Four days after their fateful exchange, Margarita uses words which convey the full import of their altered situation: 'da nun Alles anders geworden ist' (p. 188). These words take on a dual significance: they announce the end of the state of perfect trust, but they also mark a new chapter in Augustinus's life. The remaking of his life, the determination to work for his own *Heil* and that of others, here take their beginning.

Stifter's choice of the figure of a doctor allows him to explore the fruitful ambiguities contained in the terms *heilen* and *das Heil* which point to the thematic core of the work. This central motif, which occurs with varying emphasis, contains within it the nucleus of the whole design. *Heilen* implies not merely the practice of healing but also making whole and perfect; it is both restoration of health and making good what was imperfect. *Das Heil* may equally be used with religious stress, meaning the soul's salvation, the attainment of grace, as in the wider sense of well-being, good fortune or happiness. As one who practises the art of healing, Augustinus restores health to those whom he treats, but in doing so he is also working for a new humanity both among those he helps and within himself. In healing others, he is made whole. This he realizes as he begins his work: 'Da dachte ich, wirst du deine Wirksamkeit beginnen. Wird sie zu dem Heile derer sein, die dir vertrauen, und zu deinem Heile?' (p. 64).

The redemptive wholeness which Augustinus determines to pursue as his goal in opening his diary receives its vital impetus from the Obrist's tale, for the latter first gives him the idea of recording the truly significant events of his life as a means to self-knowledge. In the *Studienmappe*, the redemptive idea is even more explicitly contained in the short chapter 'Das Gelöbnis': 'Es ist eine fast traurige und sündhafte Begebenheit, die mir das Gelöbnis und Pergamentbuch eingegeben hat: aber die traurige Begebenheit wird in Heil ausgehen, wie schon das Pergamentbuch der Anfang des Heiles sein muß' (II, 150).[15] The optimistic note of moral aspiration, already clearly present here, is maintained into the final draft, although the whole practical implications, the means of attaining to a fuller humanity, are only later worked out. The details of the doctor's daily routine, the extension and improvement of the family farm, the arrangement of rooms, the building of a house, road-making and afforestation would, in themselves, have no higher purpose or meaning, but for that earnest dedication to create wholeness in every sphere of human activity. It is this moral design, this self-appointed plan of life, which informs and sustains the narrative.

The human wholeness which Augustinus consciously strives for, consists in a fundamental change of attitude, a new way of seeing the world; it implies a shift of emphasis from the subjective to the objective view. It involves self-denial and service, the suppression of personal desires, patience and the bearing of personal loss. The many severe trials and tragic blows to the doctor's life, events which might well have brought him to despair, ultimately work for his salvation in becoming part of a process of purification and moral growth. The *Letzte Mappe* represents a pattern of human life which is the exact opposite to that shown in *Abdias*, for it takes as its theme the growth of understanding, above all of self-knowledge, and gives emphasis to the guiding role of reason; it reveals a purposiveness in existence in which man actively exercises freedom of choice. It is noteworthy that the selfsame notion of *Heil* is also explicitly referred to in *Abdias* when he holds his newly-born daughter in his hands and at last it seems to him: 'als fühle er drinnen bereits den Anfang des Heiles, das nie gekommen war, und von dem er nie gewußt hatte, wo er es denn suchen sollte' (III, 28). But Abdias's passionate defiance and unrepentant rebellious-ness is directed at an obscure destiny which binds him under a perpetual chain of calamity and produces in him that inner blindness which deprives him of moral bearings. Augustinus, on the other hand, transforms his anguish into a meaningful sacrifice on his road to self-perfection. The willing acceptance of distress as part of the God-given design of existence and as a trial which should call forth the noblest human response, proves the most difficult solution but offers the greatest reward. The

Obrist's moving tale delineating, as it does, a conversion from blind egotism to altruism and the rule of reason, from rebellious-ness to *Sanftmut*, serves within the novel as the exemplar of endurance, self-mastery and ultimate acquiescence of the will in the great design of existence. The death of the Obrist's wife provides the purest model of self-sacrifice for the sake of others. The 'rosenrote Lämmerwolken' which cast a glow over her dead features suggest the workings of a comforting grace which comes as a reward once the full meaning of human sacrifice has been grasped. In a parallel instance, the Obrist draws attention to the ripening corn as he gently calls Augustinus back to life from suicidal thoughts: 'Es ist doch ein wunderbarer Segen, darüber der Mensch manches kleine Leid vergißt' (p. 194). Towards evening, after the turmoil of passions within him is allayed and his eyes can once more respond to the splendour of the world, Augustinus notes: 'Ich sah das Korn des Friedmeier an, von dem der Obrist gesagt hatte. Es war sehr schön, und seine Bärte glühten in dem Abendsonnenscheinfeuer' (p. 195). Here the fire of the passions is again symbolically transfigured into the warm glow of the sunset. The wisdom that springs from such consummate humanity as is here exemplified consists in gaining a true perspective, a balanced view, in which the subjective element is weighed against the variety and fullness of phenomenal reality, is given proper meaning by measure-ment against the passage of time. It is the wisdom of harmoniously seeing all things *sub specie aeternitatis*.

Only when measured against so profoundly detached and contemplative a view of human existence can the Obrist's remarkable words on the loss of his beloved wife or that strange note of triumphalism in the final passage of Book 1 be adequately understood. The Obrist recalls his loss in these terms: 'Und der Tag verging, und der nächste verging, und immer mehrere vergingen, und die Sonne stand am Himmel, die Getreide wuchsen, die Bäche rauschten, nur daß sie dahin war, und daß es war wie der Verlust einer goldenen Müke' (p. 219). The passage which concludes the First Book is essentially a parabolic restatement of the above:

Das Geschik fährt in einem goldenen Wagen. Was durch die Räder nieder gedrükt wird, daran liegt nichts. Wenn auf einen Mann ein Felsen fällt oder der Bliz ihn tödtet, und wenn er nun das Alles nicht mehr wirken kann, was er sonst gewirkt hätte, so wird es ein anderer thun. Wenn ein Volk dahin geht, und zerstreut wird, und das nicht erreichen kann, was es sonst erreicht hätte, so wird ein anderes Volk ein Mehreres erreichen. Und wenn ganze Ströme von Völkern dahin gegangen sind, die Unsägliches und Unzähliges getragen haben, so werden wieder neue Ströme kommen, und Unsägliches und Unzähliges tragen, und wieder neue, und wieder neue, und kein sterblicher Mensch kann sagen, wann das enden wird. Und wenn du deinem Herzen wehe gethan hast, daß es zuket und vergehen will, oder daß es sich ermannt und größer wird, so kümmert sich die Allheit nicht darum, und dränget ihrem Ziele zu, das die Herrlichkeit ist. Du aber hättest es vermeiden können, oder kannst es ändern, und die Änderung wird dir vergolten; denn es entsteht nun das Außerordentliche daraus. (pp. 248 f.)

Both passages are crucial in referring to the paradox at the heart of Stifter's world: the novelist's unremitting endeavour to reconcile the irrationality of being with an immutable order, the tragic with divine dispensation, to fit arbitrariness and chance to a grand Leibnizian design; ultimately, to discern wholeness in the phenomenal universe. And where that wholeness is not to be discerned, the need for propitiation becomes more urgent, the need for an act of volition which assents to order, meaning and purpose. (The distance is vast between the facile optimism which merely seeks refuge in comforting philosophies and that resilient optimism which bravely surmounts the direness of experience and draws its philosophy from it.) The belief which unites the Obrist and Augustinus is one that finds the magnanimous strength to become reconciled to even the bitterest of personal loss by relating it to abiding values and impersonal, transcending goals. The Obrist's earlier reference to 'manches kleine Leid' which dwindles in contemplation of the rich blessings of the earth must in no way be read as a belittlement of human suffering. His grief continues to afflict him, as those poignant silences which interrupt his narrative all too clearly testify. It is, rather, a challenging insistence on the greatness of super-personal values, it advocates a superior

awareness of the great design underlying the totality of life
— 'die Allheit' — an awareness which has the power to
strengthen and console. The glorious consummation to which
all things inexorably progress suggests an eventual restoration
of the perfect state on earth with definite religious overtones.
Stifter's mature faith clearly has its place in this. Yet the stress
falls squarely on the importance of the human element, on the
freedom of moral choice, on man as the instrument of his own
salvation. Man has power to effect change in the world about
him and within himself, as the progress of Augustinus's life
shows. The final reward for such endeavour is expressed in
terms of an embracing abstract: 'das Außerordentliche'. This
term, which carries wholly positive connotations, may be seen
in close approximation to the idea of wholeness so far explored.
The 'extraordinary', in Stifter's meaning, is that which is raised
above the common order of things; that which approaches the
condition of wholeness.

The figure who most completely represents the condition of
an achieved humanity ('die Vernunftwürde des Menschen in
seiner Sitte', as Stifter once expressed it), is the Obrist who, like
Risach, is a mature man tried and ennobled by experience.[16] The
words of consolation he offers Augustinus, after the latter's
threefold bereavement, are the sum of his hard-won philosophy
and the most perfect statement of the meaning of wholeness in
the novel. They have a chiasmic completeness which perfectly
complements the fullness of their import: 'Durch den Segen,
der aus dem Schmerze in die Taten fließt, kommt die Erwartung
eines Heils, und das Heil erscheint in der Empfindung der
Taten' (p. 293).[17]

REFERENCES

[1] This work is throughout referred to, by the title conventionally used, as the *Letzte Mappe*. Textual references are to Volume XII of Stifter's *Sämtliche Werke*, edited by F. Hüller (Reichenberg, 1939). This is prefaced by a detailed scholarly analysis of the text. Other references to this historical-critical edition indicate the volume number in roman numerals.

[2] Thus J. E. Lunding, in his valuable study *Adalbert Stifter* (Copenhagen, 1946), deals most peremptorily with the *Letzte Mappe*, dismissing it as 'kein einheitliches, organisches Werk' (p. 112) without really attempting to analyze it. J. P. Stern's penetrating critical survey of Stifter in *Reinterpretations: Seven Studies in Nineteenth-Century German Literature* (London, 1964) would seem to imply a value judgement by making no mention of Stifter's unfinished novel. Among the vast volume of Stifter criticism I list only those studies which I have found especially helpful on this work: E. A. Blackall, *Adalbert Stifter* (Cambridge, 1948) includes a detailed and sensitive account of the work (Chapter 12) calling it 'one of Stifter's very greatest achievements' (p. 419); C. Hohoff, *Adalbert Stifter: Seine dichterischen Mittel und die Prosa des neunzehnten Jahrhunderts* (Düsseldorf, 1949) places Stifter's late novel 'im Brennpunkt seines Wesens' (p. 202), and provides searching critical comment on the style of the work, which he evaluates as a creative achievement that attains to 'die schwebende Freiheit antiker Dichtungen' (p. 219); H. Kunisch, *Adalbert Stifter: Mensch und Wirklichkeit* (Berlin, 1950) has produced a full and empathetic critique of the work. It is especially valuable in the qualification of key concepts (though *das Heil* is omitted) and in evaluation of stylistic features; J. Müller, 'Heilen und Wissen. Die Gestalt des Arztes und das Problem der Humanität in Adalbert Stifters "Letzter Mappe"', *Sinn und Form*, 6 (1954), 867–79. This excellent commentary relates the themes of knowing and healing to that of 'Menschwerdung' seeing in this a continuation of the humanist tradition; also his *Adalbert Stifter: Weltbild und Dichtung* (Halle/Saale, 1956), pp. 53–64; and 'Einige Gestaltenzüge in Stifter's "Letzter Mappe"', in *Adalbert Stifter: Studien und Interpretationen*, edited by L. Stiehm (Heidelberg, 1968), pp. 227–70; Th. C. van Stockum, '"Die Mappe meines Urgroßvaters" und ihre Bedeutung im Zusammenhang von Stifters Werk und Weltanschauung', *Neophilologus*, 30 (1946), 172–84.

[3] Letter to G. Heckenast of 12 February 1864.

[4] Letter to G. Heckenast of 17 December 1864.

[5] Letter to A. Piepenhagen of 23 December 1864.

[6] Letter to H. Bürkel of 21 November 1864. All the above pronouncements stem from the year in which Stifter resumed work on *Die Mappe* after an interval of some twenty years.

[7] Letter to A. Buddeus of 21 August 1847. See also letter to Heckenast of 16 February 1847: 'Ich wollte drei Gestalten darstellen, in denen sich die Einfachheit, Größe und Güte der menschlichen Seele spiegelt'.

[8] *Erzählungen in der Urfassung*, edited by M. Stefl (Augsburg, 1952), I, 200.

[9] See F. Gundolf, *Adalbert Stifter* (Halle, 1931), p. 37; P. Küpper, 'Literatur und Langeweile', in *Adalbert Stifter: Studien und Interpretationen* (Heidelberg, 1968), pp. 171–88; J. P. Stern, 'Adalbert Stifters ontologischer Stil', ibid., pp. 103–20.

[10] For a discussion of the motif of astonishment and recognition in face of beauty see my article 'Stifter's Early Portraits of the Artist. Stages in the Growth of an Aesthetic', *FMLS*, 11 (1975), 149 ff.

[11] For a highly illuminating discussion of the significance of the garden in *Der Nachsommer* see C. E. Schorske, 'The Transformation of the Garden', *American Historical Review*, 72 (1966–67), 1283–1320.

[12] It would be impossible to do justice to the niceties of Schiller's model in a few sentences. For a full scholarly discussion of Schiller's idea of the whole man see Elizabeth M. Wilkinson and L. A. Willoughby, '"The Whole Man" in Schiller's

Theory of Culture and Society', in *Essays in German Language, Culture and Society*, edited by S. S. Prawer, R. Hinton Thomas and L. Forster (London, 1969), pp. 177–210. This carefully argued analysis of Schiller's thought points to his distinctive contribution to the concept of wholeness and takes issue with other thinkers and critics who have neglected the subtleties of Schiller's arguments. Stifter, who was not a thinker but solely an artist, was wont to adopt Schiller's concepts but give them his own, emotive rather than intellectual emphasis. This is borne out by a workmanlike thesis by Waldtraut Hörmann, 'Der Einfluß Schillers auf Adalbert Stifter' (unpublished D.Phil. Dissertation, University of Innsbruck, 1946).

[13] From 'The Tables Turned', in *The Poetical Works of William Wordsworth*, edited by T. Hutchinson (Oxford, 1923), p. 481. Like Wordsworth, Stifter firmly believes in the restorative powers of nature, in nature as the healer of human ills, as the pure source which mediates between the human and the divine. A detailed account of the close affinity between these two writers has still to be written.

[14] J. P. Stern, *Reinterpretations*, pp. 289 ff. has drawn attention to 'a certain unclarity' in Stifter's treatment of Risach's and Mathilda's story in relation to the tenor of the rest of the novel. Though I cannot agree on the point that Stifter attributes to Risach 'the taming of a passion he never felt' (p. 291), it is clearly characteristic of his art to leave far more to interpretation than the psychologically interested reader demands. In both novels Stifter is much more concerned to portray the unalterable fact of a broken relationship than to explore the misunderstandings from which it arose. In both he also concentrates on the subsequent ordering of life through self-discipline and restraint and pays little regard to the nature of past guilt.

[15] A remarkable parallel may be found in the words Kafka commits to his diary in the entry of 25 February 1912: 'Das Tagebuch von heute an festhalten! Regelmäßig schreiben! Sich nicht aufgeben! Wenn auch keine Erlösung kommt, so will ich doch jeden Augenblick ihrer würdig sein' (Franz Kafka, *Tagebücher 1910–1923*, edited by M. Brod (Frankfurt, 1951), p. 249). The agony of Kafka's need for some kind of salvation, whatever psychological, philosophical or religious meaning the term may contain for him, of course remains a quest and never finds the images of wholeness which Stifter's novel embodies.

[16] See the letter to G. Heckenast of 29 July 1858: 'was mir das Höchste Herrlichste Wünschenswerteste dieses Lebens erscheint, die Vernunftwürde der Menschen in seiner Sitte in seiner Wissenschaft in seiner Kunst, soll dauern soll verehrt werden, und soll die reinste Herrschaft führen.'

[17] J. Müller, 'Heilen und Wissen', p. 873 stresses particularly the humanist, hither-worldy sense of *das Heil* and overlooks the religious dimensions of the work when he writes of this passage: 'Das Heil liegt im tatkräftigen Wirken für andere. Tätigkeit heilt Wunden. Heilendes Tun ist das Heil.' My argument throughout has been that the vocabulary of wholeness in the novel is interfused with biblical connotations which have paradigmatic force and greatly broaden its meaning.

To my printer

ATE of a world now remote
When to give was reward in itself,
When the giver gave with his heart
And matched type to words that he loved;
You who unremittingly seek
To serve others with skills of your own,
To work on behalf of my own
Resolve to match word and deed;
Co-creator not solely concerned
With appearance of outward form,
Whose care knows no *faute de mieux*
But loves and lives in the aim;
True to the smallest nuance,
You guardian of care, to the point
Where it strays into *excès de zèle*,
From inchoate founts of type
You achieve such marvels of sense
That even those who curse its invention
May see print as a magic pure white:
O! you who confirm my belief
That, in calling, craft weds creation,
Who through sharing my doubts and despairs
Could lift the dread curse of inaction:
Stout heart of the moors and dales,
Be thanked by our county's child.

The original German by Karl Kraus for Georg Jahoda on his sixtieth birthday.
Freely translated, adapted, and presented to her own printer by
Professor Elizabeth M. Wilkinson, M.A., PH.D., F.B.A., editor, for twenty years,
of the Publications of the English Goethe Society.

A list of the publications
of Elizabeth M. Wilkinson

By ANN C. WEAVER

In order to reflect Professor Wilkinson's development as scholar, the items are arranged in chronological order of publication. Reprints and second editions have normally been indicated under the original entry. However, when an item has been reproduced — whether in English or in German — at the request of the editor of an anthology, or of a foreign publisher, a new entry has been made under the later date.

(with LAW)   denotes work written in collaboration with Professor Leonard Ashley Willoughby

*   denotes articles reprinted in *Goethe: Poet and Thinker* (1962, no. 61)

†   denotes articles reprinted in *Models of Wholeness* (in the press, no. 90)

1939
1   'Some Unpublished Letters from the Correspondence of Johann Elias Schlegel', *MLR*, 34, 396–414.

1942
2†   Review of F. O. Nolte, *Lessing's Laokoon*, *MLR*, 37, 230–32.

1944
3   Thomas Mann, *Tonio Kröger*, edited with Introduction and Notes, Blackwell's German Texts (Oxford), xliv + 112 pp. (Numerous reprints, and second edition, 1968. See also 1964, no. 66 below.)
4   (with LAW)   Friedrich Schiller, *Kabale und Liebe*, edited with Introduction and Notes, Blackwell's German Texts (Oxford), lvi + 165 pp.
5   Review of F. O. Nolte, *Art and Reality*, *MLR*, 39, 401–02.

178

1945

6   *Johann Elias Schlegel: A German Pioneer in Aesthetics* (Oxford),
[ii] + viii + 148 pp. (Awarded the Robertson Prize. Reprinted
1973, see no. 81 below.)

7   Review of S. L. Wormley, *Heine in England*, MLR, 40, 326–27.

1946

8* 'Goethe's *Tasso*: The Tragedy of a Creative Artist', *PEGS*,
NS, 15, 96–127. (German version, see 1958, no. 47, and 1967,
no. 71 below.)

1947

9   Review of Agnes Arber, *Goethe's Botany*; Maria Schindler and
Eleanor C. Merry, *Pure Colour*; and L. A. Willoughby, *Unity
and Continuity in Goethe*, PEGS, NS, 16, 120–24.

1948

10 (with LAW) 'Wandrers Sturmlied: A Study in Poetic
Vagrancy' [includes the poem and translation *en face*], *GLL*,
NS, 1, 94–116.

11 Review of Barker Fairley, *A Study of Goethe*, PEGS, NS, 17,
173–85.

12 Review of Agnes Arber, *Goethe's Botany*, MLR, 43, 556–58.

1949

13 'A Further Note on the Meaning of "Neid" in Werther's Letter
of 1 July 1771', *MLR*, 44, 243–46.

14* ' "Tasso — ein gesteigerter Werther" in the light of Goethe's
Principle of "Steigerung": An Inquiry into Critical Method',
MLR, 44, 305–28. (German version, see 1952, no. 27 below.)

15* 'The Relation of Form and Meaning in Goethe's *Egmont*', *PEGS*,
NS, 18, 149–82. (German version, see 1972, no. 79 below.)

16* 'Goethe's Poetry', *GLL*, NS, 2, 316–29.

17 Review of Emil Staiger, *Grundbegriffe der Poetik*, MLR, 44,
433–37.

18 'Goethe's *Egmont* might have been written for us', *Radio Times*,
22 April 1949, p. 4.

19 'Goethe's Art and Practice of Living', *Listener*, 10 November
1949, pp. 801–02.

1950

20 'Schiller for the English', review of H. B. Garland, *Schiller*,
and W. Witte, *Schiller*, *Spectator*, 6 January 1950, pp. 24–26.

21   'The Youth of a Poet', review of Goethe, *Truth and Fantasy from My Life*, edited by J. M. Cohen, *Spectator*, 5 March 1950, pp. 622–24.

1951

22   'Neuere Strömungen der angelsächsischen Ästhetik in ihrer Beziehung zur vergleichenden Literaturwissenschaft', in *Forschungsprobleme der vergleichenden Literaturgeschichte*, Volume 1, edited by Kurt Wais (Tübingen), pp. 141–57.

23   'Group Work in the Interpretation of a Poem by Hölderlin', *GLL*, NS, 4, 248–60. (German version, see 1952, no. 28 below.)

24   (with G. A. Wells) 'German Literature, 1700–1832', *YWML*, 11, 319–44.

25   'The First of the Hallucinated', review of *Tales from Hoffmann*, edited by J. M. Cohen, *Spectator*, 16 March 1951, pp. 350–52.

1952

26*   'The Poet as Thinker: On the Varying Modes of Goethe's Thought', in *German Studies Presented to Leonard Ashley Willoughby* (Oxford), pp. 217–42.

27   ' "Tasso — ein gesteigerter Werther" im Licht von Goethes Prinzip der Steigerung: Eine Untersuchung zur Frage der kritischen Methode', translated by Ernst Grumach, *Goethe: Neue Folge des Jahrbuchs der Goethe-Gesellschaft*, 13 (1951), 28–58 (see no. 14 above).

28   'Gemeinschaftsarbeit bei der Textinterpretation eines Hölderlin-Gedichtes', translated by K. W. Maurer, *Studium Generale*, 5, 74–82 (see no. 23 above).

1953

29*   'Goethe's Conception of Form', Henriette Hertz Trust Annual Lecture on a Master Mind (11 July 1951), *Proceedings of the British Academy*, 37 (1951), 175–97. (Reprinted 1968, see no. 75 below.)

1954

30   Review of *Goethe's Botanical Writings*, translated by Bertha Mueller, *GLL*, NS, 7, 152–53.

31   Review of W. H. Bruford, *Literary Interpretation in Germany*, *GLL*, NS, 7, 218–19.

32   Review of P. Demetz, *Goethes 'Die Aufgeregten': Zur Frage der politischen Dichtung in Deutschland*, *GLL*, NS, 7, 225–26.

1955

33 Review of Klaus Dockhorn, *Deutscher Geist und angelsächsische Geistesgeschichte*, GLL, NS, 8, 228–29.

34 'Schiller's Concept of *Schein* in the Light of Recent Aesthetics', *GQ*, 28, 219–27.

35 Translation of Thomas Mann, 'Friedrich Schiller: An Oration pronounced at Stuttgart on May 8th, 1955 . . .', GLL, NS, 9, 1–14.

1956

36 'Literature and Science' [a review of lectures delivered at the Sixth Triennial Congress of the I.F.M.L.L.], GLL, NS, 9, 246–49.

37 Review of Helmut Prang, *Irrtum und Mißverständnis in den Dichtungen Heinrich von Kleists*, GLL, NS, 9, 320–21.

38 'Aesthetic Excursus on Thomas Mann's *Akribie*', *GR*, 31, 225–35.

39 Speech to P.E.N. Club Memorial Meeting for Thomas Mann (5 October 1955), *P.E.N. News*, 192, 27–32.

1957

40 Edward Bullough, *Aesthetics: Lectures and Essays* [includes his hitherto unpublished Cambridge lectures of 1907/8 on 'The Modern Conception of Aesthetics', and his articles ' "Psychical Distance" as a Factor in Art and an Aesthetic Principle' and 'Mind and Medium in Art'], edited with an Introduction (London), xliii + 158 pp.

41 Transcription, translation and annotation of German entries in *The Notebooks of Samuel Taylor Coleridge*, edited by Kathleen Coburn, Volume 1, *1794–1804* (London), two parts.

42 *Goethes Trilogie der Leidenschaft als Beitrag zur Frage der Katharsis*, Freies Deutsches Hochstift, Reihe der Vorträge und Schriften, 18 (Frankfurt), 31 pp. (Reprinted in Japan, see 1958, no. 48 below.)

43 'Über den Begriff der künstlerischen Distanz: Von Schiller und Wordsworth bis zur Gegenwart', *Deutsche Beiträge zur geistigen Überlieferung*, 3, 69–88.

44 Review of Wolfdietrich Rasch, *Goethes "Torquato Tasso": Die Tragödie des Dichters*, GR, 32, 155–57.

45 'The Theological Basis of Faust's *Credo*', GLL, NS, 10, 229–39. (German version, see 1972, no. 80, and 1974, no. 85 below.)

1958

46 'Coleridge und Deutschland, 1794–1804: Zum ersten Band der Gesamtausgabe seiner *Notebooks*', in *Forschungsprobleme der vergleichenden Literaturgeschichte*, Volume II, edited by Fritz Ernst and Kurt Wais (Tübingen), pp. 7–23.

47 'Goethe: Tasso', in *Das deutsche Drama vom Barock bis zur Gegenwart: Interpretationen*, edited by Benno von Wiese, 2 vols (Düsseldorf), I, 193–214 and 486–89 (see no. 8 above).

48 'Goethes Trilogie der Leidenschaft', *Jahrbuch der Goethe-Gesellschaft [in Japan]*, 4, 1–33 (see no. 42 above).

1959

49 ' "Form" and "Content" in the Aesthetics of German Classicism', in *Stil- und Formprobleme in der Literatur: Vorträge des VII. Kongresses der Internationalen Vereinigung für moderne Sprachen und Literaturen in Heidelberg*, edited by Paul Böckmann (Heidelberg), pp. 18–27.

50 'Zur Sprache und Struktur der Ästhetischen Briefe', *Akzente*, 6, 389–418. (German version of no. 52 below.)

51 'The Great Contemporary' [excerpts from lunch-hour lectures on Schiller at University College London in 1945], *Adam. International Review*, 27, 22–23.

1960

52 'Reflections after Translating Schiller's *Letters on the Aesthetic Education of Man*', in *Schiller: Bicentenary Lectures*, edited by F. Norman, University of London, Institute of Germanic Studies, Publications (London), pp. 46–82. (German version, see 1959, no. 50 above.)

53 'Schiller und die Idee der Aufklärung', *Jahrbuch der deutschen Schillergesellschaft*, 4, 42–59.

54 Review of Bruno Markwardt, *Geschichte der deutschen Poetik*, II, *GLL*, NS, 14, 76–77.

1961

55† *Schiller: Poet or Philosopher?*, Special Taylorian Lecture (17 November 1959) (Oxford), 36 pp.

56 'Verse into Poetry' [an autobiographical interpretation of Goethe's two poems entitled 'Die Jahre'], in *Festschrift Presented to Harriet Minskers on her Seventieth Birthday by Pupils, Colleagues and Friends* (privately printed), pp. 15–16.

57 Transcription, translation and annotation of German entries in *The Notebooks of Samuel Taylor Coleridge*, edited by Kathleen Coburn, Volume II, *1804–1808* (New York), two parts.

58 (with B. A. Rowley) 'Testing Candidates for a University Course in Language and Literature', *ML*, 42, 56–64.

59† (with LAW) 'Goethe to Herder, July 1722: Some Problems of Pedagogic Presentation' [includes English translation of Goethe's letter], *GLL*, NS, 15, 110–22.

1962

60† (with LAW) 'The Blind Man and the Poet: An Early Stage in Goethe's Quest for Form', in *German Studies Presented to Walter Horace Bruford* (London &c), pp. 29–57. (German version, see 1974, no. 86 below.)

61 (with LAW) *Goethe: Poet and Thinker* (London), 248 pp. (Reprinted 1970; German version, see 1974, no. 83 below.)

1963

62 *In Praise of Aesthetics*, Inaugural Lecture, University College London (25 October 1962) (London), 26 pp.

63 'Vox Collegii' [thoughts provoked by teaching American and English students], *New Phineas*, 22, no. 2, 2–5.

64† 'The Inexpressible and the Un-speakable: Some Romantic Attitudes to Art and Language', *GLL*, NS, 16, 308–20.

1964

65 'Goethe, Johann Wolfgang von', in *Encyclopaedia Britannica*, x, 522–29. (Reprinted in all subsequent editions to date.)

66 '*Tonio Kröger*: An Interpretation', in *Thomas Mann: A Collection of Critical Essays*, edited by Henry Hatfield, Twentieth Century Views (Englewood Cliffs, New Jersey), pp. 22–34 (reprinted from Introduction to no. 3 above).

67 'On Being Seen and Not Heard', Presidential Address to the Modern Language Association (3 January 1964), *ML*, 45, 4–13.

1965

68† 'Schiller and the Gutenberg Galaxy: A Question of Appropriate Contexts', *GLL*, NS, 18, 309–18.

1967

69   (with LAW)   Friedrich Schiller, *On the Aesthetic Education of Man: In a Series of Letters*, edited and translated, with an Introduction, Commentary, Glossary of Terms, and 4 Appendices (Oxford), [ii] + cxcvi + 372 pp. (German version, see 1977, no. 89 below.)

70   'Dankesworte der ausländischen Germanisten', in *Nationalismus in Germanistik und Dichtung: Dokumentation des Germanistentages in München vom 17.-22. Oktober 1966*, edited by Benno von Wiese and Rudolf Henß (Berlin), pp. 361–63.

71   'Torquato Tasso', in *Goethe im XX. Jahrhundert: Spiegelungen und Deutungen*, edited by Hans Mayer (Hamburg), pp. 98–119 (reprinted from no. 47 above).

72   (with LAW)   'Nachlese zu Schillers Ästhetik. Auf Wegen der Herausgeber', *Jahrbuch der deutschen Schillergesellschaft*, 11, 374–403.

73   Review of Schiller, *Werke*, edited by Gerhard Fricke and Herbert G. Göpfert, *GQ*, 40, 253–56.

74   Review of Johann Elias Schlegel, *On Imitation and Other Essays*, translated by Edward Allen McCormick, *GQ*, 40, 437–39.

1968

75   'Goethe's Conception of Form', in *Goethe: A Collection of Critical Essays*, edited by Victor Lange, Twentieth Century Views (Englewood Cliffs, New Jersey), pp. 110–31 (reprinted from no. 29 above).

76†   (with LAW)   'Having and Being, or Bourgeois versus Nobility: Notes for a Chapter on Social and Cultural History or for a Commentary on *Wilhelm Meister*', *GLL*, NS, 22, 101–05.

1969

77†   (with LAW)   ' "The Whole Man" in Schiller's Theory of Culture and Society: On the Virtue of a Plurality of Models', in *Essays in German Language, Culture and Society*, edited by Siegbert S. Prawer, R. Hinton Thomas and Leonard Forster, University of London, Institute of Germanic Studies, Publications (London), pp. 177–210.

1971

78   'Faust in der Logosszene — Willkürlicher Übersetzer oder geschulter Exeget? Wie, zu welchem Ende — und für wen — schreibt man heutzutage einen Kommentar?', in *Dichtung, Sprache, Gesellschaft: Akten des IV. Internationalen Germanisten-Kongresses 1970 in Princeton*, edited by Victor Lange and Hans-Gert Roloff (Frankfurt), pp. 115–24.

1972

79   'Sprachliche Feinstruktur in Goethes "Egmont": Zur Beziehung zwischen Gestalt und Gehalt', in *Begriffsbestimmung der Klassik und des Klassischen*, edited by Heinz Otto Burger, Wege der Forschung, 210 (Darmstadt), pp. 353–90 (German version of no. 15 above).

80   'Theologischer Stoff und dichterischer Gehalt in Fausts sogenanntem Credo', in *Goethe und die Tradition*, edited by Hans Reiss, Wissenschaftliche Paperbacks, Literaturwissenschaft, 19 (Frankfurt), pp. 242–58 (German version of no. 45 above).

1973

81   *Johann Elias Schlegel: A German Pioneer in Aesthetics*, with a second Preface to the New Edition (Darmstadt), xvii + 148 pp. (see no. 6 above).

82   'Goethe's *Faust*: Tragedy in the Diachronic Mode', *PEGS*, NS, 42, 116–74.

1974

83   (with LAW) *Goethe: Dichter und Denker* (Frankfurt), xii + 323 pp. (German version of no. 61 above).

84   (with LAW) 'Missing Links or Whatever Happened to Weimar Classicism?', in *'Erfahrung und Überlieferung': Festschrift for C. P. Magill*, edited by Hinrich Siefken and Alan Robinson, Trivium Special Publications, 1 (Cardiff), pp. 57–74.

85   'Theologischer Stoff und dichterischer Gehalt in Fausts sogenanntem Credo', in *Aufsätze zu Goethes "Faust I"*, edited by Werner Keller, Wege der Forschung, 145 (Darmstadt), pp. 551–71 (reprinted from no. 80 above).

86   (with LAW) 'Der Blinde und der Dichter: Der junge Goethe auf der Suche nach der Form', translated by Peter Hasler, *Goethe Jahrbuch*, 91, 33–57 (German version of no. 60 above).

87   'On Teaching Prescribed Texts: Further to the "Form-Content" Problem', *ML*, 55, 105–16.

1976
88   'Preis für Germanistik im Ausland: Dankrede', *Deutsche Akademie für Sprache und Dichtung Darmstadt: Jahrbuch*, 1975, 18–23.

1977
89   (with LAW) *Schillers Ästhetische Erziehung des Menschen: Eine Einführung* (Munich), 312 pp. (adapted from the Introduction, Glossary and Appendices to no. 69 above).

IN THE PRESS
90   *Models of Wholeness: Some Attitudes to Language, Art and Life in the Age of Goethe* (Bern).
91   'Perception as Process: Goethe's Treatment of "Auf dem See" — with an Excursus on Emblematics', Presidential Address to the English Goethe Society (6 May 1976), *PEGS*.
92   'Sexual Attitudes in Goethe's Life and Work.'

Tabula Gratulatoria

Jeremy Adler
Westfield College, London

Mary Alexander
Queen Mary College, London

Alice Apt
London

Stuart and Sally Atkins
Santa Barbara, California

Alan Bance
University of St Andrews

Caroline M. Bareham
Woking

Pamela Barnett
Portsmouth Polytechnic

E. M. Batley
Goldsmiths' College, London

Roger Bauer
München

Walter Baumann
New University of Ulster

Mary Beare
London

G. F. Benham
London

Clifford Albrecht Bernd
University of California

Eric A. Blackall
Cornell University

Bernhard Blume
La Jolla, California

C. V. Bock
Westfield College, London

Hermann Boeschenstein
Toronto

C. E. Bond
Shaftesbury

Alexander von Bormann
Universiteit van Amsterdam

Nicholas Boyle
Magdalene College, Cambridge

Peter Branscombe
University of St Andrews

Nancy C. Bressey
London

John T. Brewer
Washington State University

Richard Brinkmann
Tübingen/Berkeley

N*

Kenneth Brooke
University of Keele

W. H. Bruford
Edinburgh

Klaus Bung
London

G. P. Butler
University of Bath

Richard F. M. and
Lilias W. Byrn
University of Leeds

Caroline M. Cooper
London

Marianne Cowan
Glen Ridge, New Jersey

Mary C. Crichton
University of Michigan

Joyce Crick
University College, London

Geoffrey Cubbin
University of Cambridge

Joseph B. Dallett
Carleton University, Ottawa

Alexander J. Dickson
London

Liselotte Dieckmann
St Louis, Missouri

Richard W. Dorn
Wiesbaden

Martin Dyck
Cambridge, Massachusetts

Denys Dyer
Exeter College, Oxford

Joan Edwards
London

Oliver Edwards
Belfast

Hans Eichner
University of Toronto

John M. Ellis
University of California

Barker Fairley
Toronto

R. B. Farrell
Cremorne, New South Wales

R. G. Finch
University of Glasgow

Evelyn Scherabon Firchow
University of Minnesota

M. Kay Flavell
University College, London

Seymour L. Flaxman
City University, New York

Leonard Forster
University of Cambridge

Frank M. Fowler
Queen Mary College, London

Sylvia P. Fowles
Woking

Wilfred Franz
Plön/Holstein

Margaret Freeman
King's College, London

Wolfgang Frommel
Amsterdam

Albert Fuchs
Strasbourg

Joe K. Fugate
Kalamazoo College, Michigan

H. M. L. Garland
University of Exeter

Piers Gascoigne
Bath

Tom Geddes
London

Marion E. Gibbs
Royal Holloway College,
London

Luise Gilde
London

Sander L. and Marina Gilman
Cornell University

Johanna Ingeborg Glier
Yale University

Robert Gould
Carleton University, Ottawa

Ilse Graham
King's College, London

Penelope R. Graham
Windsor

Pierre Grappin
Paris

R. F. Green
Keble College, Oxford

Ernst I. Grunfeld
London

William Haas
University of Manchester

Diether H. Haenicke
Wayne State University

Karl-Heinz Hahn
Goethe-Gesellschaft, Weimar

Käte Hamburger
Stuttgart

Michael Hamburger
Saxmundham

Sylvia C. Harris
Birkbeck College, London

R. B. Harrison
King's College, London

Henry Hatfield
Harvard University

Arthur T. Hatto
London

Heidi Heimann
London

Robert and Polly Heitner
River Forest, Illinois

Erich Heller
Northwestern University,
Illinois

Heinrich Henel
Yale University

Arthur Henkel
Universität Heidelberg

Helmut Henne
Braunschweig

Cedric Hentschel
Harrow

Ruth H. G. Herring
High Wycombe

Ida Herz
London

U. M. D. Howlett
Birmingham

Valentine Charles Hubbs
University of Michigan

Ortrud Huttrop
Lichtenau

Inge Huyssen-Mable
University College, London

Raymond Immerwahr
University of Western Ontario

Margaret C. Ives
University of Lancaster

Sidney M. Johnson
Indiana University

Charlotte Jolles
Birkbeck College, London

Trevor Jones
Jesus College, Cambridge

Sven-Aage Jørgensen
Snekkersten

Ida M. Kimber
Edinburgh

Kenneth Knight
University of Kent, Canterbury

F. J. Lamport
Worcester College, Oxford

Victor Lange
Princeton University

William Larrett
University College, London

Harry Law-Robertson
Edinburgh

D. G. Little
Trinity College, Dublin

Carl Lofmark
St David's College, Lampeter

Detlev Lüders
Frankfurt am Main

Paul Michael Lützeler
Washington University

C. P. Magill
Aberystwyth

Rudolf and Kate Majut
Leicester

A. S. Maney
Leeds

Steven D. Martinson
Northwestern University,
Illinois

Eve Mason
Newnham College, Cambridge

Hans Mayer
Universität Tübingen

Lynda G. McAllister
Kingston-upon-Thames

Lorna McLeod
Sevenoaks, Kent

David McLintock
Royal Holloway College,
London

Bertha Meyer
Montreal

Herman Meyer
Universiteit van Amsterdam

Humphrey Milnes
University of Toronto

S. Minamiozi
Osaka City University

Basil Mogridge
Carleton University, Ottawa

Katharina Mommsen
Stanford University

Michael and Estelle Morgan
University of Bristol

Irene V. Morris
University of Nottingham

Hugo Moser
Universität Bonn

Etha Nichols
Polytechnic of the South Bank,
London

H. B. Nisbet
University of St Andrews

Otto Oberholzer
Kiel

John Osborne
University of Sussex

David L. Paisey
London

Edmund Papst
University of Southampton

Roy Pascal
Birmingham

Ronald Peacock
Gerrards Cross

Wendy Philipson
Universität München

F. P. Pickering
Arborfield Cross

Heinz Politzer
University of California

Hans Popper
University College, Swansea

Edith Potter
Scripps College, California

Helga and Siegbert Prawer
University of Oxford

Ulrich Pretzel
Hamburg

Judith Purver
Manchester

H. S. Reiss
University of Bristol

F. V. Rhodes
London

Anthony W. Riley
Queen's University,
Kingston, Ontario

Heidi Robinson
University College, London

W. D. and Elaine Robson-Scott
London

Eduard Rosenbaum
London

Brian and Peggy Rowley
University of East Anglia

Josa Morgan Ruffner
London

Colin A. H. Russ
University of Kent, Canterbury

Kathleen S. Russell
Enfield

Lawrence and Judith Ryan
University of Massachusetts
and Smith College, Mass.

Hugh Sacker
Donard, Co. Wicklow

Paul Salmon
University of Edinburgh

Elizabeth Samson
Cambridge

Richard Samuel
Brighton, Victoria

Konrad Schaum
University of Notre Dame,
Indiana

Bruni Schling
London

Hans Joachim Schrimpf
Ruhr-Universität Bochum

W. Schwarz
London

D. F. S. Scott
Durham

Herbert Seidler
Wien

Friedrich Sengle
Starnberg-Söcking

Elinor Shaffer
Cambridge

Hinrich Siefken
St David's College, Lampeter

Susan Powell Sirc
University of Glasgow

J. F. Slattery
University of Nottingham

Christopher J. Smith
University College, London

N. Horton Smith
University of Nottingham

Hanna Spencer
University of Western Ontario

M. B. Stafford
London

C. N. Stanley
Wolverhampton

Roger Stephenson
University of Glasgow

E. J. Stevenson
Cambridge

Corbet Stewart
Queen Mary College, London

Alexander Stillmark
University College, London

Birgit Stolt
Uppsala

F. J. and E. C. Stopp
Caius College and Girton
College, Cambridge

Arrigo Subiotto
University of Birmingham

Martin Swales
University College, London

Bruce Thompson
University of Stirling

R. B. Tilford
University of Bradford

Masami Tobari
University of Tokyo

Roger Tomalin
Cinderford

James Trainer
University of Stirling

John L. M. Trim
Selwyn College, Cambridge

J. M. Tudor
University of Durham

R. V. Tymms
Royal Holloway College,
London

Margaret Vallance
London

Derek Van Abbé
Sutton, Cambs.

Wilhelm Vosskamp
Universität Bielefeld

A. B. Wachsmuth
Berlin-Dahlem

H. A. Wage
's Gravenhage

M.-L. Waldeck
Westfield College, London

Bruce Watson
Bedford College, London

Ann C. Weaver
High Wycombe

G. A. Wells
Birkbeck College, London

Joachim Whaley
Christ's College, Cambridge

John Whaley
Bexleyheath

Ann and John White
Kew

Olive M. White
London

Benno von Wiese
Bonn-Ippendorf

John Ritchie Wilkie
Leeds

J. F. Williams
University of Keele

Rhys W. Williams
University of Manchester

L. A. Willoughby
Berkhamsted

Marianne Winder
London

Roy Wisbey
King's College, London

William Witte
Aberdeen

Wolfgang Wittkowski
Ohio State University

Marianne Wynn
Westfield College, London

Michael Yaxley
University College, London

W. E. Yuill
Bedford College, London

Bernhard Zeller
Deutsches Literaturarchiv,
Marbach

Lieselotte Zettler de Vareschi
Caracas

Margot Zutshi
London

———

Library
University College of Wales,
Aberystwyth

Library
University College of
North Wales, Bangor

Tysk institutt
Universitetet i Bergen

Library
University of Birmingham

Germanistisches Institut
Ruhr-Universität Bochum

Germanistisches Seminar
Universität Bonn

Library
University of Bristol

Department of German
Bryn Mawr College

Library, Christ's College
Cambridge

Modern and Medieval
Languages Libraries
University of Cambridge

Library
University College, Cardiff

Library
Carleton University

Department of Germanic
Languages and Literatures
University of Chicago

Libraries
Cornell University

Deutsche Bibliothek
Frankfurt am Main

Library
University of East Anglia

Library
Goethe Institute, London

Istituto Italiano di Studi
Germanici
Rome

Department of Germanic and
Slavic Languages and
Literatures
Kent State University

Institut für
Literaturwissenschaft
Universität Kiel

Department of German
St David's University College,
Lampeter

Library
University of Lancaster

Library
Laurentian University

Brotherton Library
University of Leeds

London Library

Department of Modern
Languages
City of London Polytechnic

Institute of Germanic Studies
University of London

Library
University of London

Library
University of London,
Bedford College

Library
University of London,
Goldsmiths' College

Library
University of London,
King's College

Library
University of London,
Queen Mary College

Department of German
University of London,
University College

Library
University of London,
University College

Library
University of London,
Westfield College

Department of German
University of Manchester

John Rylands Library
University of Manchester

Department of Germanic
Studies
University of Melbourne

Department of German
Monash University

Library
University of North Carolina

Library
University of Nottingham

Modern Languages
Faculty Library
University of Oxford

Institut d'Études Germaniques
Université de Paris-Sorbonne

Institut für deutsche Sprache
und Literatur
Universität Salzburg

Library
University of Sheffield

Bibliothek
Gesamthochschule Siegen

Department of German
Language and Literature
Smith College, Massachusetts

Library
University of Southampton

Department of German
University of Strathclyde

Library
University College of Swansea

Modern Language Department
Swarthmore College

Department of Germanic
Languages
University of Texas at Austin

German Department
Trinity College, Dublin

Bibliothek
Universität Tübingen

Library
New University of Ulster

Department of German Studies
University of Warwick

Library
University of Warwick

Library, Wesleyan University

Germanistisches Institut
Universität Wien

Library
University of the Witwatersrand

B. H. Blackwell
Oxford

Dillon's University Bookshop
London

Slatner & Starkmann Ass.
London

James Thin
Edinburgh

Index of Names

By ANN C. WEAVER